THE HASH

Volume One

50952

Bishop Otter College
LIBRARY

ALSO EDITED BY PETER HAINING

The Hashish Club Volume Two:
The Psychedelic Era: From Huxley to Lennon
The Magicians: Occult Stories
A Thousand Afternoons: An Anthology of Bullfighting

THE HASHISH CLUB
An Anthology of Drug Literature

*

Volume One

THE FOUNDING OF THE MODERN TRADITION:
FROM COLERIDGE TO CROWLEY

*

Edited by
PETER HAINING

Preface by
BRIAN W. ALDISS

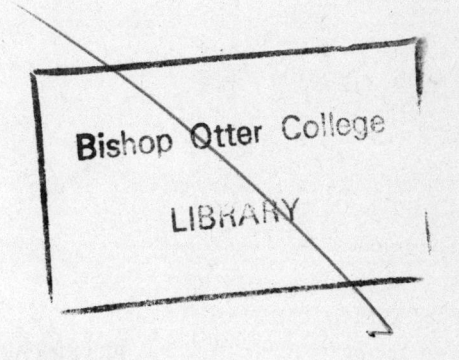

PETER OWEN · LONDON

ISBN 0 7206 0303 X

All Rights Reserved. No part of this publication
may be reproduced in any form or by any means
without the prior permission of the publisher.

PETER OWEN LIMITED
20 Holland Park Avenue London W11 3QU

First British Commonwealth edition 1975
This edition © 1975 Peter Haining
© Preface Brian Aldiss 1975

Printed in Great Britain by
Daedalus Press Stoke Ferry King's Lynn Norfolk

To the memory of
JAMES MANGAN (1803-1849)
Lost – but not forgotten

Contents

Acknowledgments   10

Preface by Brian W. Aldiss   13

Introduction   17

I

1. The Wanderings of Cain   27
   SAMUEL COLERIDGE

2. Dream Fugue   33
   THOMAS DE QUINCEY

3. A Tale of the Ragged Mountains   43
   EDGAR ALLAN POE

4. An Extraordinary Adventure in the Shades   54
   JAMES MANGAN

5. The Candlestick Ghost   68
   WILLIAM WILKIE COLLINS

II

6. The Hashish-Eaters' Club   84
   THEOPHILE GAUTIER

7. The Double Room   101
   CHARLES BAUDELAIRE

8. Hashish   105
   GERARD DE NERVAL

9. The Time of Assassins   115
   ARTHUR RIMBAUD

III

10	*Drugs and the Man* B. L. PUTNAM WEALE	120
11	*The House in Boulevard Thiers* CLAUDE FARRERE	134
12	*Torn Letters* LAFCADIO HEARN	142
13	*Finis Coronat Opus* FRANCIS THOMPSON	151
14	*A Walk Abroad* JAMES THOMSON	165

IV

15	*A New Artificial Paradise* HAVELOCK ELLIS	176
16	*The Adoration of the Magi* W. B. YEATS	191
17	*The Dying of Francis Donne* ERNEST DOWSON	198
18	*A Psychical Invasion* ALGERNON BLACKWOOD	208
19	*The Stratagem* ALEISTER CROWLEY	253

Illustrations

1 Samuel Coleridge

2 Thomas De Quincey

3 James Mangan on his death-bed

4 Wilkie Collins

5 Edgar Allan Poe

6 An interpretation of De Quincey's 'Confessions'

7 Gérard de Nerval

8 Théophile Gautier

9 Charles Baudelaire

10 A drawing by Baudelaire

11 'The Nights of Monsieur Baudelaire'

12 'The Death of Gérard de Nerval'

13 James Thomson

14 Lafcadio Hearn

15 Claude Farrère

16 Francis Thompson

17 Ernest Dowson

18 Havelock Ellis

19 W. B. Yeats

20 Algernon Blackwood

Acknowledgments

The Editor acknowledges his gratitude to the following authors, agents and executors for permission to include copyright material in this volume: The executors of the Estate of Claude Farrère for 'The House in Boulevard Thiers'. *The Contemporary Review* and the Estate of Havelock Ellis for 'A New Artificial Paradise'. Macmillan & Co. for 'The Adoration of the Magi' by W. B. Yeats. A. P. Watt Ltd for 'A Psychical Invasion' by Algernon Blackwood. John Symons, executor of the Estate of Aleister Crowley, for 'The Stratagem' by Aleister Crowley.

The Editor is also particularly indebted to Mrs Pamela Chamberlaine for the new translations of the stories by Théophile Gautier, Charles Baudelaire, Gérard de Nerval and Arthur Rimbaud which appear in Section II. Similarly to Lawrence Ferlinghetti in San Francisco, Terry Southern in New York and Alexander Trocchi in London for their help and advice in the compiling of this anthology. Finally, thanks are due to Mrs Philippa Haining for so carefully typing the manuscript and Dan Franklin at Peter Owen for his painstaking editing of the work.

If you have formed a Circle
to go into
Go into it yourself and see
how you would do.

WILLIAM BLAKE

*

Laudanum: from *laudare,* to praise, this drug being one of the most praiseworthy.

Dr William Cullen
(1710-1790)

Hashish reveals deeps of rapture and experience which natural faculties could never sound.

Bayard Taylor
(1825-1878)

Preface
BRIAN W. ALDISS

Just as we sometimes become aware that we are in a gathering of people which consists, in effect, of few who are perceptually alive; just as we sometimes become aware—and this is the beginning of love—that we are in the presence of somebody whose thought and body can immensely enrich our own; so we sometimes wish for an awareness that transcends our own limited consciousness. The present becomes our prison. We have to escape, even if that escape means moving deeper into our selves.

Means of escape are legion; life hath ten thousand several doors for men to take their exits, as Webster almost said. This anthology concerns one particular exit: that baroque, mysterious doorway marked Drugs; and some particular people: those baroque, mysterious writers who have chosen to make their way through it, from Samuel Taylor Coleridge to William Burroughs.

For every writer who allies himself with a drug—for every Wilkie Collins quaffing down laudanum by the tumblerful, for every Anna Kavan on snow for thirty-five years—there are many whom the alliance destroys. Writers probably have a better survival rate than other people, since they have their writing and the objectivity it requires to keep them on an even keel. Given an element of self-destruction in their natures, they utilize the drug to present some *outré* vision of the world—a vision which ordinary mortals without the fold are prompt to recognize as one more immensely convincing version of the truth.

And why not? For a third of every day of our lives, we are out of our minds, convinced utterly by the thousand charades of sleep in which logic, time, our very selves, undergo distortions or annihilations which must make any surrealist grit his teeth with envy. Modern theories, such as those advanced by Dr Christopher Evans, suggest that our dreams may be the brain's efforts to order the events of the day, as it comes off-line like a computer after a particular programme. I believe that, further, these witty distortions of thought-power are very much the cicatrices left by man's evolution from the animal, which will heal in a few million years, as we become fully human. If this is so, then what Sir Thomas Browne called 'the famous Nations of the dead' all dreamed more richly than we. Perhaps the present-day interest in the use of drugs can be accounted for by our trying to compensate for this unacknowledged loss at a time when evolution may be making one of its gear-shifts within us.

However that may be, drugs, as Mr Haining points out in his Introduction, are as old as mankind itself. Which is to say (if guessing is not cheating) that drug-induced states were there at the birth of religion, art, and science, all of which spring from the same creative impulse.

Of course, a book entitled 'The Hashish Club' has a great deal more romantic appeal than one entitled 'The Whisky Club', although we recognize that alcohol, tobacco, aspirin and so on are merely socially acceptable drugs. As we can control, at least to some degree, the effects of alcohol, so with other drugs: LSD in particular is an accomplice, a symbiote, not an assassin. It seems that the brain on occasions secretes its own psychedelic chemicals, as an aid to perception.

Certain so-called psychotic states are known to be the result of such internal dosages. Recent research indicates that schizophrenics suffer a much lower incidence of cancer than the rest of the population; what are they secreting? Or could it be that cancers originally developed to cure man's schizophrenic state? As these stories remind us, there is much we do well to be unsure about.

The stories work at doing directly what all forms of fiction do less directly: they allow the reader a freedom in charades in which logic, time, his very self, undergoes a distortion or annihilation which otherwise he experiences only in sleep. Just to take the time element—the fall of the House of Atreus can be played out before us in a single evening, or the Fall of the House of Usher in a single hour; or, on the other hand, James Joyce's Bloom enjoys a Dublin day which may take us a week to travel. In the cinema or on TV, we can see the triumph and destruction of the Third Reich whilst smoking a couple of cigars. This element of time-distortion in art is one of its great unconscious attractions for us. In our art galleries, we find moments and scenes frozen for ever, much as

> The sweet, sad years, the melancholy years,
> Those of my own life,

as one opium eater expressed it, become embalmed in our memory.

When Aldous Huxley first took mescaline, one morning in the spring of 1953, he found himself in 'a timeless bliss of seeing'. Experiencing a complete indifference to time, he says this: 'I could, of course, have looked at my watch; but my watch, I knew, was in another universe. My actual experience had been, was still, of an indefinite duration or alternatively of a perceptual present made up of one continually changing apocalypse'.

The time factor was banished. Could this be, I wonder, the predominant reason why we turn to drugs, that they lend us an illusory immortality?

If the clock in the mind is stilled which first started when man, alone among living things, discovered death, then other faculties awake, chief among which seems to be the visual sense. (Even beer can bring its hallucinations!)

'This is how one ought to see, how things really are,' exclaims Huxley from his trance. It is the cry of artists everywhere, seeking to convince their fellow men and women of the wonder of the world, of the lies of mundane life. Always at the basis of the cry lies an implicit condemnation of the way in which the world moves too fast. We must, says the artist, stop and stare, stop and dream, or stop and drowse.

Proust, speaking of Gérard de Nerval, who is represented in this volume, refers to the way in which one's life may be compressed into the few minutes before sleeping. Of these hypnoid visions, Proust says 'Sometimes in the moment of falling asleep we see them, and try to seize and define them. Then we wake up and they are gone, we give up the pursuit, and before we can be sure of their nature we are asleep again as though the sight of them were forbidden to the waking mind. The inhabitants of these pictures are themselves the stuff of dreams.'

And he goes on to quote from a poem of Nerval's:

> Puis une dame, à sa haute fenêtre,
> Blonde aux yeux noirs, en ses habits anciens . . .
> Que, dans une autre existence peut-être,
> J'ai déjà vue—et dont je me souviens!

There are many women, many life-styles, which would suit us; ordinary waking life defeats them.

To conclude on a note of speculation. Drugs, by abolishing that enervating sense of time from our minds, can give us the chance to touch on impossible things, as these stories show; we can move into the past, the future, or, as Nerval says, into other existences.

A research group in the Maryland Psychiatric Research Centre in the United States has recently discovered that LSD can help people who are dying, particularly those who have an extreme fear of death. For some of these patients, the LSD trip proves extremely horrifying; but the importance of the experience lies with how a patient integrates it with his previous life-experiences. In effect, he receives a lesson in how to die (Huxley needed no such lesson, although he went out on a tide of LSD).

The brain under LSD is in some respects—for instance, as regards oxygenation—under similar circumstances to the brain approaching death. So the trip represents a physical as well as a spiritual lesson.

These stories also come from undiscovered territories within the mind. I wonder if, in throwing up their distorted and magnified images of life, they are not also bringing us word from the lurid worlds of death.

Heath House B.W.A.
Southmoor
England

December 1973

Introduction

Man's desires are limited by his perceptions.
None can desire what he has not perceived.

WILLIAM BLAKE

Mankind's use of certain drugs as a stimulant to artistic creativity is a tradition almost as ancient as man himself. Records of the oldest civilizations indicate that stimulants which took the user 'out of himself' and created new fields of experience in his mind were much valued, and some of the earliest art and literature bear strong traces of these effects. In classical literature, for instance, one has only to turn to Homer to discover his story of Helen and her use of 'nepenthe' (a form of opium) to overcome grief, while Virgil gives the subject an interesting examination in the *Aeneid*. These are but two instances of a tradition which, as we shall see, has endured right to the present day.

Opium and hashish, the two drugs which primarily concern us in this first volume, are of considerable antiquity. The opium poppy, so legend has it, first grew in Egypt and Asia Minor, and was one of the very earliest standbys used by doctors to overcome pain. The Greeks knew of the plant, too, and in conjunction with the Arabs were responsible for its spread through Persia, India, China and even further afield. The Crusaders were the first to bring the plant to Europe and with them came tales of its use as a 'wonder substance' which could cure all ills, fortify soldiers against despair and fatigue, and—most important of all—induce a state of euphoria and pleasant well-being.

Through the Middle Ages we find frequent mention in the records of the use of both drugs, sometimes in the most bizarre circumstances. The witches of Europe, for instance, who were credited with the ability to fly, in fact used preparations of these drugs in the ointments and unguents with which they anointed themselves before going to the infamous 'Sabbats'. Despite the firmly-held conviction of both the witches themselves and those who went in fear of them that they could fly, they often did not even leave their beds, where the stimulating effects of the drug-laden aromas rising from their bodies 'carried' them off on wild flights of fancy. Chaucer, like his literary predecessors in Greece, knew of this drug usage and records it in several of his tales, while 200 years later Shakespeare put a similar reference into the mouth of Iago when he talks of 'poppy, mandragora and all the drowsy syrups of the world'.

However, it is not really the use of drugs—an established phenomenon that has been more than fully covered in other scholarly works—which concerns us here, but their use specifically as a stimulant to creativity and the results thereof. Nor are we concerned with the entire span of history, but rather with the 'modern' phase which began some 150 years ago and for which accurate records on both the users and their social climates exist in substantial enough detail to make objective study and suitably illustrative examples of their work readily available for a modern audience.

Although records indicate earlier literary users of drugs, it is not until the eighteenth century that anything like a continuous pattern begins to emerge. The man credited with being the first known *English* opium addict-writer—and an English example is selected purely because it happens to be the nationality of the editor—is Thomas Shadwell (1642-1692), the playwright and dramatist. Today Shadwell's work is almost completely unknown and he only really lives on in memory through being characterized in Dryden's famous *Absalom and Achitophel.* Daniel Defoe also knew of opium and may well have taken it himself. In *Robinson Crusoe,* published in 1719, he has his renowned hero take opium from the straits to China, but cautiously refrains from any detailed mention of its use. After this we progress almost naturally to the grandiloquent era of the 'Romantic Poets' where we find a widespread development of drug usage and the awakening of interest in why and how drug stimulation can affect a writer's work. By the beginning of the nineteenth century experience with drugs was to produce the significant works which form the starting point of this collection—the poems of Samuel Coleridge, the 'Confessions' of Thomas De Quincey, and the experiments of the French 'hashish eaters'.

On examining the social climates in which these men took drugs, it is interesting to note how laudanum (a liquid derivative of opium), opium itself, and hashish, were so readily available. They were considerably cheaper than other stimulants such as beer, gin and tobacco, and could be purchased from any chemist or pharmacist. Indeed, doctors frequently prescribed them for all manner of illnesses and many a contemporary writer informs us of how even children from the cradle were coddled or cured with potions heavily laced with opium and its derivatives! (Some patent medicines available today still contain extracts of opium and morphine in liquid form and hallucinogenic substances in tablets.) Horace Walpole, who had frequently seen the use of opium among the young and old, referred to it in his diary in the closing years of his life. 'The taking of opium is much spread through the country,' he wrote. 'I believe it will continue so as many now seek to be in its particular spirits throughout their days.' Specific examples of this practice could be found almost anywhere in the country. Take, for instance, East Anglia, where I spend much of the year. Here old people can still remember their grandparents referring to folk who bought 'a pennyworth o' elevation' from the chemist on market day—'a pennyworth' being a bottle of laudanum big enough to last one until the next market day came around! Use of drugs, then, was a pursuit of all classes, though only the better-off and the educated could actually record their experiences—but what they underwent personally and what they knew was happening to others was clearly reflected in their work.

Although, as I have indicated, this anthology of drug-inspired literature begins with Samuel Coleridge, it was in fact Thomas De Quincey who made the general public *as a whole* aware of both the pleasures and the pains of drug usage, and indicated to scientists and philosophers that this was an area of human experience which required detailed study to determine all the effects of these ancient 'balms of the gods'. The statements he made and the questions he posed have remained with us, in the main unsolved but mostly more clearly defined, to this day.

In the collection which you are about to read—presented in two volumes—I have drawn together those writers I consider most significant and revealing in a time span that divides neatly into two periods, each of four sections. Each writer is represented by such biographical details as I believe to be necessary to an understanding of his work, and by short stories or essays written either directly under the influence of drugs or drawn vividly from drug experiences at some period shortly thereafter. They all reflect what Alethea Hayter has called the author's 'restless mental curiosity about strange and novel mental experiences'. (*Opium and the Romantic Imagination*, 1968.)

The collection is not, let me add immediately, an attempt to justify or to condemn the use of drugs for creativity or any other experience. It was conceived and has been executed as simply the compilation of a series of 'bizarre and fantastic fragments' from the imagination of writers of accredited distinction which I hope will throw new light on them and their work. Needless to say the majority of the items here are of considerable rarity, and a few have been altogether unobtainable for years. I believe, too, that all underline the one constant fact that has reappeared time and time again during my research into drug-inspired literature: that only interesting minds can produce interesting experiences under stimulation—a dull mind is only made duller still.

Of course, a collection such as this cannot hope to be anything like exhaustive nor to cover the world scene as fully as it might. There are many other writers mentioned only in passing or in footnotes (the quotes that introduce each section, for instance, are all by people with profound knowledge of drugs who might well have been included), but repetition had to be avoided and the breadth of the period covered allowed only for the most significant writers of each generation. One should perhaps record, just to underline the continuing tradition, that places could have been found here for such writers as Lamb, Shelley, Southey and Byron, who took the opium derivative 'Black Drop'; that Sir Walter Scott wrote *The Bride of Lammermor* while taking 200 drops of laudanum a day to sustain him; and that both Charlotte Brontë and Elizabeth Barrett Browning wrote of drugs and had more than a passing knowledge of them. (Strangely there is little evidence of drug usage by women writers. Apart from the two ladies mentioned above, Mary Shelley — who indulged lightly with Shelley in Switzerland — and Anna Kavan, who died in 1968, few others of any distinction are on record.)

The reader will find that the drugs which have inspired these stories and their authors fall neatly into three categories, and are what are usually classified as the 'soft drugs'. The first group consists of the users of opium and its derivatives (the main one being laudanum, a solution of opium in alcohol which looks reddish-brown according to its consistency); the second is made up of the hashish eaters and smokers (cannabis, marijuana, *kif*, grass and pot being just a few of its many names); the third comprises writers using the hallucinogens (including the 'psychedelic' drugs such as mescaline, peyote, LSD etc.). I have made no attempt to go further and include work resulting from the use of the 'hard drugs' such as heroin and cocaine, as in the main it is of such a specialized nature as to need far more explanation than I have space available and also because I personally have found it uninspired and of only minor literary value.

The circumstances under which the authors came to indulge in drugs and the creative use to which they put these experiences are covered in appropriate detail before each item. Some of the men — George Crabbe, the poet, is a typical example — kept writing-materials close at hand so that when they awoke from their sleep or reverie, they immediately committed their 'dream impressions' to paper in diary, fictional or poetic form; others actually wrote while the drug was still coursing through their minds, like De Quincey and Poe. What they experienced varied according to the drug taken, of course, and also according to the personality, expectations and environment of the drug-taker. It is not possible to define exact differences in effect between the drugs used by the writers in this collection, as the four favourites — cannabis, opium and LSD or mescaline — could be said to affect the user in similar ways, although varying greatly in the strength of the effect achieved. Cannabis could be said to be the mildest in effect, and LSD or mescaline the strongest. All four drugs enable the user to concentrate on minute details and all of them have an effect on his experience of the time-space continuum. The hallucinogens have the power to create a multi-dimensional consciousness which almost literally takes man 'beyond his body'.

Perhaps a word of explanation is also needed about the title of this book. 'The Hashish Club' was the name given to the group of French writers and artists who first banded together in the years just before the Second Republic to experiment with, and record their experiences of, hashish. However, it seemed to me throughout my work on the collection that there was a kind of *camaraderie* about all the men I encountered, whatever their nationality. All were united in a search for new forms of expression and enlightenment — despite the different ages they lived in and their varying degrees of success and failure — and so I felt there was no more suitable sobriquet for them all than 'The Hashish Club'. That I had made a wise choice seemed to be emphasized still further when I came across the following comment by Alethea Hayter. Writing of Baudelaire, Gautier, Nerval and the other French *hachisch* eaters she says, 'There must have been a very great deal of talk about drugs —the assembled writers (and painters) comparing their symptoms under hashish or opium, and speculating on how their imagination and the writer's art might be stimulated or betrayed by drugs.' That, in effect, is what I have tried to recreate in the pages which follow.

In Morocco, where I came to complete this book, one can find perhaps the clearest visible indication of the continuing tradition of drug usage for new experience. (Until recently this might have been true of Turkey and Nepal, but earlier this summer the respective governments placed a ban on the cultivation of hashish and opium, effectively ending the appeal of these places to users and in particular the 'hippie' communities who had settled there.)

In North Africa the people use drugs — hashish and opium in particular — as they have done for centuries and many of the old storytellers still to be found surrounded by their enraptured audiences in the Berber markets of the Rif mountains or in the back streets of the *medinas* and *casbahs* of Tangier, Casablanca, Marrakesh and Fez, embellish their tales with accounts of drug experience. This is hardly surprising, for is there not an old legend which records how the patron saint of *kif*, Sidi Hidi, first brought the seeds of the hemp plant to North Africa from Asia in those dim days of the past? And how, from him, it was to spread by various routes throughout all the world so that today pilgrims journey from many countries to pay homage at his ancient tomb? It is said, too, that the hashish grown in certain high regions is the best to be found anywhere in the world.

Tangier, more than any of the other cities, probably best symbolizes the old and the new and is certainly still 'the city of madness and illusion' referred to by St Francis of Assisi in the thirteenth century. In this former free port (it became part of Morocco in 1960), both the native Moroccans and the large European and American communities use *kif* openly (although it is supposed to be illegal) and the white, hard sunlight seems to create architectural visions from the ramshackle peasant shanties that are constantly permeated by the sweet-smelling haze of the smoke from the pipe. Because of its high quality, the Moroccans use the drug as a powerful and rapidly acting stimulant for their daily work, while the foreign residents employ it to 'widen their experience'. Some of the most famous modern drug users have stayed in Tangier at one time or another and people still remember William Burroughs who lived here for nearly eight years and was nick-named by the Spaniards 'El Hombre Invisible'. Now Paul Bowles is the major author-in-residence and his observations of the drug and its usage are as keen and illuminating as those of any of his predecessors.

While it is certainly possible to debate and experience all the issues of drug stimulation far more easily in North Africa, the question has become one of international interest. Dr Daniel Freedman, Professor of Psychiatry at the University of Chicago, has already declared that we are living in the 'great stoned age', and that the government of drugs will eventually depend on how we wish to manage them. 'Drug use,' he says, 'impinges on the management of pain and pleasure.' An English colleague, Dr Thomas Beverley, has added weight to this argument by stating that when deciding on the dangers of drugs, it is important to remember that it is not the drug, but the way it is used by particular groups that makes the problem.

But, as I stated earlier, this book is not the place for a debate of this topic; it is merely a presentation of those famous writers who have experienced drug sensations and recorded their emotions in short story or essay form. To me their work points to an exploration of another dimension of the human soul, that topic so dear to us all, and summarized so appositely by Oscar Wilde: 'We have merely touched the surface of the soul, that is all. In one single ivory cell of the brain there are stored away things more marvellous and more terrible than ever we have dreamed of, or those who have sought to track the soul into its most secret places, and to make life confess its dearest sins.'

Tangier   PETER HAINING
August 1973

I

Soon as the real World I lose,
Quick Fancy takes her wonted way,
Or Baxter's sprites my soul abuse —
For how it is I cannot say,
I feel such bliss, I fear such pain;
But all is gloom, or all is gay,
Soon as the ideal World I gain.

GEORGE CRABBE
(1754-1832)

Records show that widespread addiction to laudanum, the liquid derivative of opium, was first noted in Britain during the eighteenth century. The great upsurge in its use had undoubtedly been brought about by the Industrial Revolution : by unscrupulous factory owners and employers to keep their workers going for inordinately long hours in wretched conditions; and by parents to tranquillize their children while they were at their jobs. It was perhaps most prevalent in the north; writing to a friend at the turn of the century, Samuel Coleridge remarked: 'Throughout Lancashire and Yorkshire it is the common Dram of the lower orders of people — in the small town of Thorpe the druggist informed me that he commonly sold on market days two or three pounds of Opium and a gallon of Laudanum — all among the labouring classes.' The use of opium began in the cradle and many of the popular cordials for illness and anxiety for children had a strong opium base — 'Mother Bailey's Quieting Syrup' being one of the most widely used and most powerful. As the child grew to man, he turned to 'Dr Bate's Pacific Pill' or 'Venice Treacle' which were more toxic still, and while they may have had very little effect on the particular complaint they were supposed to be curing, certainly they blanketed the pain for a time and gave a feeling of elation. But the use of laudanum and opium was not restricted to the poor; people in all walks of life used it freely, and the diaries of the rich and famous are dotted with references to its employment against gout, upset stomachs, toothache, piles and the hundred and one other complaints of the time for which none of the simple cures of today were available. Both drugs were easy to obtain and cheap to buy, and doctors were quick to prescribe them, being unaware of any after-effects. It was De Quincey's 'Confessions' which first highlighted the real 'pleasures and pains' of the drugs. In America the picture was much the same, although one doctor who warned the populace in 1790 that over-use of laudanum on children 'would soothe many a luckless infant into a state of quiet that knows no after disturbing' was literally regarded as a crank ! In the big industrial cities of New York, Chicago, and Pittsburgh both forms of the drug were in plentiful supply and there was hardly a man or woman who had not had frequent recourse to the famous 'Mrs Winslow's Soothing Syrup' with its strong content of Morphine Sulphate. On both sides of the Atlantic, then, opium and laudanum were as much a part of daily life as beer and cigarettes are today; it was to take the work of several distinguished writers who progressed from being mere imbibers to actual addicts to make the public as a whole aware that there was another side to the coin.

I

The story of literature inspired and influenced by the taking of drugs begins, in modern times, with the work of *Samuel Taylor Coleridge* (1772-1834). Although some might feel his contribution to be less than that of his younger contemporary, Thomas De Quincey, this may be because Coleridge, the poet, has enjoyed an enduring and international fame in which his life perhaps plays a less important role than his work, whereas the reverse is true of De Quincey. The youngest of fourteen children of a comfortably-off Devonshire vicar, Coleridge was a lonely child, much taken to 'dreaming' and temperamentally unsuited to discipline, which made his education at Christ's Hospital, London and Jesus College, Cambridge as frustrating to him as it was to his tutors who realized his great promise. At university his life-style fell into the pattern of the young 'rebel'; as well as beginning to write poetry, he became interested in politics and also took opium for the first time — ostensibly for rheumatic pains.

Coming down from Cambridge in 1794 without a degree, he became friendly with the equally radical young poet, Robert Southey, and both men began to plan a 'pantisocracy' or literary-agrarian settlement which was to be established in America. As part of his plans, Coleridge made an unsuitable marriage and when the scheme foundered he was left with a wife he did not want and restrictions on his freedom. Writing, both journalism and poetry, now dominated his days, while at night he began to resort more frequently to opium. In March 1795, he confessed to a friend that 'I have been obliged to take laudanum almost every night', and in November of the following year he told the same man 'I am now taking twenty-five drops of laudanum every five hours'. Certainly, Coleridge was using the drug mainly to combat the physical pains he was undergoing, but in a letter to his brother, George, he confessed that it had attractions for him too, adding: 'Opium has never had any disagreeable effects on me'. At this time he had become friendly with William Wordsworth, settled near him in the Lake District, and together the two poets literally revolutionized English verse with their work.

For a few short months this was the pinnacle of Coleridge's life, but even as he worked, the opium which had earlier sustained him began to become more and more of a necessity. By 1800 he was 'indulging' himself far above the normal — and not only with opium. A cryptic letter to an intimate acquaintance at this period reads, almost amusingly, 'Last night I received a four ounce parcel letter by post. ... On opening it, it contained my letter from Gunville, and a parcel, a small one, of *Bang* [hashish] from Purkis.... We will have a fair trial of *Bang* — do bring down some of the Hyosycamine Pills, and I will give a fair trial of Hensbane and Nepenthe, too.' By 1802 he had finally become aware of the extent of his addiction. His poem 'Ode to Dejection' (1802) clearly mirrors his feelings of failure, and however much he reproached himself, he felt unable to stop his drug use. His subsequent struggles and attempts to match the inspiration of earlier works such as 'Christabel' and 'Kubla Khan' have already been so fully discussed as to need no further mention here. Suffice it to say that in 1816 his mental and physical health was so poor that he needed to seek medical advice and thereafter was under treatment by a Dr Gillman for the rest of his life. Even he could not save the poet, however, for Coleridge was still secretly obtaining the drug by deception and trickery—a fact he admitted in several now-famous letters to friends. Throughout his life, the poet remained a great dreamer, and his notebooks contain scores of references to his dreams, carefully documented. A great many of these were obviously influenced by opium and provided the source material for some of his best poems, including the magnificent 'Pains of Sleep' (1803). The last phase of his life did see him working on literary and politico-sociological criticism and much of this writing was of the highest standard, showing him as an important member of the group of nineteenth-century writers who reacted against current religious and authoritarian standards. To represent Coleridge—and thereby begin this anthology—I have selected one of his very few 'prose poems'. It is a legendary fantasy written in 1798, which, as several authorities have pointed out, clearly shows the influence of an opium 'vision' and reflects the poet's own attitudes towards laudanum—the drug which, he once wrote, enabled him to 'sop the Cerberus'.

*

Laudanum gave me repose, not sleep; but you, I believe, know how divine that repose is, what a spot of enchantment, a green spot of fountain and flowers and trees in the very heart of a waste of sands!

Letter to George Coleridge, April 1798

The Wanderings of Cain
SAMUEL COLERIDGE

'A little further, O my father, yet a little further, and we shall come into the open moonlight.' Their road was through a forest of fir-trees; at its entrance the trees stood at distances from each other, and the path was broad, and the moonlight and the moonlight shadows reposed upon it, and appeared quietly to inhabit that solitude. But soon the path winded and became narrow; the sun at high noon sometimes speckled, but never illumined it, and now it was dark as a cavern.

'It is dark, O my father!' said Enos, 'but the path under our feet is smooth and soft, and we shall soon come out into the open moonlight.'

'Lead on, my child!' said Cain; 'guide me, little child!' And the innocent little child clasped a finger on the hand which had murdered the righteous Abel, and he guided his father. 'The fir branches drip upon thee, my son.' 'Yea, pleasantly, father, for I ran fast and eagerly to bring thee the pitcher and the cake, and my body is not yet cool. How happy the squirrels are that feed on these fir-trees! they leap from bough to bough, and the old squirrels play round their young ones in the nest. I clomb a tree yesterday at noon, O my father, that I might play with them, but they leapt away from the branches, even to the slender twigs did they leap, and in a moment I beheld them on another tree. Why, O my father, would they not play with me? I would be good to them as thou art good to me: and I groaned to them even as thou groanest when thou givest me to eat, and when thou coverest me at evening, and as often as I stand at thy knee and thine eyes look at me?' Then Cain stopped, and stifling his groans he sank to the earth, and the child Enos stood in the darkness beside him.

And Cain lifted up his voice and cried bitterly, and said, 'The Mighty One that persecuteth me is on this side and on that; he pursueth my soul like the wind, like the sand-blast he passeth through me; he is around me even as the air! O that I might be utterly no more! I desire to die—yea, the things that never had life, neither move they upon the earth—behold! they seem precious to mine eyes. O that a man might live without the breath of his nostrils. So I might abide in darkness, and blackness, and an empty space! Yea, I would lie down, I would not rise, neither would I stir my limbs till I became as the rock in the den of the lion, on which the young lion resteth his head whilst he sleepeth. For the torrent that roareth far off hath a voice: and the clouds in heaven look terribly on me; the Mighty One who is against me speaketh in the wind of the cedar grove; and in silence am I dried up.' Then Enos spake to his father, 'Arise, my father, arise, we are but a little way from the place where I found the cake and the pitcher.' And Cain said, 'How knowest thou!' and the child answered—'Behold the bare rocks are a few of thy strides distant from the forest; and while even now thou wert lifting up thy voice, I heard the echo.' Then the child took hold of his father, as if he would raise him: and Cain being faint and feeble rose slowly on his knees and pressed himself against the trunk of a fir, and stood upright and followed the child.

The path was dark till within three strides' length of its termination, when it turned suddenly; the thick black trees formed a low arch, and the moonlight appeared for a moment like a dazzling portal. Enos ran before and stood in the open air; and when Cain, his father, emerged from the darkness, the child was affrighted. For the mighty limbs of Cain were wasted as by fire; his hair was as the matted curls on the bison's forehead, and so glared his fierce and sullen eye beneath: and the black abundant locks on either side, a rank and tangled mass, were stained and scorched, as though the grasp of a burning iron hand had striven to rend them; and his countenance told in a strange and terrible language of agonies that had been, and were, and were still to continue to be.

The scene around was desolate; as far as the eye could reach it was desolate: the bare rocks faced each other, and left a long and wide interval of thin white sand. You might wander on and look round and round, and peep into the crevices of the rocks and discover nothing that acknowledged the influence of the seasons. There was no spring, no summer, no autumn: and the winter's snow, that would have been lovely, fell not on these hot rocks and scorching sands. Never morning lark had poised himself over this desert; but the huge serpent often hissed there beneath the talons of the vulture, and the vulture screamed, his wings imprisoned within the coils of the serpent. The pointed and shattered summits of the ridges of the rocks made a rude mimicry of human concerns, and seemed to prophecy mutely of things that then were not; steeples, and battlements, and ships with naked masts. As far from the wood as a boy might sling a pebble of the brook, there was one rock by itself at a small distance from the main ridge. It had been precipitated there perhaps by the groan which the Earth uttered when our first father fell. Before you approached, it appeared to lie flat on the ground, but its base slanted from its point, and between its point and the sands a tall man might stand upright. It was here that Enos had found the pitcher and cake, and to this place he led his father. But ere they had reached the rock they beheld a human shape: his back was towards them, and they were advancing unperceived, when they heard him smite his breast and cry aloud, 'Woe is me! woe is me! I must never die again, and yet I am perishing with thirst and hunger.'

Pallid, as the reflection of the sheeted lightning on the heavy-sailing night-cloud, became the face of Cain; but the child Enos took hold of the shaggy skin, his father's robe, and raised his eyes to his father, and listening whispered, 'Ere yet I could speak, I am sure, O my father, that I heard that voice. Have not I often said that I remembered a sweet voice? O my father! this is it': and Cain trembled exceedingly. The voice was sweet indeed, but it was thin and querulous, like that of a feeble slave in misery, who despairs altogether, yet can not refrain himself from weeping and lamentation. And, behold! Enos glided forward, and creeping softly round the base of the rock, stood before the stranger, and looked up into his face. And the Shape shrieked, and turned round, and Cain beheld him, that his limbs and his face were those of his brother Abel whom he had killed! And Cain stood like one who struggles in his sleep because of the exceeding terribleness of a dream.

Thus as he stood in silence and darkness of soul, the Shape fell at his feet, and embraced his knees, and cried out with a bitter outcry, 'Thou eldest born of Adam, whom Eve, my mother, brought forth, cease to torment me! I was feeding my flocks in green pastures by the side of quiet rivers, and thou killedst me; and now I am in misery.' Then Cain closed his eyes, and hid them with his hands; and again he opened his eyes, and looked around him, and said to Enos, 'What beholdest thou? Didst thou hear a voice, my son?' 'Yes, my father, I beheld a man in unclean garments, and he uttered a sweet voice, full of lamentation.' Then Cain raised up the Shape that was like Abel, and said:—'The Creator of our father, who had respect unto thee, and unto thy offering, wherefore hath he forsaken thee?' Then the Shape shrieked a second time, and rent his garment, and his naked skin was like the white sands beneath their feet; and he shrieked yet a third time, and threw himself on his face upon the sand that was black with the shadow of the rock, and Cain and Enos sat beside him; the child by his right hand, and Cain by his left. They were all three under the rock, and within the shadow. The Shape that was like Abel raised himself up, and spake to the child, 'I know where the cold waters are, but I may not drink, wherefore didst thou then take away my pitcher?' But Cain said, 'Didst thou not find favour in the sight of the Lord thy God?' The Shape answered, 'The Lord is God of the living only, the dead have another God.' Then the child Enos lifted up his eyes and prayed; but Cain rejoiced secretly in his heart. 'Wretched shall they be all the days of their mortal life,' exclaimed the Shape, 'who sacrifice worthy and acceptable sacrifices to the God of the dead; but after death their toil ceaseth. Woe is me, for I was well beloved by the God of the living, and cruel wert thou, O my brother, who didst snatch me away from his power and his dominion.' Having uttered these words, he rose suddenly, and fled over the sands: and Cain said in his heart, 'The curse of the Lord is on me; but who is the God of the dead?' and he ran after the Shape, and the Shape fled shrieking over the sands, and the sands rose like white mists behind the steps of Cain, but the feet of him that was like Abel disturbed not the sands. He greatly outrun Cain, and turning short, he wheeled round, and came again to the rock where they had been sitting, and where Enos still stood; and the child caught hold of his garment as he passed by, and he fell upon the ground. And Cain stopped, and beholding him not, said, 'he has passed into the dark woods,' and he walked slowly back to the rocks; and when he reached it the child told him that he had caught hold of his garment as he passed by, and that the man had fallen upon the ground: and Cain once more sate beside him, and said, 'Abel, my brother, I would lament for thee, but that the spirit within me is withered, and burnt up with extreme agony. Now, I pray thee, by thy flocks, and by thy pastures, and by the quiet rivers which thou lovedst, that thou tell me all that thou knowest. Who is the God of the dead? where doth he make his dwelling? what sacrifices are acceptable unto him? for I have offered, but have not been received; I have prayed, and have not been heard; and how can I be afflicted more than I already am?' The Shape arose and answered, 'O that thou hadst had pity on me as I will have pity on thee. Follow me, Son of Adam! and bring thy child with thee!'

And they three passed over the white sands between the rocks, silent as the shadows.

2

Thomas De Quincey (1785-1859) is without doubt the most famous of all literary addict-writers; and while we began this collection with Coleridge, De Quincey should perhaps more fittingly have preceded him as his work was really the forerunner and inspiration of the modern tradition. However, he was the younger of the two men (Coleridge always called him 'My dear young friend') and the poet's addiction had become public knowledge first. Like Coleridge, De Quincey came from a comfortable background—his father was a Manchester merchant—and similarly, though a good pupil, found the romantic appeal of rebellion too much to resist. He ran away from school in his early teens and wandered for several months in Wales before going to London where he rapidly became destitute and was only saved from starvation by a kindly prostitute. Admitting failure, De Quincey returned to Manchester and thereafter was sent to Oxford. Here, too, he led a solitary, friendless life, turning to opium for relief in 1804. Unknowingly he had found the motivating force of his life and work. Despite showing tremendous potential at Oxford, he grew dissatisfied again and left in 1808. One of the few friends he had made was Samuel Coleridge, whose work he greatly admired, and their joint interest in opium (Coleridge was by now a confirmed addict) was to prove the focal point of their discussions. While each accused the other of 'indulging' in drugs—a fact which only De Quincey would really accept—each man valued the other's opinion on his work. In a letter in 1808 Coleridge asked his young friend for his opinion on several poems as he felt De Quincey had experienced much the same emotions and 'your views will be valuable to me far more indeed than those criticisms in which the feeling is not stated'. In return, De Quincey was later to spend several years studying Coleridge's work and was to publish a series of essays on the poet after his death which remain to this day among the most sympathetic and authoritative.

De Quincey was at this time living in close proximity to Coleridge in the Lake District and had also become an intimate of the Wordsworth household. Another turning point in De Quincey's life seems to have occurred when he was at this house: he had become deeply fond of little Kate Wordsworth and when the child died suddenly in 1812 he was literally heart-broken. To relieve his despair he began to increase his dosage of opium and within three years was firmly addicted. Only the love of a neighbouring farmer's daughter, Margaret Simpson, sustained him and when she gave birth to a daughter in 1816, De Quincey decided to marry her. Urged by her to write, he drove himself—liberally aided by laudanum—to produce his masterwork, *The Confessions of an English Opium Eater,* which was published in two parts in *The London Magazine* in 1821. It was an immediate sensation and marked him as the first writer to study deliberately from his own experience the results and effects of taking opium. He believed its use could not only form the material for literature, but also play a part in its creation. Critics the world over were of the opinion that this was exactly what he had demonstrated with the book. Some ordinary readers were deeply impressed by the work, others were enraged. For instance, a group of American doctors dealing especially with opium addicts thought the book should be banned and the author's name 'consigned to oblivion'. De Quincey was furious at the assumption that the ills of these patients were his fault in any way, and replied in 1822: 'Teach opium-eating! Did I teach wine-drinking? Did I reveal the mystery of sleeping? No man is likely to adopt opium or lay it aside in consequence of anything he may read in a book!' Nonetheless, the influence of the 'Confessions' was far reaching, and De Quincey did come to see himself as the 'Pope of the Church of Opium'.

Although he was now firmly established as a writer, little but the few, short sequels to the 'Confessions' which he published were to have anything like its impact or durability. Nor was his struggle with opium to become any the less intense despite several attempts to reduce his enormous dosage. (At his peak, in 1813-16, he was taking between 10,000 to 12,000 drops per day—enough to kill several ordinary men!) His day-to-day life was also a shambles; haunted by debts and his inability to meet publishers' deadlines, his situation was further undermined by the death of his wife in 1837, leaving him six children —the youngest only four—to look after. He died, totally exhausted and an opium-eater to the end, in 1859. Of the short pieces which De Quincey wrote subsequent to the publication of the 'Confessions', all were inspired by his further 'discoveries' under the influence of opium, and we know from the author's own admission that there were more pieces which were either burnt by careless handling of candles or lost in the debris of his study when he was working under a particularly heavy dose of laudanum. Of the pieces that have survived, none is perhaps more suitable for our purpose than 'Dream Fugue', the third and final part of the novella, *The English Mail Coach.* Alethea

Hayter in her excellent study, *Opium and the Romantic Imagination,* has called the whole essay a 'prose poem patterned like music and incorporating all the main themes and images of his dreams, and among them the theme of opium itself, and his slavery to it and hope of restoration at the last'. Of the 'Dream Fugue' she adds succinctly that 'much of the mythology of opium dreams is in this frugal vision'.

*

I took it, and in an hour, Oh Heavens! what a revulsion! what an upheaving, from its lowest depths, of the inner spirit! what an apocalypse of the world within me. What had opened before me—an abyss of divine enjoyment suddenly revealed. Here was a panacea for all human woes. Here was the secret of happiness, about which philosophers had disputed for so many ages, at once discovered. Happiness might now be bought for a penny, and carried in the waistcoat pocket; portable ecstacies might be had, corked up in a pint-bottle, and peace of mind could be sent down in gallons by the mail-coach.

Essay, 1849

Dream Fugue
THOMAS DE QUINCEY

Passion of sudden death! that once in youth I read and interpreted by the shadows of thy averted signs![1]—rapture of panic taking the shape (which amongst tombs in churches I have seen) of woman bursting her sepulchral bonds—of woman's Ionic form bending forward from the ruins of her grave with arching foot, with eyes upraised, with clasped adoring hands—waiting, watching, trembling, praying for the trumpet's call to rise from dust for ever! Ah, vision too fearful of shuddering humanity on the brink of almighty abysses!—vision that didst start back, that didst reel away, like a shrivelling scroll from before the wrath of fire racing on the wings of the wind! Epilepsy so brief of horror, wherefore is it that thou canst not die?

[1] *'Averted signs'*: I read the course and changes of the lady's agony in the succession of her involuntary gestures; but it must be remembered that I read all this from the rear, never once catching the lady's full face, and even her profile imperfectly.

Passing so suddenly into darkness, wherefore is it that still thou sheddest thy sad funeral blights upon the gorgeous mosaics of dreams? Fragment of music too passionate, heard once, and heard no more, what aileth thee, that thy deep rolling chords come up at intervals, through all the worlds of sleep, and after forty years, have lost no element of horror?

I

Lo, it is summer—almighty summer! The everlasting gates of life and summer are thrown open wide; and on the ocean, tranquil and verdant as a savannah, the unknown lady from the dreadful vision and I myself are floating—she upon a fairy pinnace, and I upon an English three-decker. Both of us are wooing gales of festal happiness within the domain of our common country, within that ancient watery park, within that pathless chase of ocean, where England takes her pleasure as a huntress through winter and summer, from the rising to the setting sun. Ah, what a wilderness of floral beauty was hidden, or was suddenly revealed, upon the tropic islands through which the pinnace moved! And upon her deck what a bevy of human flowers—young women how lovely, young men how noble, that were dancing together, and slowly drifting towards *us* amidst music and incense, amidst blossoms from forests and gorgeous corymbi[2] from vintages, amidst natural carolling, and the echoes of sweet girlish laughter. Slowly the pinnace nears us, gaily she hails us, and silently she disappears beneath the shadow of our mighty bows. But then, as at some signal from heaven, the music, and the carols, and the sweet echoing of girlish laughter—all are hushed. What evil has smitten the pinnace, meeting or overtaking her? Did ruin to our friends couch within our own dreadful shadow? Was our shadow the shadow of death? I looked over the bow for an answer, and, behold! the pinnace was dismantled; the revel and the revellers were found no more; the glory of the vintage was dust; and the forests with their beauty were left without a witness upon the seas. 'But where,' and I turned to our crew—'where are the lovely women that danced beneath the awning of flowers and clustering corymbi? Whither have fled the noble young men that danced with *them*? Answer there was none. But suddenly the man at the mast-head, whose countenance darkened with alarm, cried out, 'Sail on the weather beam! Down she comes upon us: in seventy seconds she also will founder.'

---

[2] *Corymbus,* a cluster of fruit or flowers.

II

I looked to the weather side, and the summer had departed. The sea was rocking, and shaken with gathering wrath. Upon its surface sat mighty mists, which grouped themselves into arches and long cathedral aisles. Down one of these, with the fiery pace of a quarrel from a cross-bow,[3] ran a frigate right athwart our course. 'Are they mad?' some voice exclaimed from our deck. 'Do they woo their ruin?' But in a moment, as she was close upon us, some impulse of a heady current or local vortex gave a wheeling bias to her course, and off she forged without a shock. As she ran past us, high aloft amongst the shrouds stood the lady of the pinnace. The deeps opened ahead in malice to receive her, towering surges of foam ran after her, the billows were fierce to catch her. But far away she was borne into desert spaces of the sea: whilst still by sight I followed her, as she ran before the howling gale, chased by angry sea-birds and by maddening billows; still I saw her, as at the moment when she ran past us, standing amongst the shrouds, with her white draperies streaming before the wind. There she stood, with hair dishevelled, one hand clutched amongst the tackling—rising, sinking, fluttering, trembling, praying—there for leagues I saw her as she stood, raising at intervals one hand to heaven, amidst the fiery crests of the pursuing waves and the raving of the storm; until, at last, upon a sound from afar of malicious laughter and mockery, all was hidden for ever in driving showers; and afterwards, but when I know not, nor how.

III

Sweet funeral bells from some incalculable distance, wailing over the dead that die before the dawn, awakening me as I slept in a boat moored to some familiar shore. The morning twilight even then was breaking; and, by the dusky revelations which it spread, I saw a girl, adorned with a garland of white roses about her head for some great festival, running along the solitary strand in extremity of haste. Her running was the running of panic; and often she looked back as to some dreadful enemy in the rear. But when I leaped ashore, and followed on her steps to warn her of a peril in front, alas! from me she fled as from another peril, and vainly I shouted to her of quicksands that lay ahead. Faster and faster she ran; round a promontory of rocks she wheeled out of sight; in an instant I also wheeled round it, but only to see the treacherous sands gathering above her head. Already her person was buried; only the fair young head and the diadem of

---

[3] *Quarrel,* a cross-bow bolt, an arrow with a four-square head; connected with *quadratus,* made square.

white roses around it were still visible to the pitying heavens; and, last of all, was visible one white marble arm. I saw by the early twilight this fair young head, as it was sinking down to darkness—saw this marble arm, as it rose above her head and her treacherous grave, tossing, faltering, rising, clutching, as at some false deceiving hand stretched out from the clouds—saw this marble arm uttering her dying hope, and then uttering her dying despair. The head, the diadem, the arm—these all had sunk; at last over these also the cruel quicksand had closed; and no memorial of the fair young girl remained on earth, except my own solitary tears, and the funeral bells from the desert seas, that, rising again more softly, sang a requiem over the grave of the buried child, and over her blighted dawn.

I sat, and wept in secret the tears that men have ever given to the memory of those that died before the dawn, and by the treachery of earth, our mother. But suddenly the tears and funeral bells were hushed by a shout as of many nations, and by a roar as from some great king's artillery, advancing rapidly along the valleys, and heard afar by echoes from the mountains. 'Hush!' I said, as I bent my ear earthwards to listen—'hush!—this either is the very anarchy of strife, or else'—and then I listened more profoundly, and whispered as I raised my head—'or else, oh heavens! it is *victory* that is final, victory that swallows up all strife.'

IV

Immediately, in trance, I was carried over land and sea to some distant kingdom, and placed upon a triumphal car, amongst companions crowned with laurel. The darkness of gathering midnight, brooding over all the land, hid from us the mighty crowds that were weaving restlessly about ourselves as a centre: we heard them, but saw them not. Tidings had arrived, within an hour, of a grandeur that measured itself against centuries; too full of pathos they were, too full of joy, to utter themselves by other language than by tears, by restless anthems, and *Te Deums* reverberated from the choirs and orchestras of earth. These tidings we that sat upon the laurelled car had it for our privilege to publish amongst all nations. And already, by signs audible through the darkness, by snortings and tramplings, our angry horses, that knew no fear of fleshly weariness, upbraided us with delay. Wherefore *was* it that we delayed? We waited for a secret word, that should bear witness to the hope of nations, as now accomplished for ever. At midnight the secret word arrived; which word was—Waterloo and Recovered Christendom! The dreadful word shone by its own light; before us it went; high above our leaders' heads it rode, and spread a golden light over the paths which we traversed.

Every city, at the presence of the secret word, threw open its gates. The rivers were conscious as we crossed. All the forests, as we ran along margins, shivered in homage to the secret word. And the darkness comprehended it.

Two hours after midnight we approached a mighty Minster. Its gates, which rose to the clouds, were closed. But when the dreadful word, that rode before us, reached them with its golden light, silently they moved back upon their hinges; and at a flying gallop our equipage entered the grand aisle of the cathedral. Headlong was our pace; and at every altar, in the little chapels and oratories to the right hand and left of our course, the lamps, dying or sickening, kindled anew in sympathy with the secret word that was flying past. Forty leagues we might have run in the cathedral, and as yet no strength of morning light had reached us, when before us we saw the aerial galleries of organ and choir. Every pinnacle of the fretwork, every station of advantage amongst the traceries, was crested by white-robed choristers, that sang deliverance; that wept no more tears, as once their fathers had wept; but at intervals that sang together to the generations, saying,

'Chant the deliverer's praise in every tongue,'

and receiving answers from afar,

'Such as once in heaven and earth were sung.'

And of their chanting was no end; of our headlong pace was neither pause nor slackening.

Thus, as we ran like torrents—thus, as we swept with bridal rapture over the Campo Santo[4] of the cathedral graves—suddenly we became aware of a vast necropolis rising upon the far-off horizon—a city of sepulchres, built within the saintly cathedral for the warrior dead that rested from their feuds on earth. Of purple granite was the necropolis; yet, in the first minute, it lay like a purple stain upon the horizon, so mighty was the distance. In the second minute it trembled through many changes, growing into terraces and towers of wondrous

---

[4] *'Campo Santo'*: It is probable that most of my readers will be aquainted with the history of the Campo Santo (or cemetery) at Pisa, composed of earth brought from Jerusalem from a bed of sanctity, as the highest prize which the noble piety of crusaders could ask or imagine. To readers who are unacquainted with England, or who (being English) are yet unacquainted with the cathedral cities of England, it may be right to mention that the graves within-side the cathedrals often form a flat pavement over which carriages and horses *might* run; and perhaps a boyish remembrance of one particular cathedral, across which I had seen passengers walk and burdens carried, as about two centuries back they were through the middle of St Paul's in London, may have assisted my dream.

altitude, so mighty was the pace. In the third minute already, with our dreadful gallop, we were entering its suburbs. Vast sarcophagi rose on every side, having towers and turrets that, upon the limits of the central aisle, strode forward with haughty intrusion, that ran back with mighty shadows into answering recesses. Every sarcophagus showed many bas-reliefs—bas-reliefs of battles and of battle-fields; battles from forgotten ages—battles from yesterday—battle-fields that, long since, nature had healed and reconciled to herself with the sweet oblivion of flowers—battle-fields that were yet angry and crimson with carnage. Where the terraces ran, there did *we* run; where the towers curved, there did *we* curve. With the flight of swallows our horses swept round every angle. Like rivers in flood, wheeling round headlands—like hurricanes that ride into the secrets of forests—faster than ever light unwove the mazes of darkness, our flying equipage carried earthly passions, kindled warrior instincts, amongst the dust that lay around us—dust oftentimes of our noble fathers that had slept in God from Créci to Trafalgar. And now had we reached the last sarcophagus, now were we abreast of the last bas-relief, already had we recovered the arrow-like flight of the illimitable central aisle, when coming up this aisle to meet us we beheld afar off a female child, that rode in a carriage as frail as flowers. The mists, which went before her, hid the fawns that drew her, but could not hide the shells and tropic flowers with which she played—but could not hide the lovely smiles by which she uttered her trust in the mighty cathedral, and in the cherubim that looked down upon her from the mighty shafts of its pillars. Face to face she was meeting us; face to face she rode, as if danger there were none. 'Oh, baby!' I exclaimed, 'shalt thou be the ransom for Waterloo? Must we, that carry tidings of great joy to every people, be messengers of ruin to thee!' In horror I rose at the thought; but then also, in horror at the thought, rose one that was sculptured on a bas-relief—A Dying Trumpeter. Solemnly from the field of battle he rose to his feet; and, unslinging his stony trumpet, carried it, in his dying anguish, to his stony lips—sounding once, and yet once again; proclamation that, in *thy* ears, oh baby! spoke from the battlements of death. Immediately deep shadows fell between us, and aboriginal silence. The choir had ceased to sing. The hoofs of our horses, the dreadful rattle of our harness, the groaning of our wheels, alarmed the graves no more. By horror the bas-relief had been unlocked unto life. By horror we, that were so full of life, we men and our horses, with their fiery fore-legs rising in mid air to their everlasting gallop, were frozen to a bas-relief. Then a third time the trumpet sounded; the seals were taken off all pulses; life, and the frenzy of life, tore into their channels again; again the choir burst forth in sunny grandeur, as from the muffling of storms and darkness;

again the thunderings of our horses carried temptation into the graves. One cry burst from our lips, as the clouds, drawing off from the aisle, showed it empty before us—'Wither has the infant fled?—is the young child caught up to God?' Lo! afar off, in a vast recess, rose three mighty windows to the clouds; and on a level with their summits, at height insuperable to man, rose an altar of purest alabaster. On its eastern face was trembling a crimson glory. A glory was it from the reddening dawn that now streamed *through* the windows? Was it from the crimson robes of the martyrs painted *on* the windows? Was it from the bloody bas-reliefs of earth? There, suddenly, within that crimson radiance, rose the apparition of a woman's head, and then of a woman's figure. The child it was—grown up to woman's height. Clinging to the horns of the altar, voiceless she stood —sinking, rising, raving, despairing; and behind the volume of incense, that, night and day, streamed upwards from the altar, dimly was seen the fiery font, and the shadow of that dreadful being who should have baptized her with the baptism of death. But by her side was kneeling her better angel, that hid his face with wings; that wept and pleaded for *her*; that prayed when *she* could *not*; that fought with Heaven by tears for *her* deliverance; which also, as he raised his immortal countenance from his wings, I saw, by the glory in his eye, that from Heaven he had won at last.

V

Then was completed the passion of the mighty fugue. The golden tubes of the organ, which as yet had but muttered at intervals— gleaming amongst clouds and surges of incense—threw up, as from fountains unfathomable, columns of heart-shattering music. Choir and anti-choir were filling fast with unknown voices. Thou also, Dying Trumpeter!—with thy love that was victorious, and thy anguish that was finishing—didst enter the tumult; trumpet and echo—farewell love, and farewell anguish—rang through the dreadful *sanctus*. Oh, darkness of the grave! that from the crimson altar and from the fiery font wert visited and searched by the effulgence in the angel's eye—were these indeed thy children? Pomps of life, that, from the burials of centuries, rose again to the voice of perfect joy, did ye indeed mingle with the festivals of Death? Lo! as I looked back for seventy leagues through the mighty cathedral, I saw the quick and the dead that sang together to God, together that sang to the generations of man. All the hosts of jubilation, like armies that ride in pursuit, moved with one step. Us, that, with laurelled heads, were passing from the cathedral, they overtook, and, as with a garment, they wrapped us round with thunders greater than our own. As brothers we

moved together; to the dawn that advanced—to the stars that fled;
rendering thanks to God in the highest—that, having hid His face
through one generation behind thick clouds of War, once again was
ascending—from the Campo Santo of Waterloo was ascending—in
the visions of Peace; rendering thanks for thee, young girl! whom,
having overshadowed with His ineffable passion of death, suddenly
did God relent; suffered thy angel to turn aside His arm; and even in
thee, sister unknown! shown to me for a moment only to be hidden
for ever, found an occasion to glorify His goodness. A thousand times,
amongst the phantoms of sleep, have I seen thee entering the gates of
the golden dawn—with the secret word riding before thee—with the
armies of the grave behind thee; seen thee sinking, rising, raving, despairing; a thousand times in the worlds of sleep have seen thee
followed by God's angel through storms; through desert seas; through
the darkness of quicksands; through dreams—only that at the last,
with one sling of His victorious arm, He might snatch thee back from
ruin, and might emblazon in thy deliverance the endless resurrections
of His love!

3

The question of drugs and the extent to which *Edgar Allan Poe* (1809-49) indulged in them is one of the most debated issues in the life of this controversial and enduring author. At least six of his short stories feature drugs and drug-takers while others of his tales and poems contain passages and descriptions bearing the unmistakable traces of drug 'visions'. For me, the evidence is undeniable that he did take drugs—in particular opium—and while he may well not be classed as an addict, had imbibed seriously and long enough to know both its 'pains and pleasures'.

Poe, the originator of the detective story, the founder of the modern school of horror fiction and one of the widest influences on writers in the subsequent 'decadent' period, was a lonely, inwardly-tortured and basically unstable person all his short life. Orphaned while a very small child, he was adopted by a wealthy family and spent some of his formative years with them in England. Returning to America, he was for a short time a student at the University of Virginia, but his already developing affinity for dissipation and gambling caused his patron to remove him and put him in employment. The next few years were a record of one failure after another due to his instability: the culmination being his expulsion from the West Point Military Academy in 1831 for deliberately neglecting his duty. Thrown on his own resources, he again took up the poetry he had started in youth and at last found an aim in life, if not a curb on his eccentricity. Short stories followed his poems—now being published to some acclaim—and in 1833 he began writing for the newspapers. Even the appointment as assistant editor of the *Southern Literary Messenger* in Richmond was short-lived, his irregularity and quarrelsome nature, not to mention his excessive drinking, forcing him to move on for a brief stay in New York, and then Philadelphia. Despite the erratic nature of his life, Poe was nevertheless producing some of his finest poems and stories—several of these winning literary competitions. The remainder of his life was a rapid decline in both mental and physical health, culminating in an attempted suicide in 1848 (by taking an ounce of laudanum) and an attack of delirium tremens in the following spring. On a trip north that autumn he was found in a debilitated condition in a street in Baltimore and died almost immediately in hospital.

Sketchy though this short biography is, it does show Poe's unstable nature and underlines how it seemed so appropriate for him to turn to opium and laudanum for relief from his ills. America at this period, like Britain and Europe, had plentiful supplies of these drugs and, indeed, they were in the main cheaper than wine or spirits. A contemporary of Poe, a young parson, Walter Colton, had provided the population with its first detailed descriptions of a native-born imbiber, although he and a great many other people had already read and been much impressed by De Quincey's 'Confessions'. Apart from the evidence of usage of drugs in his work, Poe was also known by several of his friends and relatives to be a user; his cousin, Elizabeth Herring, for instance, noted in her diary that she had had 'the misfortune to see him often in sad conditions from the use of opium'. Poe was also a renowned dreamer and several of his stories are based on these visions— 'Liegia' being probably the most famous and containing perhaps Poe's fullest study of an imbiber who had become 'a bounden slave in the trammels of opium'. Other of Poe's stories, such as 'Berenice', 'The Fall of the House of Usher' and the bizarre 'Loss of Breath' contain drug references, and it is interesting to note that when Poe later prepared a collected edition of his stories, he deleted several of the references to opium. Two other famous admitted drug addicts, the Frenchman Charles Baudelaire and Francis Thompson (both of whom are represented in this collection), were firmly of the opinion that Poe was an actual addict, and published lengthy studies to that effect. The controversy will doubtless go on as long as his work is published; but here, as a clue, is perhaps the most interesting of all Poe's opium stories, with its truly memorable description of the effects of morphine —a derivative of opium—on an addict.

*

At length I bethought me of a little packet of opium which lay with my tobacco in the hookah-case; for I had acquired the habit of smoking the weed with the drug. I sought and found the narcotic. But when about to cut off a portion, I felt the necessity of hesitation. In smoking it was a matter of little importance *how much* was employed. Usually I had half filled the bowl of the hookah with opium and tobacco cut and mingled, half and half. Sometimes when I had used the whole of this mixture I experienced no very peculiar effect; at other times I would not have smoked the pipe more than two-thirds out, when symptoms of mental derangement, which were even alarming, warned me to desist. But the effect proceeded with an easy gradation which deprived the indulgence of all danger. Here, however, the case was different. I had never *swallowed* opium before. Laudanum and morphine I had occasionally used, and about *them* should have had no reason to hesitate. But the solid drug I had never seen employed. I was left altogether to conjecture. Still I felt no especial uneasiness, for I resolved to proceed by *degrees*. I would take a *very* small dose in the first instance. Should this prove impotent, I would repeat it: and so on, until I should find an abatement of the fever, or obtain that sleep which was so pressingly requisite, and with which my reeling senses had not been blessed for now nearly a week. No doubt it was this very reeling of my senses—it was the dull delirium which already oppressed me, that prevented me from perceiving the incoherence of my reason—which blinded me to the folly of defining anything as either large or small where I had no preconceived standard of comparison.

'Life in Death', 1849

A Tale of the Ragged Mountains
Edgar Allan Poe

During the fall of the year 1827, while residing near Charlottesville, Virginia, I casually made the acquaintance of Mr Augustus Bedloe. This young gentleman was remarkable in every respect, and excited in me a profound interest and curiosity. I found it impossible to comprehend him either in his moral or his physical relations. Of his family I could obtain no satisfactory account. Whence he came, I never ascertained. Even about his age—although I call him a young gentleman—there was something which perplexed me in no little degree. He certainly *seemed* young — and he made a point of speaking about his youth—yet there were moments when I should have had little trouble in imagining him a hundred years of age. But in no regard was he more peculiar than in his personal appearance. He was singularly tall and thin. He stooped much. His limbs were exceedingly long and emaciated. His forehead was broad and low. His complexion was absolutely bloodless. His mouth was large and flexible, and his teeth were more wildly uneven, although sound, than I had ever before seen teeth in a human head. The expression of his smile, however, was by no means unpleasing, as might be supposed; but it had no variation whatever. It was one of profound melancholy—of a phaseless and unceasing gloom. His eyes were abnormally large, and round like those of a cat. The pupils, too, upon any accession or diminution of light, underwent contraction or dilation, just such as is observed in the feline tribe. In moments of excitement the orbs grew bright to a degree almost inconceivable; seeming to emit luminous rays, not of a reflected, but of an intrinsic lustre, as does a candle or the sun; yet their ordinary condition was so totally vapid, filmy and dull, as to convey the idea of the eyes of a long-interred corpse.

These peculiarities of person appeared to cause him much annoyance, and he was continually alluding to them in a sort of half explanatory, half apologetic strain, which, when I first heard it, impressed me very painfully. I soon, however, grew accustomed to it, and my uneasiness wore off. It seemed to be his design rather to insinuate than directly to assert that, physically, he had not always been what he was—that a long series of neuralgic attacks had reduced him from a condition of more than usual personal beauty, to that which I saw. For many years past he had been attended by a physician, named Templeton—an old gentleman, perhaps seventy years of age—whom he had first encountered at Saratoga, and from whose attention, while there, he either received, or fancied that he received, great benefit. The result was that Bedloe, who was wealthy, had made an arrangement with Doctor Templeton, by which the latter, in consideration of a liberal annual allowance, had consented to devote his time and medical experience exclusively to the care of the invalid.

Doctor Templeton had been a traveller in his younger days, and, at Paris, had become a convert, in great measure, to the doctrines of Mesmer. It was altogether by means of magnetic remedies that he had succeeded in alleviating the acute pains of his patient; and this success had very naturally inspired the latter with a certain degree of confidence in the opinions from which the remedies had been educed. The doctor, however, like all enthusiasts, had struggled hard to make a thorough convert of his pupil, and finally so far gained his point as to induce the sufferer to submit to numerous experiments. By a frequent repetition of these a result had arisen, which of late days has become so common as to attract little or no attention, but which, at the period of which I write, had very rarely been known in America. I mean to say, that between Doctor Templeton and Bedloe there had grown up, little by little, a very distinct and strongly marked *rapport,* or magnetic relation. I am not prepared to assert, however, that this *rapport* extended beyond the limits of the simple sleep-producing power; but this power itself had attained great intensity. At the first attempt to induce the magnetic somnolency, the mesmerist entirely failed. In the fifth or sixth he succeeded very partially, and after long continued effort. Only at the twelfth was the triumph complete. After this the will of the patient succumbed rapidly to that of the physician, so that, when I first became acquainted with the two, sleep was brought about almost instantaneously, by the mere volition of the operator, even when the invalid was unaware of his presence. It is only now, in the year 1845, when similar miracles are witnessed daily by thousands, that I dare venture to record this apparent impossibility as a matter of serious fact.

The temperature of Bedloe was, in the highest degree, sensitive, excitable, enthusiastic. His imagination was singularly vigorous and creative; and no doubt it derived additional force from the habitual use of morphine, which he swallowed in great quantity, and without which he would have found it impossible to exist. It was his practice to take a very large dose of it immediately after breakfast, each morning—or rather immediately after a cup of strong coffee, for he ate nothing in the forenoon—and then set forth alone, or attended only by a dog, upon a long ramble among the chain of wild and dreary hills that lie westward and southward of Charlottesville, and are there dignified by the title of the Ragged Mountains.

Upon a dim, warm, misty day, towards the close of November, and during the strange *interregnum* of the seasons which in America is termed the Indian Summer, Mr Bedloe departed as usual for the hills. The day passed, and still he did not return.

About eight o'clock at night, having become seriously alarmed at his protracted absence, we were about setting out in search of him, when he unexpectedly made his appearance, in health no worse than usual, and in rather more than ordinary spirits. The account which he gave of his expedition, and of the events which had detained him, was a singular one indeed.

'You will remember,' said he, 'that it was about nine in the morning when I left Charlottesville. I bent my steps immediately to the mountains, and about ten, entered a gorge which was entirely new to me. I followed the windings of this pass with much interest. The scenery which presented itself on all sides, although scarcely entitled to be called grand, had about it an indescribable, and to me, a delicious aspect of dreary desolation. The solitude seemed absolutely virgin. I could not help believing that the green sods and the gray rocks upon which I trod, had been trodden never before by the foot of a human being. So entirely secluded and in fact inaccessible, except through a series of accidents, is the entrance of the ravine, that it is by no means impossible that I was indeed the first adventurer—the very first and sole adventurer who had ever penetrated its recesses.

'The thick and peculiar mist, or smoke, which distinguishes the

Indian Summer, and which now hung heavily over all objects, served, no doubt, to deepen the vague impressions which these objects created. So dense was this pleasant fog, that I could at no time see more than a dozen yards of the path before me. This path was excessively sinuous, and as the sun could not be seen, I soon lost all idea of the direction in which I journeyed. In the meantime the morphine had its customary effect—that of enduing all the external world with an intensity of interest. In the quivering of a leaf—in the hue of a blade of grass—in the shape of a trefoil—in the humming of a bee—in the gleaming of a dew-drop—in the breathing of the wind—in the faint odours that came from the forest—there came a whole universe of suggestion—a gay and motley train of rhapsodical and immethodical thought.

'Busied in this, I walked on for several hours, during which the mist deepened around me to so great an extent, that at length I was reduced to an absolute groping of the way. And now an indescribable uneasiness possessed me—a species of nervous hesitation and tremor. I feared to tread, lest I should be precipitated into some abyss. I remembered too, strange stories told about these Ragged Hills, and of the uncouth and fierce races of men who tenanted their groves and caverns. A thousand vague fancies oppressed and disconcerted me—fancies the more distressing because vague. Very suddenly my attention was arrested by the loud beating of a drum.

'My amazement, was, of course, extreme. A drum in these hills was a thing unknown. I could not have been more surprised at the sound of the trump of the Archangel. But a new and still more astounding source of interest and perplexity arose. There came a wild rattling or jingling sound, as if of a bunch of large keys—and upon the instant a dusky-visaged and half-naked man rushed past me with a shriek. He came so close to my person that I felt his hot breath upon my face. He bore in one hand an instrument composed of an assemblage of steel rings, and shook them vigorously as he ran. Scarcely had he disappeared in the mist, before, panting after him, with open mouth and glaring eyes there darted a huge beast. I could not be mistaken in its character. It was a hyena.

'The sight of this monster rather relieved than heightened my terrors—for I now made sure that I dreamed, and endeavoured to arouse myself to waking consciousness. I stepped boldly and briskly forward. I rubbed my eyes. I called aloud. I pinched my limbs. A small spring of water presented itself to my view, and here, stooping, I bathed my hands and my head and neck. This seemed to dissipate the equivocal sensations which had hitherto annoyed me. I arose, as I thought, a new man, and proceeded steadily and complacently on my unknown way.

'At length, quite overcome by exertion, and by a certain oppressive closeness of the atmosphere, I seated myself beneath a tree. Presently there came a feeble gleam of sunshine, and the shadow of the leaves of the tree fell faintly but definitely upon the grass. At this shadow I gazed wonderingly for many minutes. Its character stupified me with astonishment. I looked upward. The tree was a palm.

'I now arose hurriedly, and in a state of fearful agitation—for the fancy that I dreamed would serve me no longer. I saw—I felt that I had perfect command of my senses—and these senses now brought to my soul a world of novel and singular sensation. The heat became all at once intolerable. A strange odour loaded the breeze.—A low continuous murmur, like that arising from a full, but gently flowing river, came to my ears, intermingled with the peculiar hum of multitudinous human voices.

'While I listened in an extremity of astonishment which I need not attempt to describe, a strong and brief gust of wind bore off the incumbent fog as if by the wand of an enchanter.

'I found myself at the foot of a high mountain, and looking down into a vast plain, through which wound a majestic river. On the margin of this river stood an Eastern-looking city, such as we read of in the Arabian Tales, but of a character even more singular than any there described. From my position, which was far above the level of the town, I could perceive its every nook and corner, as if delineated on a map. The streets seemed innumerable, and crossed each other irregularly in all directions, but were rather long winding alleys than streets, and absolutely swarmed with inhabitants. The houses were wildly picturesque. On every hand was a wilderness of balconies, of verandahs, of minarets, of shrines, and fantastically carved oriels. Bazaars abounded; and in these were displayed rich wares in infinite variety and profusion—silks, muslins, the most dazzling cutlery, the most magnificent jewels and gems. Besides these things, were seen, on all sides, banners and palanquins, litters with stately dames close veiled, elephants gorgeously caparisoned, idols grotesquely hewn, drums, banners and gongs, spears, silver and gilded maces. And amid the crowd and the clamour, and the general intricacy and confusion —amid the million of black and yellow men, turbaned and robed, and of flowing beard, there roamed a countless multitude of holy filleted bulls, while vast legions of the filthy but sacred ape clambered, chattering and shrieking, about the cornices of the mosques, or clung to the minarets and oriels. From the swarming streets to the banks of the river, there descended innumerable flights of steps leading to bathing places, while the river itself seemed to force a passage with difficulty through the vast fleets of deeply burdened ships that far and wide encountered its surface. Beyond the limits of the city arose, in frequent majestic groups, the palm and the cocoa, with other gigantic and weird trees of vast age; and here and there might be seen a field of rice, the thatched hut of a peasant, a tank, a stray temple, a gipsy camp, or a solitary graceful maiden taking her way, with a pitcher upon her head, to the banks of the magnificent river.

'You will say now, of course, that I dreamed, but not so. What I saw—what I heard—what I felt—what I thought—had about it nothing of the unmistakable idiosyncrasy of the dream. All was rigorously self-consistent. At first, doubting that I was really awake, I entered into a series of tests, which soon convinced me that I really was. Now, when one dreams, and, in the dream, suspects that he dreams, the suspicion *never fails to confirm itself*, and the sleeper is almost immediately aroused. Thus Novalis errs not in saying that "we are near waking when we dream that we dream." Had the vision occurred to me as I describe it, without my suspecting it as a dream, then a dream it might absolutely have been, but, occurring as it did, and suspected and tested as it was, I am forced to class it among other phenomena.'

'In this I am not sure that you are wrong,' observed Dr Templeton, 'but proceed. You arose and descended into the city.'

'I arose,' continued Bedloe, regarding the Doctor with an air of profound astonishment, 'I arose, as you say, and descended into the city. On my way, I fell in with an immense populace, crowding through every avenue, all in the same direction, and exhibiting in every action the wildest excitement. Very suddenly, and by some inconceivable impulse, I became intensely imbued with personal interest in what was going on. I seemed to feel that I had an important part to play, without exactly understanding what it was. Against the crowd which environed me, however, I experienced a deep sentiment of animosity. I shrank from amid them, and, swiftly, by a circuitous path, reached and entered the city. Here all was the wildest tumult and contention. A small party of men, clad in garments half Indian, half European, and officered by gentlemen in a uniform partly British, were engaged, at great odds, with the swarming rabble of the alleys. I joined the weaker party, arming myself with the weapons of a fallen officer, and fighting I knew not whom with the nervous ferocity of despair. We were soon overpowered by numbers, and driven to seek refuge in a species of kiosk. Here we barricaded ourselves, and, for the present, were secure. From a loop-hole near the summit of the kiosk, I perceived a vast crowd, in furious agitation, surrounding and assaulting a gay palace that overhung the river. Presently, from an upper window of this palace, there descended an effeminate-looking person, by means of a string made of the turbans of his attendants. A boat was at hand, in which he escaped to the opposite bank of the river.

'And now a new object took possession of my soul. I spoke a few hurried but energetic words to my companions, and, having succeeded in gaining over a few of them to my purpose, made a frantic sally from the kiosk. We rushed amid the crowd that surrounded it. They retreated, at first, before us. They rallied, fought madly, and retreated again. In the meantime we were borne far from the kiosk, and became bewildered and entangled among the narrow streets of tall overhanging houses, into the recesses of which the sun had never been able to shine. The rabble pressed impetuously upon us, harassing us with their spears, and overwhelming us with flights of arrows. These latter were very remarkable, and resembled in some respects the writhing creese of the Malay. They were made to imitate the body of a creeping serpent, and were long and black, with a poisoned barb. One of them struck me upon the right temple. I reeled and fell. An instantaneous and dreadful sickness seized me. I struggled—I gasped—I died.'

'You will hardly persist *now*,' said I, smiling, 'that the whole of your adventure was not a dream. You are not prepared to maintain that you are dead?'

When I said these words, I of course expected some lively sally from Bedloe in reply; but, to my astonishment, he hesitated, trembled, became fearfully pallid, and remained silent. I looked towards Templeton. He sat erect and rigid in his chair—his teeth chattered, and his eyes were starting from their sockets. 'Proceed!' he at length said hoarsely to Bedloe.

'For many minutes,' continued the latter, 'my sole sentiment—my sole feeling—was that of darkness and nonentity, with the consciousness of death. At length, there seemed to pass a violent and sudden shock through my soul, as if of electricity. With it came the sense of elasticity and of light. This latter I felt—not saw. In an instant I seemed to rise from the ground. But I had no bodily, no visible, audible, or palpable presence. The crowd had departed. The tumult had ceased. The city was in comparative repose. Beneath me lay my corpse, with the arrow in my temple, the whole head greatly swollen and disfigured. But all these things I felt—not saw. I took interest in nothing. Even the corpse seemed a matter in which I had no concern. Volition I had none, but appeared to be impelled into motion, and flitted buoyantly out of the city, retracing the circuitous path by which I had entered it. When I had attained that point of the ravine in the mountains at which I had encountered the hyena, I again experienced a shock as of a galvanic battery; the sense of weight, of volition, of substance, returned. I became my original self, and bent my steps eagerly homewards — but the past had not lost the vividness of the real — and not now, even for an instant, can I compel my understanding to regard it as a dream.'

'Nor was it,' said Templeton, with an air of deep solemnity, 'yet it would be difficult to say how otherwise it should be termed. Let us suppose only, that the soul of the man of to-day is upon the verge of some stupendous psychal discoveries. Let us content ourselves with this supposition. For the rest I have some explanation to make. Here is a water-colour drawing, which I should have shown you before, but which an unaccountable sentiment of horror has hitherto prevented me from showing.'

We looked at the picture which he presented. I saw nothing in it of an extraordinary character; but its effect upon Bedloe was prodigious. He nearly fainted as he gazed. And yet it was but a miniature portrait —a miraculously accurate one, to be sure—of his own very remarkable features. At least this was my thought as I regarded it.

'You will perceive,' said Templeton, 'the date of this picture—it is here, scarcely visible, in this corner—1780. In this year was the portrait taken. It is the likeness of a dead friend—a Mr Oldeb—to whom I became much attached at Calcutta, during the administration of Warren Hastings. I was then only twenty years old. When I first saw you, Mr Bedloe, at Saratoga, it was the miraculous similarity which existed between yourself and the painting which induced me to accost you, to seek your friendship, and to bring about those arrangements which resulted in my becoming your constant companion. In accomplishing this point, I was urged partly, and perhaps principally, by a regretful memory of the deceased, but also, in part, by an uneasy, and not altogether horrorless curiosity respecting yourself.

'In your detail of the vision which presented itself to you amid the hills, you have described, with the minutest accuracy, the Indian city of Benares, upon the Holy River. The riots, the combats, the massacre, were the actual events of the insurrection of Cheyte Sing, which took place in 1780, when Hastings was put in imminent peril of his life. The man escaping by the string of turbans was Cheyte Sing himself. The party in the kiosk were sepoys and British officers, headed by Hastings. Of this party I was one, and did all I could to prevent the rash and fatal sally of the officer who fell, in the crowded alleys, by the poisoned arrow of a Bengalee. That officer was my dearest friend. It was Oldeb. You will perceive by these manuscripts,' (here the speaker produced a note-book in which several pages appeared to have been freshly written) 'that at the very period in which you fancied these things amid the hills, I was engaged in detailing them upon paper here at home.'

In about a week after this conversation, the following paragraphs appeared in a Charlottesville paper:—

'We have the painful duty of announcing the death of Mr AUGUSTUS BEDLO, a gentleman whose amiable manners and many virtues have long endeared him to the citizens of Charlottesville.

'Mr B., for some years past, has been subject to neuralgia, which has often threatened to terminate fatally; but this can be regarded only as the mediate cause of his decease. The proximate cause was one of especial singularity. In an excursion to the Ragged Mountains, a few days since, a slight cold and fever were contracted, attended with great determination of blood to the head. To relieve this, Dr Templeton resorted to topical bleeding. Leeches were applied to the temples. In a fearfully brief period the patient died, when it appeared that in the jar containing the leeches had been introduced, by accident, one of the venomous vermicular sangsues which are now and then found in the neighbouring ponds. This creature fastened itself upon a small artery in the right temple. Its close resemblance to the medicinal leech caused the mistake to be overlooked until too late.

'N.B. The poisonous sangsue of Charlottesville may always be distinguished from the medicinal leech by its blackness, and especially by its writhing or vermicular motions, which very nearly resemble those of a snake.'

I was speaking with the editor of the paper in question, upon the topic of this remarkable accident, when it occurred to me to ask how it happened that the name of the deceased had been given as Bedlo.

'I presume,' said I, 'you have authority for this spelling, but I have always supposed the name to be written with an *e* at the end.'

'Authority?—no,' he replied. 'It is a mere typographical error. The name is Bedloe with an *e* all the world over, and I never knew it to be spelt otherwise in my life.'

'Then,' said I, mutteringly, as I turned upon my heel; 'then, indeed, has it come to pass that one truth is stranger than any fiction—for Bedlo without the *e*, what is it but Oldeb conversed? And this man tells me it is a typographical error.'

4

'Poe's career was dark enough, but it was not all unhappy. However, Mangan's life is one of unmitigated gloom. He walked the dark way of his life alone. His comrades were strong shadows, the bodyless creations wherein his ecstasy was most cunning.' So wrote Justin McCarthy in his *Hours With Great Irishmen* of perhaps the most mysterious, talented and yet least understood man of letters of the nineteenth century, *James Clarence Mangan* (1803-49). The life story of this son of an Irish grocer runs an almost uncanny parallel with that of his transatlantic counterpart, Edgar Allan Poe, and even in their work there is a bizarre similarity, although it would have been impossible for one to have copied the other. Both, too, were obsessed with opium and laudanum, leaving strong traces of it in their lifestyles and their writing.

Mangan was born the eldest son of a sacrilegious and drunken Dublin grocer who would give his last penny to any scrounger that asked for it, yet kept his wife and children in want, and in fear of him. The family lived in one of the poorer quarters of the city in a house belonging, most appropriately for the gloomy bent of young Mangan, to a family named Usher. The young man seemed to sense the unstable course his life was going to take. 'In my boyhood,' he wrote later, 'I was haunted by an indescribable feeling of something terrible. It was as though I strove in the vicinity of some tremendous danger, to which my apprehensions could give neither form nor outline.' During his brief schooling, Mangan shunned contact with other boys and buried himself in books. Then, at fifteen, his father had become so impoverished that he had to leave school and take a job as a clerk. For the next ten years he worked an exhausting ten-hour day, seven days a week, and undoubtedly ruined his already poor health. But the condition of the family did not improve and they had to move to still poorer quarters; Mangan, in his few moments of rest, began to write poetry as a relief from the drudgery, and had obviously also begun to seek solace in laudanum and alcohol. By the time he was thirty and his poems were first being published, he was already a haggard figure, his hair having turned prematurely grey. He had also read De

Quincey's 'Confessions' and his biographer, D. J. O'Donoghue, tells us that at this time he was 'strongly under De Quincey's influence'. A story which originated from this period is 'An Extraordinary Adventure in The Shades' (1833) which I have reprinted here, and which clearly underlines what Mr O'Donoghue says in its obsessively detailed observation of a strange encounter, and in several passages which resemble certain paragraphs to be found in the 'Confessions'. Apart from his drinking, Mangan's friends were aware that he was taking laudanum more and more frequently, although he himself was reluctant to admit it. It began to show through in some of his bizarre essays like 'A Sixty Drop Dose of Laudanum' (1839), and one of the few people who knew him, James Price, was forced to conclude: 'Poor Clarence! What a world of dreary enthusiasm was thine! The opium drug, so destructive in its ultimate effects, but oh, how delicious in its first visions, lifted thee from out of thy abode of squalor, thy associations of wretchedness. Thou became the denizen of another world—a fairy world.' But the 'fairy world' was not to sustain Mangan for long; for a brief time he fell in love with a young girl, Margaret Stackpole, only to be spurned at this one moment of happiness. The blow was too much for Mangan. The rest of his life resembles a Victorian temperance-lecture. He turned increasingly to drink and drugs, to the detriment of his already fragile health, and his life became a tortuous progression from one inn to the next. To supplement his income he put his knowledge of German to use as a translator and began to publish not only foreign poetry and short stories, but also his own work. He had a fervent interest in ghosts and spiritualism, 'a forecourt to paradise' as he called it, and many of the trappings of the strange and mysterious appeared in his tales and essays. His work met with little success and when he could no longer borrow from his publishers, he began to sleep rough, going on massive solitary drinking sprees. Mangan made two half-hearted attempts to end his addiction to alcohol and opium, but both were failures.

His decline was rapid. By 1849, the last year of his life, he resembled a skeleton, and was missing for some weeks until found in a disused building, so emaciated as to be unable to stand. He had contracted cholera. He was rushed to hospital and, although he rallied briefly, James Mangan died on June 20th—just a few months before Poe. One friend, the young painter Frederick Burton, was with him at his death (producing the one authentic portrait of Mangan which exists); the congregation at his funeral numbered five.

The acclaim that eluded him in his lifetime has barely been accorded to him in death, but his mark on literature and poetry is undeniable as this verse—which might well be his epitaph—shows:

Breakfastless, Bangless, bookless and chiboukless
Through the chill day, alone with my conscience I
Mope in some nook, and ponder my follies,
Which same were not few.

*

You know, my friend, the constitutional placidity of my temperament; how like Epictetus I am, and so forth, but coming into collision with the wrongheadedness of the age so frequently as I do, innate integrity and a sense of principle compel me to curse by bell, book and gaslight, every thing and being in the vicinity of my person. The Gorgon's head, the triple-faced hell dog, the handwriting on Belshazzar's palace wall, the into-stone metamorphosing snake locks of Medusa, the Cock Lane Ghost, the Abaddon-born visions of Quincey, the opium-eater, the devil that perpetually stood opposite to Spinello, the caverns of Dom Daniel, the fireglobe that burned below the feet of Pascal, were each and all miserable little bagatelles by the feet of the phantasmagoria that ever more haunt my brain and blast my eyes.

Very Original Correspondence, 1833

An Extraordinary Adventure in the Shades
JAMES MANGAN

The day of the week was Sunday, of the month, the first; the month itself was April, the year 1832. Sunday, first of April, 1832—*de mortuis nil nisi bonum;* but I really must say that thou wert, in very truth, a beautiful, a bland, and a balmy day. I remember thee particularly well. Ah! which of the days that the departed year gave birth to do I not remember? The history of each and of all is chronicled in the volume of my brain—written into it as with a pen of iron, in characters of ineffaceable fire! It is pretty generally admitted by the learned that an attempt to recall the past is labour in vain, else should I, for one, purchase back the bygone year with diadems and thrones (supposing that I had the diadems and thrones to barter). Under present circumstances my only feasible proceeding is to march onward rectilineally, cheek-by-jowl, with the spirit of the age, to abandon the bower of Fancy for the road-beaten pathway of Reason —renounce Byron for Bentham, and resign the brilliant and burning imagery of the past for the frozen realities of the present and the future. Be it so. Whatever may become of me my lips are sealed—a padlocked article. *Tout est perdu, mes amis;* and when the case stands thus, the unfortunate victim had much better keep his breath to cool his porridge withal; for he may stake his last cigar upon it, that anything more supremely ridiculous than his efforts to soliloquize his friends into a sympathetic feeling will never come under the cognizance of the public.

The foregoing paragraph is exclusively 'personal to myself.' I am now going to relate what will be generally interesting.

For the evening of the 1st of April, '32, I had an appointment with an acquaintance whom I had almost begun to look on as a friend. The place of rendezvous was in College Green, at the Shades Tavern —a classic spot, known to a few select persons about town. At half-past six o'clock I accordingly repaired thither. As yet my acquaintance, whom I had almost begun to regard as a friend, had not made his appearance. Taking possession of a vacant box, I ordered the waiter to bring a bottle of port and two glasses. He obeyed. Mechanically I began to sip the wine, awaiting, with some anxiety, the arrival of my acquaintance, whom I had almost begun to regard as a friend; but half-an-hour elapsed, and he came not. Now I grew fidgety and thoughtful, and began to form a variety of conjectures. At length, for very weariness, I gave this up. Suddenly I heard some one cough slightly. I raised my head and looked forth at the door. Seated at an opposite table I beheld a gentleman of tall stature and commanding aspect, striking, indeed, to a degree, in his physiognomy. He was reading a newspaper, and was apparently deeply absorbed in its contents. How was it that I had hitherto neglected to notice this man? I could not forbear wondering. I was unable to account for the circumstance, except by referring to my previous abstraction, the preoccupied nature of my thoughts, and the agitation which the anticipation of the meeting with my acquaintance, whom I had almost begun to regard as a friend, had necessarily tended to produce, in a person of my delicately nervous temperament. Now, however, I was resolved to compensate for my previous absence of mind. I examined the stranger opposite me minutely. I criticised him without saying a syllable, from hat-crown (he wore his beaver) to shoe-tie (he sported pumps). His cravat, waistcoat, frock, unutterables—all underwent a rigid analysis by my searching eye. I scrutinized all, first collectively and then consecutively; and I owe it to truth and justice to protest, that, upon my honour, the result was decidedly satisfactory; all was perfect, lofty, gentleman-like. Viewed as a whole, his countenance was, as I have remarked, peculiarly particular. I was, however, determined to institute an examination into it, *Stückweisse* (bit by bit), as they say at Vienna, and I reviewed every feature distinctively and apart. Had I been a Quarterly Reviewer, or Professor Wilson himself, I could not have discovered the slightest groundwork to erect a superstructure of censure on. Had similar perfection ever until that hour been encountered by any? Never and nowhere. I knew not what to imagine; my faculties were bewildered. The thing was too miraculous, it was over magnificent, extraordinary, super-inexplicable. Who was this man? I had always been a considerable peripatetic; but I could not recollect that in town or country he had ever until now encountered my inspection. Such a figure and such a face I could not, had I but once beheld them, possibly forget; they would have been enrolled among the archives of my memory, as treasures to be drawn largely and lavishly upon on some future night, when the current of my ideas should run darkly and low, among underwood and over brambly places, and the warehouse of my imagination be ransacked in vain for a fresh assortment of imagery, and the punchless jug stand solitary upon the dimly-lighted table, and not a human voice be heard to set that table in a roar. I had never before seen this man; of course, then, it was obvious I now saw him for the first time. As this reflection, which I conceive to be a strictly logical one, occurred, I filled my glass a fifth time, and sipped as usual. The stranger continued to peruse his paper. His attitude was half recumbent and wholly motionless. It was a reasonable inference from this, that he must be an individual of steady habits and unchangeable principles, whom it might be exceedingly difficult to detach from a favourite pursuit, or draw aside from the path of prudence or duty. Rectitude of conduct is a quality that commands my esteem. If I had before admired the stranger, this consideration annexed to my admiration a feeling of respect. Yes; he was evidently a cautious and forethoughtful character—perhaps a little too inflexible in his determinations; but, then, has not inflexibility ever been the invariable concomitant of vast powers? Whether, however, this interrogatory were answered negatively or affirmatively, it was certain that adequate testimony of the positive inflexibility of this man's disposition was as yet wanting; and I should perpetrate an enormous act of injustice in condemning him, unless I had been antecedently placed in possession of every fact and circumstance exercising the remotest influence upon the question. It is essential to the passing of an upright sentence that crude and precipitate opinions be discarded; and should I, by over hastily following the dictates of a rash judgment, irrevocably commit myself in the eyes of philosophy, and eternally damn my own character as an impartial observer of the human family at large? Would it be reasonable? Would it be even polite? Should I not, in fact, deserve to be hooted down wherever I exhibited myself, and driven, like Ahasuerus the wanderer, from post to pillar; seeking refuge now in a cavern and now in a pot-house, and finding rest nowhere—a houseless wretch—a spectacle to society, and a melancholy memorial to after ages of the ruinous results of that self-conceit which prompts to a headstrong perseverance in opinions of a ridiculous order? What a doom! I shuddered as I silently contemplated the abstract possibility of such a contingency; and then filling a sixth glass went on sipping. Still my acquaintance, who was not yet a friend, had not blessed me with the light of his countenance; and my only resource was to watch, with an attentive eye, the proceedings, if any should take place, of the being at the opposite table. I felt my interest in the unknown augment moment by moment. Questionlessly, thought I, the Platonic theory is not wholly visionary —not altogether a bam. I must have known this man in some preadamite world; and the extraordinary sensations I experience are explicable only by reference to an antenatal state of existence. He and I have been ancient companions—fraternized members of the aboriginal Tuzenbund—the Orestes and Pylades of a purer and loftier sphere. Perhaps I died upon the block for him! Who shall expound me the enigma of the sympathetical feelings reciprocated between master minds, when upon earth each meets the other for the first time, unless by pointing to the electrical chain which runs dimly back through the long gallery of time, ascending from generation to generation, until it has reached the known beginning of all things, and then stretches out anew, far, far beyond that wide-a-way into the measureless deep of primary creation, the unknown, the unimaginable infinite! There is nothing incredible if we believe life to be a reality; for, to a psychologist the very consciousness that he exists at all is a mystery unfathomable in this world. An ass will attempt to illuminate us on the subject, and may produce, with an air of consequential cognoscity, a schedule of what he is pleased to call reasons; but it is all hollow humbug. So stands a leaden-visaged geologist who, up to his knees in the centre of a quagmire, and silently and sedulously pokes at the mud with his walking stick, fancying himself the while a second Cuvier; though the half-dozen clowns who act as spectators, and whom he takes for assembled Europe, perceive that the poor creature does nothing but turn up sludge eternally. As to the illuminating ass, only suffer him to proceed, and he will undertake to probe infinity with a bodkin, and measure the universe with a yard of pack thread. There are two distinguished plans for the extinction of such an annoyance—first, to cough him down; second, to empty a pot of porter against his countenance. I have tried both experiments, and can vouch that the most successful results will follow.

The stranger, as I continued to gaze, elevated his hand to his head, and slightly varied the position of his hat. Here was a remarkable event—a landmark in the desert—an epoch in the history of the evening, affording scope for unbounded conjecture. I resolved, however, by no means to allow imagination to obtain the start of judgment on this occasion. The unknown had altered the position of his hat. What was the inference spontaneously deducible from the occurrence of such a circumstance? Firstly, that anterior to the motion which preceded the change, the unknown had conceived that his hat did not sit properly on his head; secondly, that he must be gifted with the organ of order in a high degree. Individuals in whom that organ is prominently developed, rarely, if ever, are imaginative or poetical; hence it was to be inferred, that the energies of the unknown were exclusively devoted to the advancement of prosaical interests. But here again rose cause to bewilder and embarrass. I could see by a glance that the unknown was conning a column of poetry; and that his expressive countenance, as he went on, became palely illumined by a quenchless lamp from the sanctuary within. How did this harmonise with my former conclusion? I surmounted the difficulty, however, by reflecting that it is, after all, possible for a man to be at once illimitably imaginative and profoundly philosophical, as we find, said I, mentally in the instance of Dr Bowring! Ah, stupidity! thy name is Clarence. That until this moment the truth should never have struck thee! That only now shouldst thou have been made aware that Bowring himself was before thee! A thrill of joy pervaded my frame, as I reclined my brow upon my hand, and internally exclaimed: yes, it is, indeed Bowring! It must be he, because it can be no other.

As I had always been ardently desirous of an introduction to that illustrious man, whom I justly regard as one of the leading genii of Modern Europe, I shall leave the public to imagine the overpowering nature of my feelings upon discovering that the golden opportunity had at length been vouchsafed, and that I was now free to enter into oral communication with a master-spirit of the age. I paused to deliberate upon the description of address I should put forth, as well as the tone of voice which it would be most appropriate to assume; whether aristocratical or sentimental, free and easy or broken-hearted; and also upon the style of expression properest for my adoption, and best calculated to impress the mind of Bowring with a conviction that whatever my defects may prove to be in detail, I was—take me all in all—a young man of magnificent intellect and dazzling originality, and possessed a comprehensiveness of capacity discoverable in nobody else within the bills of mortality. Whether I should compress my sentiments within two bulky sentences or subdivide them into fifteen little ones was, likewise, matter of serious importance. So acute an observer of mankind and syntax as Bowring is, will infallibly, said I, detect the slenderest inaccuracy in my phraseology. To betray any philological inability would be a short method of getting myself damned in his eyes, and I should go down to the latest posterity as a bungler and a bumpkin. Mannerism is a grand thing. Let me, therefore, review this question minutely and microscopically under all the various lights and shades in which it can be presented to the mind before I pass the Rubicon irremediably.

Mannerism is a grand thing, pursued I, following the current of my reflections. It is the real heavy bullion, the geniune ore, the ingot itself; every other thing is jelly and soapsuds. You shall tramp the earth in vain for a more pitiable object than a man with genius, with nothing else to back it with. He was born to amalgamate with the mud we walk upon, and will, whenever he appears in public, be trodden over like that. Transfuse into this man a due portion of mannerism; the metamorphosis is marvellous. Erect he stands and blows his trumpet, the sounds whereof echo unto the uttermost confines of our magnificent world. Senates listen; Empires tremble; Thrones tumble down before him! He possesses the wand of Prospero, the lamp of Aladdin, the violin of Paganini, the assurance of the devil! What has conferred all the advantages upon him? Mannerism! destitute of which we are, so to speak, walking humbugs; destitute of which the long odds are, that the very best individual among us, after a life spent on the treadmill system, dies dismally in a sack.

For myself, concluded I, I tilt at Charlatanism in all its branches; but it is, nevertheless, essential that I show off with Bowring; I am nothing if not striking. It is imperative on me, therefore, to strike. Six hours of unremitting study a few weeks previously enabled me to concoct a very superior joke about the March of Intellect's becoming a Dead March on the first of April. This had never appeared. Should I suffer the diamond to sparkle? It was a debatable question whether Dr B. would not internally condemn me as an unprincipled ruffian for sneering at my own party. I know not, said I. I am buried in Egyptian darkness on this point; but, *prima facie,* I should be inclined to suppose Bowring a moral cosmopolite, who could indifferently floor friends and enemies, *con amore.* To humbug the world in the gloss is certainly a herculean achievement; but the conquest of impossibilities is the glory of genius. Both Bowring and I are living in a miraculous era—the second quarter of the 19th century, and shall I deny to him the capability of appreciating one of the loftiest efforts of the human mind? Perish the notion!

I had nearly arrived at a permanent decision when the progress of my meditation was abruptly arrested by the intervention of a new and startling consideration. Bowring was a universal linguist, a master of dead and living languages to any extent. Admirably well did he know —none better—the intrinsic nothingness of the English tongue. Its periods and phrases were, in truth, very small beer to him. Suppose that I were to accost him in the majestical cadences of the Spanish. A passage from Calderon might form a felicitous introduction; or in the French? I could draw upon Corneille, Malherbe, Voltaire, etc. to any amount; or in the German? Here, again, I was at home. To spout Opitz, Canitz, Ugo Wieland, and oh! above all, Richter—*meines herz Richter, (ach wenn Ich ein herz habe)* was as easy as to mix as a fifth tumbler. Of Latin and Greek I made no account; Timbuctooese I was slightly deficient in. As to the Hungarian and Polish they were not hastily to be sneezed at. The unknown tongues merited some attention, on account of the coal-black locks of the Rev. Ned Irving. In short, the satisfactory adjustment of this point was to be sedulously looked to. After some further deliberation I at length concluded upon doing nothing hurriedly. First ideas, said I, should be allowed time to cool into shape. A grammatical error would play the devil with me. The great Utilitarian would dub me quack, and the forthcoming number of the Westminster would nail me to the wall as a hollow-skulled pretender to encyclopediacal knowledge, a character which I am much more anxious that Oliver Yorke should fasten upon Lardner than Roland Bowring upon me.

As, however, I languidly sipped my ninth glass a heart-chilling and soul-sinking reminiscence came over me. I remembered to have somewhere read that Bowring was a Cassius-like looking philosopher. Now the stranger before me was rather plump than spare : certainly more *embonpoint* than corresponded with the portrait given of the Doctor. Thus was my basket of glass instantaneously shattered to fragments, while I, like another Alnascher, stood weeping over the brittle ruin. This, then, was not Bowring! The tide of life ran coldly to my heart; and I felt myself at that moment a conscious nonentity!

What was to be done? Hastily to discuss the remainder of my wine, to order a fresh bottle, and to drink six or eight glasses in rapid succession, was the operation of a few minutes. And oh, what a change! Cleverly, indeed, had I calculated upon a glorious reaction. Words I have none to reveal the quiescence of spirit that succeeded the interior balminess that steeped my faculty in blessed sweetness; I felt renovated, created anew! I had undergone an apotheosis; I wore the cumbrous habiliments of flesh and blood no longer; the shell, hitherto the circumscriber of my soul, was shivered; I stood out in front of the universe a visible and tangible intellect, and beheld, with giant grasp, the key that had power to unlock the deep prison which enclosed the secrets of antiquity and futurity!

The solitary thing that excited my surprise and embarrassment was

1 Samuel Coleridge at twenty-six.

2 Thomas De Quincey.

3 James Mangan on his death-bed.

4 Wilkie Collins.

5 Edgar Allan Poe.

the anomalous appearance which the nose of the stranger had assumed. But a few brief minutes before it had exhibited a symmetry the most perfect, and dimensions of an everyday character; now it might have formed a respectable rival to the Tower of Lebanon. As I concentrated the scattered energies of mind, and brought them soberly to bear upon the examination of this enormous feature, I learned from an intimate perception of too incommunicable a nature to admit of development, that the stranger was no other than a revivification of Maugraby, the celebrated oriental necromancer, whose dreaded name the romances of my childhood had rendered familiar to me, and who had lately arrived in Dublin for the purpose of consummating some hell-born deed of darkness, of the particulars of which I was, in all probability, destined to remain eternally ignorant. That there is, as some German metaphysicians maintain, idiosyncracy in some individuals, endowing them with the possession of a sixth sense or faculty to which nomenclature has as yet affixed no distinct idea (for our ideas are in fewer instances derivable from things than from names) is a position which I will never suffer any man, woman, or child, to contest. Had I myself ever at any former period been disturbed by the intrusion of doubts upon the subject, here was evidence more than sufficient to dissipate them all. Here was evidence too weighty to be kicked downstairs in a fine *de haut en bas* fashion; for, although I had never until the present evening, come into contact with Maugraby, this sixth faculty, this fine, vague, spiritual, unintelligible, lightning-like instinct had sufficed to assure me of his presence and proximity. It was even so; certainty is the sepulchre of scepticism; scepticism is the executioner of certainty. As the believer, when he begins to doubt, ceases to believe; so the doubter, when he begins to believe, ceases to doubt. These may be entitled eternal, moral axioms, philosophical aphorisms, infinitely superior to the aphorisms of Sir Morgan O'Dogherty touching the relative merits of soap and bear's grease, black pudding, *manches a gigot,* cravats, cold fish, and similar bagatelles; and I may as well take this opportunity of observing that Sir M. O'D. has by such discussions inflicted incalculable injury upon the cause of philosophy, which mankind should be perpetually instructed to look up to as the very soul of seriousness and centre of gravity.

That he whom I surveyed was identically and *bona fide* Maugraby, it would have betrayed symptoms of extravagant lunacy in me to deny; because the capability of producing so remarkable an effect, as the preternatural growth of nose which I witnessed, was one which, so far as my lucubration enabled me to judge, had always been exclusively monopolized by Maugraby. It was by no manner of means material whether what came under my inspection were a tangible reality or an optical illusion; that was Maugraby's business, not mine; and if he had juggled my senses into a persuasion of the fidelity of that appearance which confounded me, when, in point of fact, the entire thing, if uncurtained to the world, would turn out to be a lie—a shabby piece of 'Lock-and-gankel-work', a naked bamboozlement; if he had done this, upon his own head be the deep guilt, the odium, the infamy attachable to the transaction. It would be hard if I were compelled to incur any responsibility for the iniquitous vagaries of an East Indian sorcerer. To the day of my death I would protest against such injustice. The impression transmitted along the cord of the visual nerve to the external chambers of the brain, and thence conveyed by easy stages into the inner domicile of the soul, is all, quoth I, that I have to do with. Of such an impression I am the life-long slave. Whether there be other physical objects on the face of this globe as well as myself—whether there be the material of a globe at all—whether matter be an entity or an abstraction—whether it have substratum or not—and whether there be anything anywhere having any existence of any description, is a problem for Berkeleyans; but if there be any reasoning essences here below independent of myself, in circumstances parallel with my own, their opinions will corroborate mine; our feelings will be found to coalesce, our decisions to coincide. In any event, however, no argument arising from the metaphysics of the question can annihilate the identity of Maugraby. Were I to have been hanged for it in the course of the evening, at the first convenient lamp-post, I could not suppress a sentiment of envy at the superiority over his fellow-creatures which characterised the Indian juggler. Elevate me, said I, to the uppermost step of the ladder, establish me on the apex of the mountain, and what, after all, is my pre-eminence? Low is the highest! Contemptibly dwarfish the loftiest attitude! Admit my powers to be multifarious and unique; yet, am I, by comparison with this intelligence, sunk 'deeper than ever plummet sounded'. Lord of this earth, Maugraby; his breath exhales pestilence; his hand lavishes treasures! He possesses invisibility, ubiquity, tact, genius, wealth, exhaustless power undreamed of. Such is Maugraby; such is he on whom I gaze. He is worthy to be champion of England or to write the leading articles for the Thunderer.

Gradually the current of my thoughts took another course, and my mind yielded to suggestions and speculations that were anything but tranquillizing and agreeable. I am not prone to be lightly affected; legerdemain and playhouse thunder move me never; it might be even found a task to brain me with a lady's fan; and hence the mere size of Maugraby's nose, though I admitted it to be a novelty of the season, was insufficient to excite any emotion of terror within me. Viewed in the abstract, it was unquestionably no more than an additory, a bugbear to the uninitiated of the suburbs; a staggering deviation from the appearances that everyday life presents us with; and if this were the Alpha and Omega of the affair, Maugraby was a bottle of smoke. But this was not all; it was to be recollected that the nose increased each moment in longitude and latitude; here was the rub. The magnitude of a man's nose is not, *per se,* an object of public solicitude; the balance of power is not interfered with by it, and its effects upon the social system are comparatively slight; but if a progressive increase in that magnitude be discernible, such an increase becomes a subject of interest to the community with whom the owner of the nose associates, and will, in course of time, absorb the undivided attention of mankind. [See Slawkenbergius, vol. ix., chap. xxxii., p. 658, Art. Nosology]. It was apparent that in Maugraby's case dismal damage would accrue to the proprietor of the Shades. His (Maugraby's) nose would speedily become too vast for the area of the apartment; it would soon constitute a barricade, it would offer a formidable obstacle to the ingress of visitors; eventually the entrance to the tavern would be blocked up; all intercourse would be thus impracticable; business would come to a dead standstill, and an evil, whose ramifications no penetration could reach, would thus be generated.

But experience alone could testify to the absolute amount of injury that would be inflicted through the agency of this mountainous feature. Extending itself through College Green, through Dame Street, Westmoreland Street, and Grafton Street, it would by regular degrees, occupy every square foot of vacant space in this mighty metropolis. Then would ensue the prostration of commerce, the reign of universal terror, the precipitated departure of the citizens of all ranks into the interior, and Dublin would, in its melancholy destiny, be assimilated by the historian of a future age, with Persepolis, Palmyra, and Nineveh! As the phantasmagoria of all this ruin arose in shadowy horror upon my anticipations, is it wonderful that I shook as if affected with palsy, and that my heart sank into my bosom to a depth of several inches? I fell at once into a train of soliloquy.

Too intimately, Maugraby, am I acquainted with thine iron character to doubt for an instant thy rocky immovability of purpose. What thou willest that executest thou. Expostulation and remonstrance, oratory and poetry are to thee so much rigmarole; even my tears will be thy laughing stock. I have not the ghost of a chance against thee.

Maugraby! thou damned incubus! what liberty is this thou darest to take with me? Supposest thou that I will perish, as perishes the culprit at the gallows, bandaged, night-capped, hoodwinked, humbugged. Is thy horn after all so soft? I am, it is true, weaponless, unless we consider this glass decanter in my fist a weapon; but all the weapons with which nature has endowed me shall be exercised against thee. Still, and at the best, 'my final hope is flat despair.' I stand alone; like Anacharsis Clootz, I am deserted by the human race; I am driven into a box, there I am cooped up; a beggarly bottle of wine is allotted to me; *pour toute compagnie,* I am placed in juxtaposition with a hellhound, and then I am left to perish ignobly.

That I should at this moment have neither pike, poker, pitchfork, nor pickaxe, will be viewed in the light of a metropolitan calamity by the future annalist of Dublin, when he shall have occasion to chronicle the circumstance. The absence of a vat of tallow from this establishment is of the greatest detriment to me, for in such a vat it might be practicable to suffocate this demi-dæmon. There being no such vat it becomes obvious he can never be suffocated in it. How, then, good Heavens, can any man be so senseless, betray so much of the Hottentot, show himself so far sunk in stupidity, as to expect that I should find one at my elbow? How deplorably he needs the schoolmaster! How requisite it is that some friend to human perfectibility should advance him one halfpenny each Saturday, wherewith to procure a halfpenny magazine. He is this night the concentrated extract of absurdity; the force of assay can no further go. I protest with all the solemnity of my awful position that if there be a chandler's vat under this roof the fact is the most extraordinary that history records. Its existence is not to be accounted for on any commercial principle. No man can tell how it was conveyed hither, or at whose expense it was established. An impenetrable veil of mystery shrouds the proceeding; the whole thing is dark; it is an enigma, a phenomenon of great importance. I had better leave it where I found it.

My regards were now painfully fascinated by the great magician of the Dom-Daniel. To look in any direction but the one I felt to be totally impracticable. He had spell-bound me doubtlessly; his accursed jugglery had been at work while I, with the innocent unsuspiciousness which forms my distinguishing characteristic, had been occupied in draining the decanter. Was ever an inhabitant of any city in Europe so horribly predicamented? It was manifest that he had already singled me out as his first victim. I foreknew the destiny whereinto I was reserved. I saw the black marble dome, the interminable suites of chambers, the wizard scrolls, the shafts and arrows, and in dim but dreadful perspective, the bloody cage, in which, incarcerated under the figure of a bat, I should be doomed to flap my leathern wings dolefully through the sunless day.

Mere human fortitude was inadequate to the longer endurance of such agonising emotions as accompanied the portrayal of these horrors upon my intellectual retina. Nature was for once victor over necromancy. I started up, I shrieked, I shouted, I rushed forward headlong. I remember tumbling down in a state of frenzy, but nothing beyond.

> The morn was up again, the dewy morn,
>   With breath all incense and with cheek all bloom,
>   Laughing the clouds away with playful scorn,
>   And living as if earth contained no tomb.

But I could not enjoy it, for I was in bed, and my temples throbbed violently. I understood that I had been conveyed from the Shades in a carriage. Dr Stokes was at my bedside; I inquired of him whether he had seen Maugraby hovering in the vicinity of the house, As the only reply to this was a shake of the head I at once and briefly gave him an account of my adventure.

Well, said he, I can satisfy you of the individuality of your unknown. He is neither Maugraby nor Bowring, but BRASSPEN, of the *Comet* Club. I saw him there last night myself. *Tout est mystere dans ce monde-ci,* thought I, *Je ne sais trop qu'en croire.*

5

It seems most appropriate that *William Wilkie Collins* (1824-1889) should bring this first section to a close. He met Samuel Taylor Coleridge, with whom we began, when he was a young boy of nine, and retained a vivid and influential memory of the great poet throughout his life. He had learned of Coleridge's addiction at that early age from his mother, who was one of the few people to show real tolerance and understanding of the poet's condition and thereby earned his undying gratitude. The matter-of-fact way in which the young Wilkie was told of the use of laudanum undoubtedly contributed to the easy and casual manner in which he himself took it in later life and thereafter steadfastly refused to either consider it a matter of great moment or a danger to his well-being and work. The life of Wilkie Collins is, indeed, something of a striking contrast to the four other writers we have just studied—Coleridge, De Quincey, Poe and Mangan—in that he did not suffer from great variances of emotion and did not lead a life of torment and dissipation.

Born the elder son of enlightened parents—his father was a noted landscape and figure painter—he was educated in England and Italy. After a number of years of comparatively indifferent success in business and law, he began writing and thereafter rapidly became one of the most popular authors of his time. His dedication to work and his prodigious output left him little time for anything else, and his life looked destined to become one of orderly if exhausting routine until illness, in the form of gout, began to plague him in the 1860s. Laudanum was readily available and often prescribed by doctors, so Collins sought this for relief. But, in time, what had been merely a sop to pain, began to take a real grip on him. The crisis came in 1867-8, when his beloved mother fell ill. Called to her bedside as she lay raving, he knew it would be impossible to leave until the end came—yet he had a novel with an urgent deadline, *The Moonstone,* to write. Attempts to continue it proved futile and the work fell behind. In desperation he turned to laudanum for sustenance and began to dose himself in order to keep going. 'He took it not by the dram,' Dr Noel P. Davis has written in his *The Life of Wilkie Collins* (1956) 'but by the glassful from a decanter. It cleared his mind and he gathered together the complicated threads of his story. Thus, by a drugged, unnatural effort he lifted *The Moonstone* to a level of pure form never since approached.' The drug sustained him constantly until February 19th 1868 when his mother finally died, but the effect the huge doses had had on him and his work was not forgotten. Several of his later works were also to be produced under its influence, including his equally famous novel *The Woman in White* (1860), *Armadale* (1864) and *The Evil Genius* (1885)—not to mention several of his short stories, including the one I have selected here.

By 1877 Collins was in almost constant pain and carried a supply of laudanum in a silver flask wherever he went, sipping from it regularly. A friend, Squire Bancroft, noted in his *Recollections of Sixty Years* (1909) that Collins 'habitually drank at a single dose enough laudanum to kill a dozen men' and this caused his appearance to deteriorate until his flesh sagged and his eyes were 'literally enormous bags of blood'. But his work continued unabated and far from denying his need of the drug, he was even making mention of it in some of his books. Some ill-effects were inevitable, however, and in 1885 he began to see movement in the shadows of his gas-lit study. Phantoms had begun to pursue him, he told his family: he thought he could see 'a green woman with tusk teeth who stood waiting on the stairs to bite a piece from my shoulder'. He also occasionally saw a 'mysterious light' not unlike a candle, and this experience he utilized for the tale of fantasy and adventure reprinted here.

Apart from the success of *The Moonstone* and *The Woman in White*, Collins will be remembered for his friendship and collaboration with Charles Dickens[1] and his novel *Armadale* which, despite a notable lack of success in England, became a huge best-seller in America where it outsold the work of Dickens, Victor Hugo and even the local favourite, Nathaniel Hawthorne. It also played an important part in the history of American literature, for it was the serial which saved the life of *Harper's Weekly*—then the only good mass circulation magazine available and, because of falling sales, in danger of being closed. As Dr Davis has noted, 'Circulation perked up, how-

---

[1] *Editor's note.* Charles Dickens was also an occasional imbiber of laudanum in the later years of his life to sustain him through long bouts of writing and lecturing. His admissions of this are to be found in his *Collected Letters* and also John Forster's famous *Life of Charles Dickens*. Dickens was also interested in opium smoking and on one occasion visited an opium den in London to collect material for the book he was then working on, *The Mystery of Edwin Drood*. The murderer in the story, John Jaspar, is an opium addict and the book contains some memorable passages describing events under the influence of the drug.

ever, with the first instalment of *Armadale* and by the end of the story had reached its pre-Civil War level.... The truth is that Collins had much to do with teaching our grandparents to read!' And this was all achieved by a story which chronicled the activities of a drug addict, Miss Gwilt, and her experiments with laudanum, and which had a 'weird, dreamlike consistency of mood and setting'! 'The Candlelight Ghost', apart from its hallucinatory influence, is also interesting in that Collins wrote it for a popular magazine and had to sustain himself once again with laudanum to complete it within the exacting deadline he had been set. For all that, it is a fine example of the author's storytelling ability—a skill he retained to his death even under the intense pressures of demanding editors, crippling pain and massive intakes of laudanum.

*

Who was the man who invented laudanum? I thank him from the bottom of my heart, whoever he was.... I have had six delicious hours of oblivion; I have woken up with my mind composed; I have written a perfect little letter; I have drunk my cup of tea with a real relish of it; and I have dawdled over my morning toilet with an exquisite sense of relief—and all through the modest little bottle of drops which I see on my bedroom chimney-piece at this moment. Drops, you are a darling! If I love nothing else, I love you!

Note made on a spring morning, 1865

The Candlestick Ghost
WILLIAM WILKIE COLLINS

I have got an alarming confession to make. I am haunted by a Ghost.

If you were to guess for a hundred years, you would never guess what my ghost is. I shall make you laugh to begin with—and afterwards I shall make your flesh creep. My Ghost is the ghost of a Bedroom Candlestick.

Yes, a bedroom candlestick and candle or a flat candlestick and candle—put it which way you like—that is what haunts me. I wish it was something pleasanter and more out of the common way; a beautiful lady, or a mine of gold and silver, or a cellar of wine and a coach and horses, and such-like. But, being what it is, I must take it for what it is, and make the best of it—and I shall thank you kindly if you will help me out by doing the same.

I am not a scholar myself; but I make bold to believe that the haunting of any man with anything under the sun, begins with the frightening of him. At any rate, the haunting of me with a bedroom candlestick and candle began with the frightening of me with a bedroom candlestick and candle—the frightening of me half out of my life; and, for the time being, the frightening of me altogether out of my wits. That is not a very pleasant thing to confess, before stating the particulars; but perhaps you will be the readier to believe that I am not a downright coward, because you may find me bold enough to make a clean breast of it already, to my own great disadvantage, so far.

Here are the particulars, as well as I can put them :

I was apprenticed to the sea when I was about as tall as my own walking-stick; and I made good enough use of my time to be fit for a mate's berth at the age of twenty-five years.

It was in the year eighteen hundred and eighteen, or nineteen, I am not quite certain which, that I reached the before-mentioned age of twenty-five. You will please to excuse my memory not being very good for dates, names, numbers, places, and such-like. No fear, though, about the particulars I have undertaken to tell you of; I have got them all ship-shape in my recollection; I can see them, at this moment, as clear as noonday in my own mind. But there is a mist over what went before, and, for the matter of that, a mist likewise over much that came after—and it's not very likely to lift at my time of life, is it?

Well, in eighteen hundred and eighteen, or nineteen, when there was peace in our part of the world—and not before it was wanted, you will say—there was fighting, of a certain scampering, scrambling kind, going on in that old battlefield, which we seafaring men know by the name of the Spanish Main.

The possessions that belonged to the Spaniards in South America had broken into open mutiny and declared for themselves years before. There was plenty of bloodshed between the new government and the old; but the new had got the best of it, for the most part, under one General Bolivar—a famous man in his time, though he seems to have dropped out of people's memories now. Englishmen and Irishmen with a turn for fighting, and nothing particular to do at home, joined the General as volunteers; and some of our merchants here found it a good venture to send supplies across the ocean to the popular side. There was risk enough, of course, in doing this; but where one speculation of the kind succeeded, it made up for two, at the least, that failed. And that's the true principle of trade, wherever I have met with it, all the world over.

Among the Englishmen who were concerned in this Spanish-American business, I, your humble servant, happened in a small way to be one.

I was then mate of a brig belonging to a certain firm in the City, which drove a sort of general trade, mostly in queer out-of-the-way places, as far from home as possible; and which freighted the brig, in the year I am speaking of, with a cargo of gunpowder for General Bolivar and his volunteers. Nobody knew anything about our instructions, when we sailed, except the captain; and he didn't half seem to like them. I can't rightly say how many barrels of powder we had on board, or how much each barrel held—I only know we had no other cargo. The name of the brig was the *Good Intent*—a queer name enough, you will tell me, for a vessel laden with gunpowder, and sent to help a revolution. And as far as this particular voyage was concerned, so it was. I mean that for a joke, and I hope you will encourage me by laughing at it.

The *Good Intent* was the craziest old tub of a vessel I ever went to sea in, and the worst found in all respects. She was two hundred and thirty, or two hundred and eighty tons burden, I forget which; and she had a crew of eight, all told—nothing like as many as we ought by rights to have had to work the brig. However, we were well and honestly paid our wages; and we had to set that against the chance of foundering at sea, and, on this occasion, likewise, the chance of being blown up into the bargain.

In consideration of the nature of our cargo, we were harassed with new regulations which we didn't at all like, relative to smoking our pipes and lighting our lanterns; and, as usual in such cases, the captain who made the regulations, preached what he didn't practice. Not a man of us was allowed to have a bit of lighted candle in his hand when he went below—except the skipper; and he used his light, when he turned in, or when he looked over his charts on the cabin table, just as usual.

This light was a common kitchen candle or 'dip', and it stood in an old battered flat candlestick, with all the japan worn and melted off, and all the tin showing through. It would have been more seamanlike and suitable in every respect if he had had a lamp or a lantern; but he stuck to his old candlestick; and that same old candlestick has ever afterwards stuck to *me*. That's another joke, if you please, and a better one than the first, in my opinion.

Well (I said 'well' before, but it's a word that helps a man on like), we sailed in the brig, and shaped our course, first, for the Virgin Islands, in the West Indies; and, after sighting them, we made for the

Leeward Islands next; and then stood on due south, till the look-out at the mast-head hailed the deck, and said he saw land. That land was the coast of South America. We had had a wonderful voyage so far. We had lost none of our spars or sails, and not a man of us had been harassed to death at the pumps. It wasn't often the *Good Intent* made such a voyage as that, I can tell you.

I was sent aloft to make sure about the land, and I did make sure of it.

When I reported the same to the skipper, he went below, and had a look at his letter of instructions and the chart. When he came on deck again, he altered our course a trifle to the eastward—I forget the point on the compass, but that don't matter. What I do remember is, that it was dark before we closed in with the land. We kept the lead going, and hove the brig to in from four to five fathoms water, or it might be six—I can't say for certain. I kept a sharp eye to the drift of the vessel, none of us knowing how the currents ran on that coast. We all wondered why the skipper didn't anchor; but he said, No, he must first show a light at the foretop mast-head, and wait for an answering light on shore. We did wait, and nothing of the sort appeared. It was starlight and calm. What little wind there was came in puffs off the land. I suppose we waited, drifting a little to the westward, as I made it out, best part of an hour before anything happened —and then, instead of seeing the light on shore, we saw a boat coming towards us, rowed by two men only.

We hailed them, and they answered 'Friends!' and hailed us by our name. They came on board. One of them was an Irishman, and the other was a coffee-coloured native pilot, who jabbered a little English.

The Irishman handed a note to our skipper, who showed it to me. It informed us that the part of the coast we were off was not over safe for discharging our cargo, seeing that spies of the enemy (that is to say, of the old government) had been taken and shot in the neighbourhood the day before. We might trust the brig to the native pilot; and he had his instructions to take us to another part of the coast. The note was signed by the proper parties; so we let the Irishman go back alone in the boat, and allowed the pilot to exercise his lawful authority over the brig. He kept us stretching off from the land till noon the next day—his instructions, seemingly, ordering him to keep us well out of sight of the shore. We only altered our course, in the afternoon, so as to close in with the land again a little before midnight.

This same pilot was about as ill-looking a vagabond as ever I saw; a skinny, cowardly, quarrelsome mongrel, who swore at the men, in the vilest broken English, till they were every one of them ready to pitch him overboard. The skipper kept them quiet, and I kept them quiet, for the pilot being given us by our instructions, we were bound to make the best of him. Near nightfall, however, with the best will in the world to avoid it, I was unlucky enough to quarrel with him.

He wanted to go below with his pipe, and I stopped him, of course, because it was contrary to orders. Upon that, he tried to hustle by me, and I put him away with my hand. I never meant to push him down; but, somehow, I did. He picked himself up as quick as lightning, and pulled out his knife. I snatched it out of his hand, slapped his murderous face for him, and threw his weapon overboard. He gave me one ugly look, and walked aft. I didn't think much of the look then; but I remembered it a little too well afterwards.

We were close in with the land again, just as the wind failed us, between eleven and twelve that night; and dropped our anchor by the pilot's directions.

It was pitch dark, and a dead airless calm. The skipper was on deck with two of our best men for watch. The rest were below, except the pilot, who coiled himself up, more like a snake than a man, on the forecastle. It was not my watch till four in the morning. But I didn't like the look of the night, or the pilot, or the state of things generally, and I shook myself down on deck to get my nap there, and be ready for anything at a moment's notice. The last I remember was the skipper whispering to me that he didn't like the look of things either, and that he would go below and consult his instructions again. That is the last I remember, before the slow, heavy, regular roll of the old brig on the ground swell rocked me off to sleep.

I was awoke by a scuffle on the forecastle, and a gag in my mouth. There was a man on my breast, and a man on my legs; and I was bound hand and foot in half a minute.

The brig was in the hands of the Spaniards. They were swarming all over her. I heard six heavy splashes in the water, one after another. I saw the captain stabbed to the heart as he came running up the companion—and I heard a seventh splash in the water. Except myself, every soul of us on board had been murdered and thrown into the sea. Why I was left, I couldn't think, till I saw the pilot stoop over me with a lantern, and look, to make sure of who I was. There was a devlish grin on his face, and he nodded his head at me, as much as to say, *You* were the man who hustled me down and slapped my face, and I mean to play the game of cat and mouse with you in return for it!

I could neither move nor speak; but I could see the Spaniards take off the main hatch and rig the purchases for getting up the cargo. A quarter of an hour afterwards, I heard the sweeps of a schooner, or other small vessel, in the water. The strange craft was laid alongside of us; and the Spaniards set to work to discharge our cargo into her. They all worked hard except the pilot; and he came, from time to time, with his lantern, to have another look at me, and to grin and nod always in the same devilish way. I am old enough now not to be ashamed of confessing the truth; and I don't mind acknowledging that the pilot frightened me.

The fright, and the bonds, and the gag, and the not being able to stir hand or foot, had pretty nigh worn me out, by the time the Spaniards gave over work. This was just as the dawn broke. They had shifted good part of our cargo on board their vessel, but nothing like all of it; and they were sharp enough to be off with what they had got, before daylight.

I need hardly say that I had made up my mind, by this time, to the worst I could think of. The pilot, it was clear enough, was one of the spies of the enemy, who had wormed himself into the confidence of our consignees without being suspected. He, or more likely his employers, had got knowledge enough of us to suspect what our cargo was; we had been anchored for the night in the safest berth for them to surprise us in; and we had paid the penalty of having a small crew, and consequently an insufficient watch. All this was clear enough—but what did the pilot mean to do with *me*?

On the word of a man, it makes my flesh creep, now, only to tell you what he did with me.

After all the rest of them were out of the brig, except the pilot and two Spanish seamen, these last took me up, bound and gagged, as I was, lowered me into the hold of the vessel, and laid me along the floor; lashing me to it with ropes' ends, so that I could just turn from one side to the other, but could not roll myself fairly over, so as to change my place. They then left me. Both of them were the worse for liquor : but the devil of a pilot was sober — mind that ! — as sober as I am at the present moment.

I lay in the dark for a little while, with my heart thumping as if it was going to jump out of me. I lay about five minutes or so, when the pilot came down into the hold, alone.

He had the captain's cursed flat candlestick and a carpenter's awl in one hand, and a long thin twist of cotton yarn, well oiled, in the other. He put the candlestick, with a new 'dip' candle lighted in it, down on the floor, about two feet from my face, and close against the side of the vessel. The light was feeble enough; but it was sufficient to show a dozen barrels of gunpowder or more, left all round me in the hold of the brig. I began to suspect what he was after, the moment I noticed the barrels. The horrors laid hold of me from head to foot; and the sweat poured off my face like water.

I saw him go, next, to one of the barrels of powder standing against the side of the vessel, in a line with the candle, and about three feet, or rather better, away from it. He bored a hole in the side of the barrel with his awl; and the horrid powder came trickling out, as black as hell, and dripped into the hollow of his hand, which he held to catch it. When he had got a good handful, he stopped up the hole by jamming one end of his oiled twist of cotton-yarn fast into it; and he then rubbed the powder into the whole length of the yarn, till he had blackened every hairsbreadth of it.

The next thing he did—as true as I sit here, as true as the heaven above us all—the next thing he did was to carry the free end of his long, lean, black, frightful slow-match to the lighted candle alongside my face. He tied it (the bloody-minded villain!) in several folds, round the tallow dip, about a third of the distance down, measuring from the flame of the wick to the lip of the candlestick. He did that; he looked to see that my lashings were all safe; and then he put his face down close to mine, and whispered in my ear, 'Blow up with the brig!'

He was on deck again the moment after; and he and the two others shoved the hatch on over me. At the farthest end from where I lay, they had not fitted it down quite true, and I saw a blink of daylight glimmering in when I looked in that direction. I heard the sweeps of the schooner fall into the water—splash! splash! fainter and fainter, as they swept the vessel out in the dead calm, to be ready for the wind in the offing. Fainter and fainter, splash! splash! for a quarter of an hour or more.

While those sounds were in my ears, my eyes were fixed on the candle.

It had been freshly lit—if left to itself it would burn for between six and seven hours. The slow-match was twisted round it about a third of the way down; and therefore the flame would be about two hours reaching it. There I lay, gagged, bound, lashed to the floor; seeing my own life burning down with the candle by my side—there I lay, alone on the sea, doomed to be blown to atoms, and to see that doom drawing on, nearer and nearer with every fresh second of time, through nigh on two hours to come; powerless to help myself and speechless to call for help to others. The wonder to me is that I didn't cheat the flame, the slow-match, and the powder, and die of the horror of my situation before my first half-hour was out in the hold of the brig.

I can't exactly say how long I kept the command of my senses after I had ceased to hear the splash of the schooner's sweeps in the water. I can trace back everything I did and everything I thought, up to a certain point; but, once past that, I get all abroad, and lose myself in my memory now, much as I lost myself in my own feelings at the time.

The moment the hatch was covered over me, I began, as every other would have begun in my place, with a frantic effort to free my hands. In the mad panic I was in, I cut my flesh with the lashings as if they had been knife-blades; but I never stirred them. There was less chance still of freeing my legs, or of tearing myself from the fastenings that held me to the floor. I gave in, when I was all but suffocated for want of breath. The gag, you will please to remember, was a terrible enemy to me; I could only breathe freely through my nose—and that is but a poor vent when a man is straining his strength as far as ever it will go.

I gave in, and lay quiet, and got my breath again; my eyes glaring and straining at the candle all the time.

While I was staring at it, the notion struck me of trying to blow out the flame by pumping a long breath at it suddenly through my nostrils. It was too high above me, and too far away from me, to be reached in that fashion. I tried, and tried, and tried—and then I gave in again and lay quiet again; always with my eyes glaring at the candle, and the candle glaring at *me*. The splash of the schooner's sweeps was very faint by this time. I could only just hear them in the morning stillness. Splash! splash!—fainter and fainter—splash! splash!

Without exactly feeling my mind going, I began to feel it getting queer, as early as this. The snuff of the candle was growing taller and taller, and the length of tallow between the flame and the slow-match, which was the length of my life, was getting shorter and shorter. I calculated that I had rather less than an hour and a half to live.

An hour and a half! Was there a chance, in that time, of a boat pulling off to the brig from shore? Whether the land near which the vessel was anchored was in possession of our side, or in possession of the enemy's side, I made out that they must, sooner or later, send to hail the brig, merely because she was a stranger in those parts. The question for *me* was, how soon? The sun had not risen yet, as I could tell by looking through the chink in the hatch. There was no coast village near us, as we all knew, before the brig was seized, by seeing no lights on shore. There was no wind, as I could tell by listening, to bring any strange vessel near. If I had had six hours to live, there might have been a chance for me, reckoning from sunrise to noon. But with an hour and a half, which had dwindled to an hour and a quarter by this time—or, in other words, with the earliness of the morning, the uninhabited coast, and the dead calm all against me—there was not the ghost of a chance. As I felt that, I had another struggle—the last —with my bonds; and only cut myself the deeper for my pains.

I gave in once more, and lay quiet, and listened for the splash of the sweeps.

Gone! Not a sound could I hear but the blowing of a fish, now and then, on the surface of the sea, and the creak of the brig's crazy old spars, as she rolled gently from side to side with the little swell there was on the quiet water.

An hour and a quarter. The wick grew terribly, as the quarter slipped away; and the charred top of it began to thicken and spread out mushroom-shape. It would fall off soon. Would it fall off red-hot, and would the swing of the brig cant it over the side of the candle, and let it down on the slow-match? If it would, I had about ten minutes to live instead of an hour.

This discovery set my mind for a minute on a new tack altogether. I began to ponder with myself what sort of a death blowing-up might be. Painful? Well, it would be, surely, too sudden for that. Perhaps just one crash, inside me, or outside me, or both, and nothing more? Perhaps not even a crash; that and death and the scattering of this living body of mine into millions of fiery sparks, might all happen in the same instant? I couldn't make it out; I couldn't settle how it would be. The minute of calmness in my mind left it, before I had half done thinking; and I got all abroad again.

When I came back to my thoughts, or when they came back to me (I can't say which), the wick was awfully tall, the flame was burning with a smoke above it, the charred top was broad and red, and heavily spreading out to its fall.

My despair and horror at seeing it, took me in a new way, which was good and right, at any rate, for my poor soul. I tried to pray; in my own heart, you will understand, for the gag put all lip-praying out of my power. I tried, but the candle seemed to burn it up in me. I struggled hard to force my eyes from the slow, murderous flame, and to look up through the chink in the hatch at the blessed daylight. I tried once, tried twice; and gave it up. I tried next only to shut my eyes, and keep them shut—once—twice—and the second time I did it. 'God bless old mother, and sister Lizzie; God keep them both, and forgive me.' That was all I had time to say, in my own heart, before my eyes opened again, in spite of me, and the flame of the candle flew into them, flew all over me, and burnt up the rest of my thoughts in an instant.

I couldn't hear the fish blowing now; I couldn't hear the creak of the spars; I couldn't think; I couldn't feel the sweat of my own death agony on my face—I could only look at the heavy charred top of the wick. It swelled, tottered, bent over to one side, dropped—red hot at the moment of its fall—black and harmless, even before the swing of the brig had canted it over into the bottom of the candlestick.

I caught myself laughing.

Yes! laughing at the safe fall of the bit of wick. But for the gag I should have screamed with laughing. As it was, I shook with it inside me—shook till the blood was in my head, and I was all but suffocated for want of breath. I had just sense enough left to feel that my own horrid laughter, at that awful moment, was a sign of my brain going at last. I had just sense enough left to make another struggle before my mind broke loose like a frightened horse, and ran away with me.

One comforting look at the blink of daylight through the hatch was what I tried for once more. The fight to force my eyes from the candle and to get that one look at daylight, was the hardest I had had yet; and I lost the fight. The flame had hold of my eyes as fast as the lashings had hold of my hands. I couldn't look away from it. I couldn't even shut my eyes, when I tried that next, for the second time. There was the wick, growing tall once more. There was the space of unburnt candle between the light and the slow-match shortened to an inch or less.

How much life did that inch leave me? Three-quarters of an hour? Half an hour? Fifty minutes? Twenty minutes? Steady! an inch of tallow candle would burn longer than twenty minutes. An inch of tallow! the notion of a man's body and soul being kept together by an inch of tallow! Wonderful! Why, the greatest king that sits on a throne can't keep a man's body and soul together; and here's an inch of tallow that can do what the king can't. There's something to tell mother, when I get home, which will surprise her more than all the rest of my voyages put together. I laughed inwardly, again, at the thought of that; and shook and swelled and suffocated myself, till the light of the candle leaped in through my eyes and licked up the laughter, and burnt it out for me, and made me all empty, and cold, and quiet once more.

Mother and Lizzie. I don't know when they came back; but they did come back—not, as it seemed to me, into my mind this time; but right down bodily before me, in the hold of the brig.

Yes: sure enough, there was Lizzie, just as light-hearted as usual, laughing at me. Laughing! Well, why not? Who is to blame Lizzie for thinking I'm lying on my back, drunk in the cellar, with the beer barrels all round me? Steady! she's crying now—spinning round and round in a fiery mist, wringing her hands, screeching out for help—fainter and fainter, like the splash of the schooner's sweeps. Gone!—burnt up in the fiery mist. Mist? fire? no: neither one nor the other. It's mother makes the light—mother knitting, with ten flaming points at the ends of her fingers and thumbs, and slow-matches hanging in bunches all round her face instead of her own grey hair. Mother in her old armchair, and the pilot's long skinny hands hanging over the back of the chair, dripping with gunpowder. No! no gunpowder, no chair, no mother—nothing but the pilot's face, shining red hot, like a sun, in the fiery mist; turning upside down in the fiery mist; running backwards and forwards along the slow-match, in the fiery mist;

spinning millions of miles in a minute, in the fiery mist—spinning itself smaller and smaller into one tiny point, and that point darting on a sudden straight into my head—and then, all fire and all mist—no hearing, no seeing, no thinking, no feeling—the brig, the sea, my own self, the whole world, all gone together!

After what I've just told you, I know nothing and remember nothing, till I woke up (as it seemed to me) in a comfortable bed, with two rough and ready men like myself sitting on each side of my pillow, and a gentleman standing watching me at the foot of the bed. It was about seven in the morning. My sleep (or what seemed like my sleep to me) had lasted better than eight months—I was among my own countrymen in the island of Trinidad—the men at each side of my pillow were my keepers, turn and turn about—and the gentleman standing at the foot of the bed was the doctor. What I said and did in those eight months, I never have known and never shall. I woke out of it as if it had been one long sleep—that's all I know.

It was another two months or more before the doctor thought it safe to answer the questions I asked him.

The brig had been anchored, just as I had supposed, off a part of the coast which was lonely enough to make the Spaniards pretty sure of no interruption, so long as they managed their murderous work quietly under cover of night.

My life had not been saved from the shore, but from the sea. An American vessel, becalmed in the offing, had made out the brig as the sun rose; and the captain having his time on his hands in consequence of the calm, and seeing a vessel anchored where no vessel had any reason to be, had manned one of his boats and sent his mate with it, to look a little closer into the matter, and bring back a report of what he saw.

What he saw, when he and his men found the brig deserted and boarded her, was a gleam of candlelight through the chink in the hatchway. The flame was within about a thread's breath of the slow-match, when he lowered himself into the hold; and if he had not had the sense and coolness to cut the match in two with his knife, before he touched the candle, he and his men might have been blown up along with the brig, as well as me. The match caught and turned into sputtering red fire, in the very act of putting the candle out; and if the communication with the powder barrel had not been cut off, the Lord only knows what might have happened.

What became of the Spanish schooner and the pilot I have never heard from that day to this.

As for the brig, the Yankees took her, as they took me, to Trinidad, and claimed their salvage, and got it, I hope, for their own sakes. I was landed just in the same state as when they rescued me from the brig, that is to say, clean out of my senses. But, please to remember it was a long time ago; and, take my word for it, I was discharged cured, as I have told you. Bless your hearts, I'm all right now, as you may see. I'm a little shaken by telling the story, as is only natural—a little shaken, my good friends, that's all.

II

I cannot describe the thousand fantastic ideas which passed through my brain during the three hours I was under the influence of the hachisch: they appeared too odd to be believed sincere; the persons present doubted at times, and asked me if I was not making sport of them, for I had my reason in the midst of this strange madness.

DR JEAN MOREAU
(1805-1880)

Just as in Britain and America, an interest in, and studies of, the effects of drug taking were emerging in Europe. It has been suggested that Germany, with the idealistic philosophies of the German Romantics, was the birthplace of this whole movement. But while it is certainly true that many of the works produced at this time were visionary in content, and that the great masters of the Gothic genre such as Goethe, Schiller, Walpole, Beckford and Lewis, had found their inspiration in Germany, it has never been satisfactorily proved that any of these men were addicts, or even indulged in drugs for their creative processes. That their tales are so full of Eastern splendour and Oriental imaginings is probably more due to their travels and the genius of their minds than the effects of stimulants. What is certain, though, is that the French Romantics of the early years of the nineteenth century became interested in the effects of opium and, more particularly, another drug not dissimilar in effect, hashish.

From the group of poets and artists who were most absorbed in this *mode du hachisch,* three names stand high above the rest: Théophile Gautier, Charles Baudelaire and Gérard de Nerval. These men and their companions were interested in the effects of the drug both from a scientific and an aesthetic point of view, having undoubtedly been influenced by De Quincey's 'Confessions' which had been swiftly translated into French after publication in England. They were determined to conduct their own experiments not only with opium, but also with the drug hashish, which had at that time excited everyone's interest in Paris through the investigations published by the physician Dr Jean Moreau of Tours. Théophile Gautier had, some short while before this, published a short story called 'The Opium Pipe' which concerned his initiation to opium, and there had been other reports of opium and laudanum experiences. However, it was the group of men who came together to form *Le Club des Hachischins* who created most interest. It is their motivation and the stories that resulted from their activities which form this next section.

6

Théophile Gautier (1811-1872), the painter, poet, novelist and critic was one of the founder members of the famous Hashish Club in the Paris of the 1840s. The city at this time was a bohemian heaven, and as Gautier himself later remarked, 'It was the fashion to be pale and greenish looking; to appear to be wasted by the pangs of passion and remorse; to talk sadly and fantastically about death.' Against this background, Gautier got together with others of his friends and acquaintances from the world of the arts to try hashish provided by the man who had begun the *mode,* Dr Moreau. The group met in the imposing Hotel Pimodan on the Ile Saint-Louis, in a lavishly furnished room on one of the upper floors. The members assembled once a month and were organized in an Oriental order under the command of a 'Sheik' called 'The Prince of Assassins'. His word was law and he was supposed to maintain his authority by the use of a 'magic drug' made up of hashish and other narcotics. According to the members this particular preparation made 'water taste like wine, berries like meat and meat like berries'. Here, surrounded by plush Oriental furnishings, the artists would take their hashish, lie back on couches or on the floor, and then afterwards recount all they had experienced.

It seems appropriate that the best description of the club, its members and their meetings should have been provided by Gautier himself, and it is his account which I have reprinted here. Among his writing in fiction one can find several references to stimulants; certain short stories, such as 'La Morte Amoreuse' and novels like *The Cross of Berny* bear the unmistakable marks of 'visionary' writing. Gautier was a most prolific writer throughout his life, and one needs only to mention the novel *Mademoiselle de Maupin,* his poem 'Albertus', the theatrical criticism and his famous travel sketches to demonstrate the range of his work. The man himself led a life almost totally devoted to work and without great incident, though one should perhaps record that he overcame a sickly childhood by making determined efforts to improve his physique by means of overeating and drinking. (He also took a buxom mistress in preference to a thin one in this same cause!) He constantly displayed a boundless and questing appetite for life, and it is perhaps not surprising to find that his interest in hashish—important though it was—was short lived. For the best part of a year he went to the gatherings enthusiastically—even managing to talk the naturally cautious Balzac into attending one night, although he steadfastly refused to sample the drug. Then, as suddenly as he had begun, Gautier decided to abandon the quest for further sensations, 'because a real writer needs only his natural dreams and does not want his thoughts to be influenced by any external agency, whatever it may be.' So he went his own way; the Club, however, was to continue.

*

Hashish has nothing of that ignoble heavy drunkenness about it which the races of the North obtain from wine and alcohol: it offers an intellectual intoxication.

Essay, 1844

The Hashish-Eaters' Club
Theophile Gautier

I

One December evening, I obeyed a mysterious summons expressed in enigmatic terms understood by the members but unintelligible to others, and arrived in a distant district, a kind of oasis of solitude in the centre of Paris, which the river surrounds with its two arms, as if to defend it against the inroads of civilization, for it was an old house in the Ile Saint-Louis, Pimodan House, built by Lauzun, which was the monthly meeting-place of the strange club which I had recently joined, and I was going to attend my first meeting there.

Although it was not quite six o'clock, it was very dark. A mist, which the nearness of the Seine made even thicker, blurred everything with its cotton-wool, which was torn and pierced here and there by the reddish haloes of the lanterns and the threads of light escaping from lighted windows.

The pavement was wet, and shimmered under the street lamps, as water reflects a light; a bitter wind, laden with icy particles, whipped your face and its guttural whistling formed the top line of a symphony, whose bass was provided by the swollen waters breaking against the arches of the bridges; not one of the harsh poetic forms of winter was lacking on that evening.

Along the deserted quay, among the mass of dark buildings, it was difficult to find the house I was seeking; but my coachman, standing up on his seat, was able to read on a marble plaque the half-effaced name of the old house which was the meeting-place of the initiated.

I raised the carved knocker, for the rise of the brass bell-pushes had not yet reached these remote parts, and I heard the door-pull squeak several times without success; at last it yielded to a more vigorous pull and the rusty old latch opened, and the door of massive planks turned on its hinges.

Behind the yellowish glass of the window pane, as I entered, appeared the head of an old door-woman, vaguely outlined by a guttering candle, a ready-made picture by Skalken. This head made a queer grimace, and a skinny finger poked out of the porter's lodge to show me the way.

As far as I could distinguish, by the wan light which always falls, however dark the sky, the courtyard which I was crossing was surrounded by buildings of ancient architectural form, with steep gables. I felt my feet getting wet as if I had walked through a meadow, for the cracks between the paving stones were full of grass.

The tall, narrow-paned windows of the stairs, blazing against the dark façade, guided me and prevented me from losing my way.

I mounted the steps and found myself at the foot of one of those huge staircases that they built in the time of Louis XIV, in which a modern house could easily dance. An Egyptian chimera in the style of Lebrun, with a Cupid astride, lay with outstretched paws on a pedestal, holding a candle in its claws which were curved like a sconce.

The steps were shallow, the landings well placed, a witness to the skill of the old architect and the gracious living of past centuries; as I climbed that wonderful stair, I felt that in my tight black dress coat I spoilt the effect of the whole, and that I was usurping a right which I did not possess; the servants' staircase would have been good enough for me.

The walls were covered with pictures, mostly without frames, copies of masterpieces of the Italian and Spanish schools; and above, in the shadow, could be seen vaguely a great ceiling painted with frescoes of mythology.

I reached the right floor.

A drum of crushed, watered Utrecht velvet, whose yellowed braid and rounded nails told of long years of service, showed me the door I wanted.

I rang, the door was opened for me with the customary precautions, and I found myself in a great room, lit at one end by a few lamps. As you entered, you took a step backwards into two centuries ago. Time, which passes so quickly, seemed not to have flowed over that house, and like a clock which you have forgotten to wind up, its hand always pointed to the same time.

The walls were panelled and painted white, and half-covered with darkened canvases bearing the stamp of their period; on the vast stove stood a statue which looked as if it had been stolen from the arbours of Versailles. On the rounded cupola of the ceiling was daubed a twisted allegory, in the style of Lemoine, and possibly by him.

I moved towards the lighted part of the room where several human shapes were milling round a table, and as soon as the light reached me and made me recognisable, a vigorous cheer shook the old building to the echoes.

'It's he, it's he', several voices shouted simultaneously, 'give him his share!'

The doctor was standing by a sideboard on which stood a tray full of little saucers of Japanese porcelain. A piece of greenish paste or sweetmeat, about as large as my thumb, was taken out of a crystal vase by him, with the aid of a spatula, and placed beside a mother-of-pearl spoon, on each saucer.

The doctor's face glowed with enthusiasm, his eyes sparkled, his cheeks grew red, the veins on his temples stood out sharply, his dilated nostrils breathed deeply.

'This will be deducted from your share of paradise,' he said as he handed me the amount due to me.

When each one had eaten his piece, coffee was served in the Arab fashion, with the grounds and without sugar.

Then we sat down at the table.

This alteration to the usual culinary order no doubt surprises the reader; it is not, indeed, usual to take coffee before the soup, and it is normally only at dessert that sweetmeats are eaten. This certainly deserves an explanation.

II

There once existed in the East an order of formidable sectarians commanded by a sheik who went by the title of Old Man of the Mountain, or Prince of Assassins.

This Old Man of the Mountain was obeyed without question; the Assassins, who were his subjects, marched with absolute devotion to execute his orders, whatever they might be; no danger stopped them, even certain death. At a sign from their leader, they hurled themselves from the top of a tower, or went to bury their dagger in a sovereign in his palace, in the midst of his guards.

By what tricks did the Old Man of the Mountain obtain such complete surrender?

By means of a marvellous drug, of which he possessed the recipe, and which has the property of causing dazzling hallucinations.

Those who had taken it found when they awoke from their dream, that real life was so dull and colourless that they sacrificed it joyfully in order to return to the paradise of their dreams; for every man killed while carrying out the orders of the sheik, went to heaven automatically, or if he escaped death, was again allowed to enjoy the delights of the mysterious composition.

Now, the paste which the doctor had just distributed to us was exactly the same as that which the Old Man of the Mountain stuffed into his fanatics without them realising it, as he made them believe that he held in his power the heaven of Mahomet and the Louris of three shades, in other words, of hashish, from which comes hashisheen, hashish-eater, root of the word assassin, the fierce meaning of which is perfectly explained by the bloodthirsty behaviour of the followers of the Old Man of the Mountain.

To be sure, the people who had seen me leave home, at a time when simple mortals are eating, did not suspect that I was going to the Ile Saint-Louis, a virtuous and patriarchal place if ever there was one, to eat a strange food which was used several centuries ago as a means of rousing excitement by a usurping sheik, in order to drive his devotees to kill. Nothing in my patently bourgeois appearance could have made anyone suspect me of such an excess of orientalism; I looked more like a nephew going to dine with his old aunt than a believer about to taste the joys of Mahomet's heaven in the company of twelve Arabs who were as French as could be.

Before this revelation, if anyone had told you that there existed in Paris in 1845, in that period of gambling and railways, an order of hashish-eaters whose story M. de Hammer has not written, you would not have believed him, and yet nothing could be more true—as is the way with incredible things.

III

The meal was served in a strange manner and in all kinds of extravagant and picturesque dishes.

Large Venetian glasses with milky spiral decoration, German drinking-glasses with historic crests, Flemish jugs of enamelled earthenware, slim-necked flagons still wrapped in their reed covers, were used instead of glasses, bottles and carafes.

The opaque china of Louis Leboeuf, and the English flowered crockery, such as adorn a bourgeois table, were conspicuous by their absence; no two plates were alike, but each had its own worth; China, Japan, Saxony, included there samples of their most beautiful paste and their richest colours; all a little chipped, a little cracked, but in exquisite taste.

The dishes were mostly enamels of Bernard de Palissy, or Limoges china, and sometimes, when you were cutting your food, your knife met, under the real food, a reptile, a frog, or a bird, all in relief. The eel to be eaten mingled its coils with the moulded serpent.

An honest philistine would have felt some terror at the sight of these guests, hairy, bearded, moustached, or shaven in some strange way, brandishing 16th-century daggers, Malay krisses and navajas, as they bent over plates of food which the beams from the flickering lamps made to look suspicious.

Dinner was coming to an end, already some of the most fervent members were feeling the effects of the green paste; personally, I had experienced a complete transposition of taste. The water I drank seemed to me to have the flavour of the most delicious wine, the meat in my mouth was transformed into raspberry, and vice versa. I could not have distinguished a chop from a peach.

My neighbours were beginning to appear rather odd; their eyes were wide open like the pupils of an owl; their noses lengthened into probosces, their mouths stretched like the mouth of a bell. Their faces took on supernatural shades of colour.

One of them, with a pale face in a black beard, was roaring with laughter at an invisible sight, another was making incredible efforts to hold his glass to his lips, and his contortions, in order to succeed, were arousing deafening shrieks of mirth.

One man, whose movements were jerky and nervous, twiddled his thumbs at an incredible speed; another was stretched out on his chair, staring vaguely, and his arms hung limp as he let himself slide voluptuously into the bottomless sea of oblivion.

I rested my elbows on the table and watched all this with a remaining glimmer of sense, which came and went like a guttering candle. A vague warmth stole over my limbs, and a madness, like a wave breaking on a rock and retreating to hurl itself again, reached and withdrew from my brain, which it finally engulfed. Hallucination, a strange guest, had come to stay with me.

'To the drawing-room, to the drawing-room,' cried one of the guests, 'can't you hear the heavenly choir? The orchestra has been ready for a long time.'

And indeed, a delightful harmony reached us in fitful gusts through the din of conversation.

IV

The drawing-room is a huge room, with carved and gilded panels, a painted ceiling, cornices adorned with satyrs chasing nymphs among the reeds, a vast fireplace of coloured marble, heavy brocade curtains, redolent of the richness of the past.

Tapestry furniture, sofas, armchairs, and bergeres, wide enough to allow the skirts of duchesses and marchionesses to spread out comfortably, welcomed the hashish-eaters in their soft, ever-open arms. A low fireside chair in the chimney corner tempted me; I sat down and gave myself up, unresisting, to the effects of this extraordinary drug.

After a few minutes, my companions disappeared one by one, leaving no trace but their shadow on the wall, which soon absorbed it; just as the brown marks made by water on sand disappear as they dry.

And from this point, as I had no further knowledge of their movements, you will have to be satisfied for now with the story of my own personal impressions.

Solitude reigned in the room which was lit only by a few feeble lights; then suddenly, a red flash passed under my eyelids, a countless number of candles were lit as if by themselves, and I felt a warm golden light enveloping me. The place where I was was the same, but different, as a sketch is different from the finished picture; everything was larger, richer, more magnificent. Reality served only as an introduction to the splendours of hallucination.

I could not yet see anyone, and yet I felt the presence of a multitude.

I could hear materials rustling, slippers squeaking, voices whispering, murmuring, humming and buzzing, stifled bursts of laughter, noises as of a chair or table leg. China was being rattled, doors were opened and shut; something strange was happening.

An enigmatic character suddenly appeared to me.

How had he come in? I don't know; yet the sight of him did not frighten me. His nose was curved like a bird's beak, his green eyes were surrounded by three brown rings, and he kept wiping them with a huge handkerchief; a high cravat, white and starched, in the knot of which was tucked a visiting card saying 'Daucus-Carota, of the Golden Pot', was fastened tightly around his thin neck, and made his cheeks bulge over it in reddish folds; a black coat with square tails, from which hung bunches of charms, imprisoned his chest which was puffed out like a pouter pigeon. As for his legs, I must confess that they were made of a mandragore root, bifurcated, black, rough, covered with knobs and warts, and it seemed to have been recently pulled up, for lumps of earth still stuck to the hairs. These legs shook and twitched with extraordinary activity and when the small body which they upheld was right in front of me, this strange character burst into sobs and wiping his eyes on his sleeve, said in the most doleful voice: 'Today we must die of laughing.' And tears as big as peas ran down the sides of his nose. '... Of laughing ... of laughing'; like an echo this was repeated by a chorus of discordant, nasal voices.

V

Then I looked at the ceiling, and I saw a crowd of heads without bodies, like cherubs', which had such comical expressions, such cheerful, and happy faces, that I could not help sharing their hilarity—their eyes were creased, their mouths were stretched out, and their nostrils were dilated; their grimaces were enough to cheer up spleen itself. These comic masks moved in zones turning inside out, which produced a dazzling and giddying effect.

Gradually the drawing-room had filled with extraordinary figures, such as are only found in the engravings of Callot and the aquatints of Goya; a jumble of characteristic tawdry finery and rags, of human and animal shapes; in any other circumstances I might have been uneasy in such company but there was nothing threatening about these monstrosities. It was slyness, not fierceness, which gave the sparkle to these eyes. Only good humour bared these uneven fangs and these pointed teeth.

As if I had been the king of the feast each figure came in turn into the circle of light in the centre of which I sat, and mumbled in my ear, with an air of grotesque compunction, jokes of which I cannot remember a single one, but which, at the moment, seemed enormously witty to me, and roused the maddest hilarity in me.

As each one appeared, a laugh which was Homeric, Olympian, immense, bewildering, and seemed to echo to infinity, burst out round me, like the rumbling of thunder.

Voices which were alternately yapping or sepulchral, shouted: 'No, it's too funny, that's enough! Good heavens, how I am enjoying myself—better and better!

Stop—I'm worn out—Ho ho, ha-ha, hi, hi—What a good joke, what a fine pun!

Stop—I'm stifling—I can't breathe—Don't look at me like that—or hold me in—I shall burst!'

In spite of these half-humorous, half-earnest protests, the tremendous hilarity was getting more and more, the din grew more intense, the floors and walls of the house rose and palpitated like a human diaphragm, shaken by this frantic, irresistible and implacable laughter.

Soon, instead of coming up to me one by one, the grotesque figures attacked me en masse, shaking their long pierrot sleeves, stumbling in the folds of their magicians' robes, squashing their cardboard noses in ridiculous falls, scattering a cloud of powder from their wigs, and singing out-of-tune outrageous songs with impossible rhymes.

All the types invented by the mocking spirit of nations and artists were collected together there, but ten times, a hundred times more concentrated. It was a strange rabble; the Neapolitan Punchinello gave a friendly pat to the hump of the English Punch; the Harlequin of Bergamo rubbed his black nose against the floury mask of the French clown, who uttered fearful shrieks; the Bolognese Doctor threw snuff into the eyes of old Cassandra; Tartaglia galloped about, riding on a clown, and Gilles kicked Don Spavento's behind; Karagheuz, brandishing his obscene weapon, was fighting a duel with an Oscan buffoon.

Further off was a confused swarming of the fantasies of comical dreams, hybrid creatures, a shapeless mixture of humans, animals and utensils; monks with wheels for feet and saucepans for stomachs, warriors in armour made of plates and dishes, and brandishing wooden swords in birds' claws, statesmen worked by a mechanical turn-spit; kings standing half in, half out of watch-towers like pepper-pots, alchemists with heads made like bellows, with limbs twisted like alembics, ribald figures made of a collection of pumpkins with strange bulges, everything in fact that might be drawn by the feverish pencil of a cynic egged on by intoxication.

They swarmed, crawled, trotted, jumped, grunted and whistled, as Goethe says in 'The Night of the Walpurgis.'

To get away from the outrageous insistence of these extraordinary characters, I took refuge in a dark corner, from which I could watch them as they executed dances such as were never known in the Renaissance at the time of Chicard, or in the Opera in the reign of Musard, the shock-headed king of the quadrille. These dancers, a thousand times better than Molière, Rabelais, Swift and Voltaire, produced, with an entrechat or a balance, comedies that were so profoundly philosophical, satires on such a high level and so piquantly witty, that I was obliged to hold my sides as I stood there.

Daucus-Carota, still wiping his eyes, was performing unbelievable pirouettes and cabrioles, especially for one whose legs were of mandragore roots, and he kept saying in a comically pitiful voice: 'It is today that we must die of laughing.'

Oh you who have admired the sublime foolishness of Odry, the hoarse idiocy of Alcide Tousez, the complacent stupidity of Arnal, the parrot-like grimaces of Ravel and who think you know what a comic masque is, if you had been present at this 'Gustave' ball evoked by hashish, you would agree that the most side-splitting humorists of our little theatres are more suitable to be carved on the corners of a coffin or a tomb!

What strangely convulsed faces! What blinking eyes, sparkling with sarcasm under their bird's membrane! What grins like the slot of a money-box! What mouths, as if chopped out by an axe! What noses, comically twelve-sided! What paunches, huge and ridiculous like Pantaguel!

Flashing through all this higgledy-piggledy, which was a sort of painless nightmare, there appeared sudden resemblances whose effect was irresistible, caricatures which would have made Daumier and Garvarni envious, fantasies enough to make the marvellous Chinese artists swoon with delight, those Phidiases of the pot-bellied and ape-like figures.

All these visions, however, were in no way monstrous or burlesque; there was grace, too, in this carnival of forms; near the fireplace, a little head with peach-bloom cheeks rolled on its blonde hair, showing in an interminable grin thirty-two little teeth, as small as grains of rice, and laughing with a shrill, vibrating, silvery laugh, long-drawn out, embroidered with trills and organ-stops, which went through my brain, and by a sort of nervous magnetism, made me do all sorts of extravagant things.

The joyous frenzy was at its height, nothing more could be heard but convulsive sighs, inarticulate chucklings. The laughter had lost its resonance and had turned to groans, pleasure gave way to spasms; Daucus-Carota's refrain was about to come true.

Already several hashish-eaters had given in, rolling on the floor in that soft-heavy way of drunkards which makes their falls harmless; 'Good heavens, how happy I am! What joy! I am floating in ecstasy! I am in heaven! I am deep in the abyss of delight!'—exclamations like these could be heard, confused and jumbled.

Raucous cries rose from bursting breasts, arms stretched wildly towards some fugitive vision; heels and heads tapped on the floor. It was time to throw a drop of cold water on this burning mass, or the pot would have cracked.

The human frame, which has so little strength for pleasure; and so much for pain, could not have borne any higher degree of pressure of happiness.

One of the club members, who had not taken part in the voluptuous intoxication, in order to take charge and to prevent those of us who might think we had wings from flying out of the windows, got up, opened the piano, and sat down.

His two hands fell, and together pressed down the keys, and a glorious chord resounded loudly, silencing all the noise, and changing the character of the intoxication.

6 'Slowly drifting towards us amidst music and incense'; an interpretation of De Quincey's 'Confessions' by Sonia Woolf.

7 Gérard de Nerval.

8 Théophile Gautier.

VI

The tune was, I believe, Agatha's aria from the *Freischütz*; that heavenly melody had scattered the ridiculous visions that beset me, like a wind sweeping away shapeless clouds. The grimacing creatures went away, crawling under the chairs, hiding in the curtain-folds, with little stifled sighs, and once more I felt I was alone in the room.

The colossal organ of Fribourg never produced, certainly, a greater mass of sound than the piano played by the 'voyant' (that is what they call the sober member). The notes vibrated so powerfully, that they pierced my breast like arrows of light; soon the tune being played seemed to come from inside me; my fingers played on a non-existent keyboard; the sounds came out blue and red, like electric sparks; the soul of Weber was re-incarnated in me.

When the piece was finished, I continued with inward improvisations, after the German master, which gave me an ineffable thrill; what a pity there was no magic shorthand writer to collect up these inspired melodies which were heard only by me, and which with great modesty, I do not hesitate to rank above the masterpieces of Rossini, Meyerbeer, and Félicien David.

Oh Pillet! Oh Vatel! Any one of the thirty operas I composed in ten minutes, would make you rich in six months.

The somewhat convulsive gaiety of the beginning had given way to an indefinable sense of well-being, an unending calm.

I was in this blessed phase of hashish which the Orientals call 'Kief'. I could no longer feel my body; the links between matter and spirit were broken; I moved by my will alone in an atmosphere which offered no resistance.

In this way I imagine, souls behave in the world to which we shall go after death.

A bluish vapour, an Elysian light, like the reflection of a blue grotto, created in the room an atmosphere in which I could vaguely see dim, trembling contours; this atmosphere which was both fresh and warm, damp and scented, enveloped me like a warm bath, in a kiss which was so sweet that I became weak; if I wanted to move, the caressing air formed a thousand voluptuous eddies around me; a delightful languor took possession of my senses and stretched me out on the sofa, where I lay limp as a cast-off garment.

Then I realised the pleasure experienced, according to their degree of perfection, by the spirits and the angels as they pass through the ethers and the heavens, and how eternity can be spent in paradise.

There was nothing material in this ecstasy; no earthly desire sullied its purity. In any case, love itself could not have increased it; Romeo, if he had eaten hashish, would have forgotten Juliet. The poor girl, leaning over the jasmine, would have stretched out in vain her beautiful alabaster arms through the darkness, from her balcony above; Romeo would have stayed at the foot of the silken ladder, and although I am hopelessly in love with that angel of youth and beauty created by Shakespeare, I must agree that the most beautiful girl in Verona is not, in the eyes of a hashish-eater, worth the trouble of moving!

So I watched calmly, although with delight, the garland of ideally beautiful women adorning the frieze with their divine nudity; I saw the gleam of their satin shoulders, their silvery breasts shining, their little pink-soled feet adorning the ceiling, the ripple of their curving hips, but I felt no temptation. The charming apparitions which tormented St Anthony would have had no power over me.

By a strange miracle, after a few minutes of contemplation, I melted into the object I was looking at, and became myself that object.

So I had changed into the nymph Syrinx, because the frieze represented in fact the daughter of Ladon pursued by Pan.

I felt all the terror of the poor girl as she fled, and I was trying to hide behind some fantastic reeds, to avoid the cloven-hoofed monster.

VII

During my ecstasy, Daucus-Carota had come in again. Sitting cross-legged on his suitably twisted roots, he glared at me with flaming eyes; his beak clicked so sardonically, his whole misshapen person sparkled with such an air of jeering triumph, that I shivered in spite of myself.

He guessed I was afraid, and continued to grimace and contort himself all the more, and came closer, limping like a wounded daddy-long-legs, or like a legless cripple.

Then I felt a cold breath in my ear, and a voice which was well-known to me, though I could not place its owner, said to me:

'This wretched Daucus-Carota, who has sold his legs for drink, has pinched your head and replaced it, not with a donkey's head as Puck did to Bottom, but with an elephant's head.'

Extremely intrigued, I went straight to the mirror, and saw that the warning was not a lie.

I could have been taken for a hindu or javanese idol; my forehead had become uglier, my nose was lengthened to a trunk, and curved over my chest, my ears flapped down to my shoulders, and as a crowning horror, I was indigo-blue, like Shiva, the blue god.

Filled with anger and exasperation, I began to run after Daucus-Carota, who leapt and yelped and gave all the signs of extreme terror;

I managed to catch him, and banged him so hard on the edge of the table that in the end he gave me back my head which he had wrapped in his handkerchief.

Pleased with this victory, I made to go back to my sofa, but the same little unknown voice said to me :

'Take good care, you are surrounded by enemies; invisible powers are trying to draw you and hold you back. You are a prisoner here; try to go and you will see.'

A veil was torn from my spirit, and it became clear to me that the members of the club were cabalists and magicians who wished to bring about my ruin.

VIII

I got up with great difficulty, and went towards the door of the drawing-room, which I reached only after a considerable time, for an unknown force was making me go back one step in every three. According to my calculation, I took ten years to get there.

Daucus-Carota was following me, sniggering and muttering false commiseration :

'If he goest at this rate, he will be old by the time he gets there.'

However, I had managed to reach the next room, but its dimensions seemed to be changed and unrecognisable. It got longer and longer . . . ad infinitum. The light which twinkled at the end of it seemed as far away as a fixed star.

Discouragement seized me, and I was about to stop, when the little voice said to me, almost touching me with its lips :

'Courage ! she is waiting for you at eleven o'clock.'

By making a desperate appeal to my strength of mind, I succeeded, by a huge effort of will, in lifting my feet which clung to the ground, and which I had to uproot like tree-trunks. The mandragore-legged monster escorted me, parodying my efforts and singing in a sort of drawling plain-song : 'The marble is winning, the marble is winning !'

And indeed, I felt my feet petrifying, as if I was encased to the hips in marble, like the Daphne in the Tuileries. I was a statue to the waist, like the enchanted princes of the 'Arabian Nights'. My hard heels echoed heavily on the floor : I could have played the Commander in 'Don Juan'.

However, I had arrived on the landing of the stairs, which I had tried to go down; it was half-lit, and in my dream it seemed of Cyclopean and gigantic proportions. Its two ends, drowned in darkness, seemed to me to plunge into the two gulfs of heaven and hell; when I looked up, I could dimly see, in an incredible perspective, countless landings one above the other; flights of stairs to be climbed as if to reach to the top of the tower of Lylacq; looking down, I felt, rather than saw, an abyss of steps, a whirlwind of spirals, a dazzling number of convolutions.

'This staircase must pierce right through the earth,' I said to myself as I went on mechanically. 'I shall get to the bottom the day after the Last Judgement.'

The faces of the pictures looked at me pityingly, some of them moved with painful contortions, like a dumb person trying to give some important information in a crisis. It seemed as if they wanted to warn me of a trap to avoid, but an inert, dull force dragged me on; the steps were soft and sank beneath my weight, like the mysterious ladders in the trials of Freemasonry. The flabby, slippery stones collapsed like toads' bellies; new landings, new stairs, kept appearing before my resigned feet, while those I had already negotiated returned of their own accord in front of me.

This performance lasted a thousand years by my reckoning.

At last I reached the entrance hall, where another no less terrible persecution awaited me.

The dragon holding a candle in its paw, which I had noticed on entering, barred my way with evidently hostile intention; his greenish eyes twinkled with irony, his sly mouth laughed wickedly; he approached me, almost crawling, dragging in the dust his bronze armour, but it was not in submission; his lion's hindquarters trembled fiercely, and Daucus-Carota urged him on, as one does to make a dog fight:

'Bite him, bite him! Marble meat for a bronze mouth, that's a mighty feast!'

I would not let myself be frightened by this hideous beast, but passed by him.

A gust of cold wind struck my face and the night sky, clear of clouds, suddenly appeared to me. A scattering of stars was like gold dust in the veins of a great block of lapis lazuli.

I was in the courtyard.

To reproduce the effect this dark architecture had on me, I should need the point with which Piranesi streaked the black polish of his marvellous copperplate engravings; the courtyard had become as large as the Champ-de-Mars, and had in a few hours become surrounded with giant buildings which were outlined against the horizon in a lacework of spires, cupolas, towers, gables, pyramids, worthy of Rome or Babylon.

I was extremely surprised, I had never suspected that the Ile St-Louis contained so many magnificent monuments, which would in any case have covered its real area twenty times over, and I thought, not without apprehension, of the magical power which had been able in one evening, to raise such buildings.

'You are the plaything of vain illusions; this courtyard is very small,' murmured the voice, 'it is twenty-seven paces long by twenty-five paces wide.'

'Yes, yes,' grumbled the bifurcated abortion, 'paces of seven-league boots. You will never be there by eleven o'clock; it is 1500 years since you left. Half your hair is already grey.... Go back up there, it's the wisest thing to do.'

As I did not obey, the odious monster tripped me up in the tangle of his legs, and using his hands like grappling irons, dragged me back in spite of my resistance, and made me go up the stairs again, where I had suffered such anguish, and set me down, to my great despair, in the drawing-room from which I had escaped with such difficulty.

Then I was seized with utter giddiness; I became deliriously mad.

Daucus-Carota leapt to the ceiling, and said 'Fool, I gave you back your head, but before I did so, I took out your brains with a spoon.'

I felt unutterably sad, for as I put my hand to my head, I found it was open, and I fainted away.

IX

When I regained consciousness, I saw the room was full of people dressed in black, who greeted each other sadly and shook hands with a melancholy friendliness, like people afflicted with a common grief.

They said, 'Time is dead; henceforth there will be neither years nor months, nor hours; Time is dead, and we are going to his funeral.'

'It is true that he was very old, but I did not expect this to happen; he was very well for his age,' added one of the mourners whom I recognised as a painter friend of mine.

'Eternity was worn out, there has to be an end,' replied another.

'Good heavens,' I cried, struck with a sudden idea, 'if there is no more time, when will it be eleven o'clock?'

'Never,' cried Daucus-Carota in a voice of thunder, pushing his face into mine, and appearing to me in his real light. 'Never... it will always be a quarter to nine—the hand will remain on the minute when time ceased to be, and it will be your torture to come and look at the motionless hand, and to go back and sit down, and so on, until you walk your heels down to the bone.'

A greater force drew me on and I walked backwards and forwards 400 or 500 times, looking at the clock with a dreadful uneasiness.

Daucus-Carota was sitting astride the clock and making terrible faces at me.

The hand did not move.

'Wretch, you have stopped the pendulum,' I cried, wild with rage.

'No, it is swinging as usual ... but suns will crumble to dust before this steel arrow advances by a millionth of a millimetre.'

'Come, I see that I must exorcise the evil spirits, things are getting ugly,' said the 'voyant', 'let's have a little music. David's harp will be replaced this time by Erard's piano.'

And, sitting down on the piano-stool he played tunes that were lively and gay in character.

This seemed to upset greatly the mandragore-man, who became smaller, flatter, colourless, and who uttered inarticulate groans; at last he lost all human likeness and rolled on the floor in the form of a salsify with a forked root.

The spell was broken.

'Alleluia! Time has come back to life,' cried childish happy voices, 'go and look at the clock now!'

The hand marked eleven o'clock.

'Sir, your carriage is below,' said the servant to me.

The dream was over.

The hashish-eaters went off each their own way, like officers escorting Marlborough.

As for me, I went light-footed down those stairs which had caused me such agonies, and a few moments later I was in my room in very truth; the last vapours caused by the hashish had disappeared.

My reason had returned, or at least what I call my reason, for lack of any other term.

My lucidity would have made me capable of understanding a pantomime or vaudeville, or of making up rhymes with words of not more than three letters.

7

Charles Pierre Baudelaire (1821-1867) shares with Thomas De Quincey the distinction of having produced one of the two most important creative works on drugs. His *Les Paradis Artificiels,* according to Alethea Hayter, 'is with De Quincey's "Confessions" the twin peak of the literature of drug addiction.' Acclaim such as this has been accorded to the book ever since its publication in 1860, and came as perhaps the biggest surprise to Baudelaire, for he had been inspired to write it as a result of reading the 'Confessions' and felt that they had already said everything new that could be said about opium addiction. Though it was addiction to alcohol and opium that finally brought Baudelaire to destitution and death, he was for the early part of his life only an occasional imbiber.

Born in Paris, he had an unhappy childhood quarrelling with his step-father, and after a reasonably successful education at the Sorbonne—during which time he probably took opium for the first time—embarked on a world tour which was to profoundly affect his life. In Mauritius he met a beautiful half-caste girl, Jeanne Duval, who became his mistress and was to form the inspiration for much of his work. (After Baudelaire's death, his daughter Judith said of this relationship, 'He loved her because in his fancy she represented the primitive beauty of the strange lands of which he dreamed.') On his return to Paris in 1843 he began to mix with the painters and writers of the day and, with no shortage of money from his wealthy step-father, was looked upon as a rich dandy and one of the best dressed men in the city. It was one of these painters, Joseph Ferdinand Boissard, who introduced Baudelaire to the *Club des Hachischins* and thereby fired in him the enthusiasm for stimulants and the effects they produced. By this time, the Club had moved its meeting place from the Hotel Pimodan to the sumptuous flat of the playboy, Roger de Beauvoir, the 'idol of Paris'. It was here, in a Gothic room hung with black velvet, with priceless Eastern fittings and ornately-carved oaken furniture, that Baudelaire joined his contemporaries to sample hashish. In her famous biography of Baudelaire (1933), Enid Starkie writes of these gatherings: 'Any Philistine bourgeois, if he could have entered these precincts, would have been terrified and horrified, too, at the sight of the members sitting around the table waving Renaissance daggers and Eastern swords over their heads, and bending over a bowl of astonishing-looking green jam, whose colour the flickering lights of the lamps overhead made seem more ghostly still.' Baudelaire was greatly impressed by his experience, particularly the effect which the drug had of confusing one sense with another, the condition known as synaesthesia. It stirred his creative powers and led him to draw pictures (one such example is illustrated in this book) and write numerous stories and essays, culminating in Les Paradis Artificiels. He also became fascinated by the relationship between the intoxication produced by wine and that produced by hashish. 'It occurred to me,' he wrote, 'to treat wine and hashish in the same article, because they do indeed have something in common : both cause an inordinate poetic involvement in men. Man's greatness is attested by his frantic craving for all things—healthful or otherwise—that excite his individuality.' The result was his essay, 'Wine and Hashish Compared as Means to Achieve a Multiplication of the Individual's Potential' (1851), which summarized his thoughts and came out in favour of wine as the more powerful stimulant! At this time he was also taking increasing doses of laudanum for stomach pains and depression, and his notebooks record numerous opium dreams in which he saw 'strange things of rapture and gloom'.

His masterpiece, and the work which established his name for all time, Les Fleurs du Mal, appeared in 1857, but despite its critical ovation, he, the printer and the publisher were prosecuted for impropriety in 1864. Nevertheless the book was to exert an influence which has continued unabated to this day. From this same period came his masterly translations of the works of Thomas De Quincey and Edgar Allan Poe, both of whom he admired greatly, and the items which subsequently made up Petits Poemes en Prose (1869)—including the two opium poems 'Rêve Parisien' and 'L'Irrémediable'. The remainder of his life was a continuing search for the good and the evil, an obsession with the macabre, which caused some critics to label him a 'Satanist', and a steady decline into poverty—and finally paralysis—brought about by drink and opium. From this last period comes the remarkable short story 'La Chambre Double', which I have selected here. It is a vivid picture of Baudelaire, living in a sordid room, still driven by his obsession with drugs, and utilizing them to sustain himself for the labour of producing work for his publishers.

*

Hashish reveals to a man nothing but himself. It is true that the man is so to speak squared and cubed to infinity, and since it is also true that the memory of his impressions will remain when the debauch is over, those who hope to *make use* of hashish do not seem at first sight to be altogether unreasonable in their hope. But I implore them to realize that the thoughts of which they hope to make so much use are not really as beautiful as appear in the tinsel magic of their momentary disguise.... Now, even if we admit for a moment that hashish can confer genius, or at least increase it, it must not be forgotten that it is the nature of hashish to weaken the will, and so to give with one hand what it takes away with the other, that is, to bestow imagination without the power to make use of it.

Les Paradis Artificiels, 1860

The Double Room
Charles Baudelaire

A room like a daydream, a truly *spiritual* room, where the still atmosphere is faintly tinted with pink and blue.

Here the soul bathes in an idleness spiced with regret and desire—something crepuscular, bluish and rosy; a dream of delight during an eclipse.

The shapes of the furniture are elongated, prostrate, languishing. The furniture seems to be dreaming. One might suppose it to be endowed with somnambulistic life, like that of vegetation or of minerals. The stuffs speak a dumb language, like that of flowers, skies or sunsets.

The walls are defiled by no abomination of art. Juxtaposed with pure dream, with the unanalysed impression, positive and definitive art is a blasphemy. Here everything has the sufficing clarity and the delicious obscurity of harmony.

An infinitesimal perfume, most exquisitely choice, in which mingles a faint humidity, swims through this atmosphere in which the half-slumbering spirit is lulled amidst the sensations of a conservatory.

Muslin streams down by the windows and bed, gushing in snowy cascades. On the bed lies the Idol, the sovereign of dreams. But how came she here? Who brought her? What magic power has installed her on this throne of daydream and delight?

What does it matter? There she is and I recognise her.

Yes, I know those eyes whose flame pierces the dusk—those subtle and terrible 'ogles', I know them by their terrifying malice! They attract, enthral and devour the gaze of him who unwisely beholds them. I have often studied them, those black stars compelling curiosity and admiration.

To what benevolent demon do I owe these surroundings of mystery, silence, peace and perfumes? Ah bliss! That which we generally call life has not, even in its happiest extension, anything in common with this supreme life with which I have now made acquaintance, which I savour minute by minute, second by second!

But no, there are no more minutes or seconds. Time has disappeared. It is Eternity that reigns now—an eternity of delights.

But a knock, heavy and terrible, has resounded on the door, and, as one does in dreams of Hell, I feel as if a pick-axe had struck me in the stomach.

Enter a Spectre. It is a bailiff who is here to torture me in the name of law; an infamous concubine who has come to upbraid me with her poverty and add the trivialities of her life to the sorrows of mine; or perhaps a printer's devil demanding the next instalment of a manuscript.

That room of paradise, the Idol, sovereign of dreams—the *Sylphide*, as the great Rene used to call her—all that magic has disappeared at the Spectre's brutal stroke.

Horror, my memory returns—my memory! Yes, this hovel, this dwelling of everlasting dreariness, is really mine. Mine, this silly furniture, dusty and dilapidated; the hearth without flame or live coal, and befouled with spittle; the gloomy windows where the rain has traced furrows in the grime; the manuscripts unfinished or covered with erasures; the calendar, with dates of foreboding underlined in pencil!

And that other-worldly perfume, so intoxicating to my perfected senses, has been replaced, alas, by a fetid odour of tobacco, mixed with some sickening sort of dampness. The whole place has the rancid reek of desolation.

In this world of mine, narrow but crammed with disgust, only one well-known object smiles upon me: the phial of laudanum. An old and terrible mistress—lavish, like all mistresses, alas, with her caresses and betrayals.

Yes, indeed, Time is here again, Time is again the sovereign ruler; and with that hideous dotard has returned all his demoniac train of Memories, Regrets, Spasms, Fears, Agonies, Nightmares, Angers and Neuroses.

And now, you may be sure, the seconds are loudly and solemnly accentuated—each, as it leaps from the clock, saying: 'I am Life, insupportable, implacable Life!'

There is only one Second in human Life whose mission it is to announce news of happiness—that 'happy release' of which every man is so inexplicably afraid!

Yes, Time rules again; he has resumed his brutal dictatorship. He prods me like an ox, with his two-pronged goad:

'Get up, donkey! Sweat, slave! Live, creature of doom!'

8

The third famous literary member of the *Club des Hachischins* was Gérard de Nerval (1808-1855) whose unhappy, dissipated life resembles in many aspects those of his contemporaries, James Mangan in Ireland and Edgar Allan Poe in America. Nerval, apart from being an enthusiastic and regular attender at the Club, also sought hashish on his travels in the East and gained extensive knowledge of it while in Egypt, 'the font of drug-taking'. Born in Paris, he was educated at the College Charlemagne and there became friends with Théophile Gautier. Both were day-boys and their friendship developed in as well as out of school. It was to Gautier that Nerval owed not only support and consolation in his later penury and hapless love affair, but also his introduction to the 'Hashish Club'.

Nerval arrived on the French literary scene at the age of twenty with a remarkable translation of *Faust,* and in his comments about the book revealed his interest in—and probably actual experience of— necromancy and mysticism. Obviously of an unstable and gloomy nature, he began to develop into an eccentric in his twenties and stories about his bizarre exploits became the talk of Paris. On one occasion he was seen taking a lobster for a walk through the Palais-Royal gardens on a length of blue ribbon; on another he threw off all his clothes in the street at midnight and said he was 'casting off all my earthly trammels'! He was arrested for this last escapade, but his friends soon obtained his release. A trip to the Near East, which he recorded in *Voyage en Orient,* further filled his mind with thoughts of the exotic and the bizarre, and from one of his adventures he produced the story 'Hashish' which I have reprinted below. Several of the other tales in this extraordinary book are coloured by 'visionary' descriptions which seem to indicate that Nerval also indulged in opium. (This contention is further supported by two highly autobiographical short stories, 'Nuit du 31 Décembre' (1832) and 'Portrait du Diable' (1839), both of which demonstrate considerable knowledge of the effects of laudanum and opium.) The insanity into which he now declined was probably brought about chiefly by his hopeless love for an actress, Jenny Colon, who was ever-demanding of him and gave little in return. This woman obviously haunted his waking and sleeping hours and is immortalized in his novel *Aurelia* and the collection of essays, *Le Rêve et la Vie*. His last months were spent in gloomy solitude or restless pacing of the streets of Paris as he struggled to make a living from his writing. In a final depression one cold winter's evening he hanged himself with a white silk cord on the railing outside a lodging house which he had called at too late to be admitted. Later examination revealed that the 'white silk cord' was in fact the girdle of another Parisian actress, Madame de Maintenon, which he had bought from a second-hand shop.

*

After a few moments' torpor a new life begins, liberated from the conditions of space and time.... Why then should I not at last force those mystic gates, armed with all my will-power, and dominate my sensations instead of submitting to them? Is it not possible to master that alluring and terrifying chimera, to impose law on these visions which make game of our reason?

Note published posthumously, 1855

Hashish
GERARD DE NERVAL

On the right bank of the Nile, some distance from the port of Fostat, where are the ruins of Old Cairo, and not far from the mountain of Mokatam which towers above the new city, some time after the year 1000 of the Christians, which corresponds to the fourth century of the Mussulman Hegira, there was a little village, mainly inhabited by people of the sect of the Sabeans.

From the last of the houses that stand upon the river's bank there is a delightful view. The Nile, with its caressing waves, surrounds the island of Rodda, seeming to hold it as a slave would hold a basket of flowers in his arms. On the other bank is Ghizeh, and at night, when the sun has just gone down, the gigantic triangles of the pyramids tear asunder the band of violet mist which follows the sunset. Upon this clear background the tops of the palms, sycamores and Pharaoh's fig-trees stand out darkly. Stretched out upon the plain, like a crouching dog, the Sphinx seems to watch over the herds of water-buffaloes which come trailing down to the watering-place, and the lights of fishermen pierce the thick darkness of the shores with stars of gold.

In the Sabean village, the place from which this view might best be enjoyed, was a white-walled *okel*, surrounded by locust-trees. Its terrace went down to the water's edge, and there, every night, the boatmen, who were going up or coming down the Nile, could see the quivering wicks swimming in their bowls of oil.

Through the bays of the arcades, one who troubled to look from a boat in the middle of the river might easily have seen within the *okel*, travellers and customers seated before wooden tables on baskets of palm, or rug-covered divans, and would certainly have been astonished by their strange appearance. Wild gestures, succeeded by dull immobility, crazy laughter, inarticulate cries, would have enabled him to guess that this was one of those houses where, taking no heed of the prohibition, infidels came to make themselves drunk with wine, bouza (beer) or hashish.

One evening a boat, steered with the decision of a steersman who knows his bearings, touched land in the shadow of the terrace, at the foot of a staircase whose lowest steps were washed by the water, and from it there sprang a young good-looking man who seemed to be a fisherman. Mounting the steps with a strong quick step, he sat down in the corner of the room at a place which seemed to be his own. Nobody paid any attention to his coming; he was evidently an habitué of the place.

At the same moment, by the opposite door, that is to say on the land side, there entered a man dressed in a tunic of black wool, wearing, contrary to custom, long hair beneath a *takieh* (white cap).

His unexpected appearance caused some surprise. He sat down in a corner in the shadow, and the general drunkenness gaining the upperhand again, soon nobody paid any attention to him. Although he was poorly dressed, the newcomer's face did not bear the stamp of the anxious humility of extreme poverty. His clear-cut features recalled the severe lines of a lion's head. His eyes, of dark sapphire blue, had an indefinable power; they alarmed and charmed at once.

Yousouf, which was the name of the young man who had come in the boat, immediately felt a secret sympathy for the unknown whose unaccustomed presence he had noticed. Since he had not yet taken part in the orgy, he approached the divan on which the stranger was seated.

'Brother,' said Yousouf, 'you seem weary; doubtless you have come a long way. Will you take some refreshment?'

'Indeed, my way has been long,' replied the stranger. 'I came into this *okel* to rest; but what can I drink here, where only forbidden drinks are served?'

'You Mussulmans, you dare not moisten your mouths with anything but pure water; but we, who are of the sect of the Sabeans, we can, without offending our law, refresh ourselves with the generous blood of the grape, or the fair juice of the barley.'

'But I do not see any fermented drink in front of you.'

'Oh, I have long disdained their vulgar drunkenness,' said Yousouf, making a sign to a negro, who set upon the table two small glass cups surrounded by silver filigree, and a box filled with a greenish paste in which was placed an ivory spatula. 'This box contains the paradise your prophet promised to his believers, and, if you were not scrupulous, in one hour I would put you in the arms of the houris without making you pass across the bridge of Alsirat,' he said, laughing.

'But this paste is hashish, if I am not mistaken,' said the stranger, pushing aside the cup in which Yousouf had put a part of the fantastic mixture, 'and hashish is forbidden.'

'Everything pleasant is forbidden,' said Yousouf, swallowing his first spoonful.

The stranger looked at him with dark blue eyes; and his forehead contracted in folds so violent that his hair moved with the movement of the skin. For a moment one would have thought that he would spring upon the careless young man and tear him to pieces; but he contained himself, and, suddenly changing his mind, stretched out his hand, took the cup, and slowly began to sample the green paste.

After a few minutes, the effects of the hashish began to make themselves felt upon the young man and the stranger: a gentle languor spread over all their limbs, a vague smile hovered over their lips. Although they had hardly spent half an hour in each other's company, they felt as though they had known one another for a thousand years. When the effect of the drug upon them grew stronger, they began to laugh, to move about, and speak with extreme volubility, especially the stranger, who, a strict observer of all the prohibitions, had never before tasted this preparation and felt its effects strongly. He seemed a prey to extraordinary exaltation: hosts of new thoughts, unheard-of and inconceivable, traversed his soul like whirlwinds of fires. His eyes sparkled as though they were lighted from within by the reflection of some unknown world; his demeanour took on a superhuman dignity. Then the vision faded, and he collapsed limply upon the cushions.

'Well, my friend,' said Yousouf, taking advantage of this interval in the stranger's intoxication, 'what do you think now of this good pistachio jam? Will you still anathematise the good fellows who gather peacefully here to be happy in their own way?'

'Hashish makes man like to God,' said the stranger in a slow, deep voice.

'Yes,' said Yousouf eagerly. 'Water drinkers only know the common, material appearance of things. Drunkenness, while it disturbs the eyes of the body, enlightens those of the soul; the spirit, freed from the body, its stern jailer, escapes like a prisoner whose warder has gone to sleep, leaving the key in the door of the cell. Happy and free, he wanders through space and light, chatting familiarly with the genii he meets, and they delight him with sudden and exquisite revelations. He flies easily through atmospheres of unspeakable happiness, and all this in the space of a minute that seems to him an eternity, so rapidly does one sensation follow another. I have a dream which continually returns, always the same and always different. When I go back to my boat staggering beneath the splendours of my visions, closing my eyes to that continual stream of hyacinths, carbuncles, emeralds and rubies which form the basis upon which the hashish paints the most remarkable phantasies ... in the bosom of the infinite, I see, as it were, a celestial countenance, more beautiful than all the creations of the poets, which smiles upon me with a sweetness that goes all through me, and descends from the skies to come to me. Is it an angel, a fairy? I know not. She seats herself beside me in my boat, whose common wood at once is changed to mother-of-pearl, and floats upon a silver stream, driven along by a breeze laden with perfumes.'

'Strange, happy vision!' murmured the stranger, nodding his head.

'That is not all,' continued Yousouf. 'One night, when I had taken a weaker dose, I woke up from my intoxication as my boat was passing the point of the island of Rodda. A woman like that of my dream was gazing at me with eyes which, though they were human, had none the less the glory of heaven. Her half-open veil showed me a jacket covered with precious stones which sparkled in the moonlight. My hand found hers; her soft skin, smooth and fresh like the petals of a flower, her rings of which I could feel the carving, convinced me of her reality.'

'Near the island of Rodda?' said the stranger, thoughtfully.

'I was not dreaming,' continued Yousouf, without paying any attention to the remark of his confidant of the moment. 'The hashish had only brought out a memory buried in the very depths of my soul, for this divine countenance was known to me. Where had I seen it before? in what world had we met? what previous existence had brought us together? That I could not say, but this strange meeting, this bizarre adventure, caused me no surprise: it seemed quite natural that this woman, who so completely realised my ideal, should be there in my boat, in the middle of the Nile, as if she had sprung from the calyx of one of those broad blossoms which come to the surface of the waters. Without asking for any explanation, I cast myself at her feet, and spoke to her all that love in its exaltation could imagine that was most burning and most sublime: there came to me words of tremendous significance; expressions which contained a universe of thought, mysterious phrases in which vibrated the echo of vanished worlds. My soul grew greater and greater in the past and in the future; the love which I was expressing, I was sure that I had felt from all eternity.

'As I spoke, I saw her great eyes light up and send forth a mysterious force; her transparent hands came towards me tapering in rays of light. I felt myself enveloped in a net of flame, and in spite of myself I fell back from waking to dreaming. When I finally shook off the invincible delicious torpor which bound my limbs, I was on the bank opposite to Ghizeh, moored to a palm-tree, and my black boy was calmly sleeping beside the boat which he had drawn upon the sand. There was a pale red light on the horizon; day was about to break.'

'That was a love which seems little like our earthly loves,' said the stranger, without casting any doubt upon the possibility of Yousouf's story, for hashish makes men credulous of prodigies.

'I have never yet told this unbelievable story to anyone; why have I trusted it to you, whom I have never seen before? It is hard for me to explain. A mysterious attraction draws me to you. When you came into this room, a voice cried to me from the depth of my heart: "There he is at last." Your coming calmed a secret uneasiness which gave me no rest. You are he whom I have awaited without knowing. Before you, my thoughts spring from me, and I have been forced to tell you all the mysteries of my heart.'

'What you feel,' said the stranger, 'I too feel, and I will tell you something that I have never yet dared to own even to myself. You have an impossible passion, but I have one that is monstrous: you love a fairy, but I love—you will shudder—I love my own sister. Yet, strangely, I can feel no remorse for this unlawful desire. In vain I blame myself; I am absolved by some mysterious power that I feel within myself. My love has nothing in it of earthly impurity. It is not lust that drives me to my sister, though in beauty she is the equal of the phantom of my visions; it is an indefinable attraction, an affection deep as the sea, vast as the skies, and such as a god himself might feel. The idea that my sister might join herself to any other man fills me with digust and horror, as though it were a sacrilege. Through the veils of flesh I see in her a something which is of heaven. Despite the name which this earth gives her, she is the spouse of my divine soul, the virgin who was destined for me from the very first days of creation: there are moments when, through the ages and the darkness, I seem to find signs of our secret relationship. Scenes from before the appearance of men upon this earth come to my memory, and I see myself seated with her beneath the golden branches of Eden, served by obedient spirits. If I united myself with another woman, I should be afraid of prostituting and dissipating the world-soul which beats within me. By the concentration of our divine blood, I would make an immortal race, a final god, more mighty than all those who have shown themselves until now with divers names and under different appearances.'

Whilst Yousouf and the stranger were exchanging these long confidences, the customers of the *okel,* in their drunkenness, were giving way to mad contortions, wild laughter, ecstatic swoonings and convulsive dances; but little by little the power of the hemp having lessened, they recovered their calm, and lay along the divans in that prostrate condition which usually follows such excess.

A man of patriarchal appearance, whose beard fell down over his trailing robe, came into the *okel* and advanced to the middle of the room.

'Rise, my brothers,' said he in a deep-sounding voice, 'I have been to observe the heavens; this is a favourable hour for us to sacrifice before the Sphinx a white cock in honour of Hermes and Agathodæmon.'

The Sabeans rose to their feet, and seemed to be about to follow their priest; but the stranger, when he heard that suggestion, changed colour twice or even thrice. The blue of his eyes became black; terrible wrinkles furrowed his cheeks, and from his chest there came a dull roaring which made the assembly tremble with fright, as though a lion had fallen in the midst of the *okel.*

'Impious blasphemers! Impure brutes! Worshippers of idols!' he cried in a voice that resounded like thunder.

At this explosion of anger, a movement of stupor passed through the crowd. The unknown had such an air of authority, and raised the folds of his robe with such a proud gesture, that no one dared make answer to his reproaches.

The old man approached him. 'Brother,' said he, 'what is there of evil in sacrificing a cock, with all due ceremony, to the good genii Hermes and Agathodæmon?'

The sound of the two names made the stranger gnash his teeth.

'If you have not the beliefs of the Sabeans, what has brought you here? Are you a follower of Jesus or Mohammed?'

'Mohammed and Jesus are impostors,' cried the unknown, blaspheming with a hearty fearlessness.

'Then doubtless you belong to the religion of the Parsees; you worship fire. . . .'

'Phantoms, delusions . . . all that is but lies!' the man in the black smock interrupted with redoubled indignation.

'Then whom do you worship?'

'He asks me whom I worship! I worship no one, for I myself am God, the one true God, of whom the others are but shadows.'

At this inconceivable, incredible, wild assertion, the Sabeans hurled themselves upon the blasphemer, and they would have dealt with him roughly, had not Yousouf, covering him with his body, drawn him away to the terrace beside the Nile, though he fought and cried like a madman. At last, with a vigorous kick at the bank, Yousouf drove the boat out into the middle of the stream. When they were in midstream Yousouf asked his friend where he should take him.

'There, where you see the lights shining on the island of Rodda,' replied the stranger, whose excitement had been calmed by the night air.

With a few strokes of the oars, they reached the shore, and the man in the black smock, before leaping ashore, offered his saviour a ring of ancient design, saying: 'In whatever place you meet me, you have only to show me this ring and I will do whatever you desire.' Then he went off, and disappeared among the trees upon the river's bank. To make up for lost time, Yousouf, who wished to be present at the sacrifice of the cock, began to cut through the waters of the Nile with redoubled energy.

9

As can be seen from the examples of Gautier, Baudelaire and Gérard de Nerval, experimentation with drugs was widespread among the writers, artists and bohemians of Paris through much of the second half of the nineteenth century. The great Honoré de Balzac might almost be credited with having set the scene back in 1838 when he published his *Treatise on Modern Stimulants*—a work of pure theory where drugs were concerned, for he adamantly refused to sample any of them. In subsequent years, apart from those writers we have mentioned, other notable *literateurs* who took opium or hashish at one time or another included Alexandre Dumas (who belonged to the *Club des Hachischins* for a period); the doomed Prosper Mérimée; Alfred de Musset, dramatist and one of the translators of De Quincey's 'Confessions'; Pierre Loti, the voyager and 'Flower of the Pacific'; and last, but perhaps most important of all, *Arthur Rimbaud* (1854-1891).

This boy genius from Belgium, the archetype of the youthful rebel, impatient to sample life's pleasures and poisons, abandoning poetry for ever before he was out of his teens, writing 'the most remarkable poems since the death of Baudelaire', was certainly the French poet's spiritual heir in both his appetite for life and his genius. He became the friend and companion in debauchery of Paul Verlaine, the Parisian poet, and together the older man and his teenage companion idled and drank their way across the capital, eager for any new sensation. Rimbaud had fled to Paris to escape a strict and domineering mother and rebelled in the classic tradition: first steeping himself in the bohemian climate and then keenly embracing its thrills. 'He intoxicated himself, systematically, with alcohol, hashish and tobacco,' wrote his distinguished biographer, Edgell Rickword (*Rimbaud: The Boy and The Poet*, 1924). 'He would sit drowsing on the seats of the cafés and when roused would sit up rubbing his eyes with the backs of his hands. He moved among the men of letters of Paris like a drunkard or a visionary.' According to his contemporaries, he relished every impression, and one noted that he 'lived like a somnambulist at the mercy of his visions'. From hashish he was to derive one marvellously wrought prose-poem, 'The Time of Assassins', which he actually wrote under the fading influence of the drug and which is reprinted here. Another biographer, M. Ruchon, sees traces of hashish in another work, 'Anguish'. 'It is possible,' he says, 'that the phrase, "Oh, laurels! Oh diamond! Love, vigour!— high above all joys and all glory—in every shape—everywhere, demon, god—youth of this being which is Myself!" with its feeling of calm, of being far away, is about the search for inspiration, for the state of ecstasy produced by the artificial paradises.' After debauchery, however, came recriminations: Rimbaud separated from Verlaine in 1872, nearly starved to death under the bridges of Paris, and then reunited with Verlaine again, existing for a time in London in a state of uneasy friendship. Moving on to Brussels in 1873 they quarrelled once again, and this time the enraged Verlaine shot and wounded his friend. While the poet was imprisoned for attempted murder, Rimbaud went through the final phase of his creativity, producing *Les Illuminations* (from which the story here is taken) and *Une Saison en Enfer*. This last work was so badly treated by the critics that Rimbaud vowed never to write again, burned all his manuscripts, and—still only nineteen years old—set off on a life of travel during which he only once more put pen to paper (to write a short travelogue for the Geographical Society in 1887). It was suggested that Rimbaud took hashish again at the end of his life, when he was suffering intense pain in his right knee, but this has never been substantiated. Ill health forced him to return to France in 1891 and six months after his return he died in Marseilles at the age of thirty-seven.

*

I say that it is necessary to be a seer, to make oneself a seer. The poet makes himself a seer by a long, immense, and reasoned unruliness of all his senses. Every form of love, of suffering, of folly, he seeks himself; and exhausts in himself every kind of poison, retaining only the quintessentials. Ineffable torture, where he has need of all his faith, of all his supernatural strength; where, amongst other people he becomes the unhealthy one, the great criminal, the great accursed — and the supreme master—because he attains the *unknown*. Because he has cultivated his soul, which is already rich, more than any other person! He attains the unknown, and when, distracted, he loses his understanding of his visions, none the less he has seen them. Let him perish in his leapings amongst unheard-of and numberless things: there will come other horrible labourers; they will begin at those horizons where the other has succumbed.

Letter to M. Delahaye, June 1872

PENCIL SKETCH OF RIMBAUD BY VERLAINE

The Time of Assassins
ARTHUR RIMBAUD

Oh *my* Good! Oh *my* Ideal! Atrocious fanfare which does not make me lose my balance! Fantastic prop! Hurrah for the wonderful work and the marvellous body; for this initiation! It began amidst the laughter of children and it will end there too.

This poison will remain in our veins, even when—the fanfare shifting its tone—we shall have returned to the old lack of harmony.

But now let us—so worthy of these tortures—fervently recall the superhuman promise made to our body and soul at their creation. Let us recall this promise—this madness! Elegance, Science, Violence!

To us the promise was made that the Tree of Knowledge should be buried in the shade, that tyrannical respectabilities should be deported in order that our pure love should be indulged.

It began with certain aversions, and ended—we being unable to grasp eternity at the moment—with a confusion of perfumes, laughter of children, discretion of slaves, austerity of virgins, dread of earthly things and beings—holy be ye held by the memory of that evening!

It began with every sort of boorishness; it ended with angels of flame and of ice. Little evening of intoxication, blessed be you! Rule and method, we are your champions!

We do not forget how last night you glorified each one of us, young and old. We have faith in your poison. We know how to sacrifice our entire life every day.

The Time of Assassins is here!

III

The mass of evidence, Chinese and foreign, points to a fascinating, enthralling power in opium.

WILLIAM H. BRERETON
(1840-1908)

Although opium smoking is widely thought to have had its origins in China, it in fact began in Egypt and was probably not introduced into the Orient until the late 1700s. History indicates that the opium poppy, *Papaver somniferum*, was first cultivated in Egypt during the time of the Pharaohs and was then taken by the Arab traders on their journeys through Turkey, Persia, India and so on, to the far corners of the earth. In China, opium is first recorded as having been used for medical purposes; then, during the reign of Keinlung (1736-1796), it was found to be smokable and so began the enduring tradition. The British, who for years tried unavailingly to get foreign trade allowed in China, were for a time accused of actually introducing opium smoking into the country as part of their campaign to further their interests. The animosity of the two nations culminated in the Opium Wars of 1839-42, when China banned the importation of the drug across her borders and destroyed the British-owned opium stores in Canton. This was the excuse the British had been seeking for an all-out confrontation, and their superior troops easily won the ensuing battles. The Treaty of Nanking (1842) granted free access for British traders to the major Chinese ports and ceded Hong Kong to the Crown.

In the years that followed, opium smoking increased enormously, and by the turn of the century it was virtually commonplace among people in all walks of life. The Chinese who emigrated took the habit with them, and the major colonies to be found in Hong Kong, America and Europe were often centres for the introduction of the drug to the indigenous population. In China itself, at the close of the nineteenth century, several charitable organizations were becoming concerned about the effects of the drug and began to campaign for its prohibition. Although there was a certain amount of sympathy in mandarin circles towards these 'foreign do-gooders', very little, apart from the occasional perfunctory attempts to stop the most blatant abuses, was done by the local authorities. It was not until the emergence of Mao tse-Tung and the Revolution that major changes were brought about. Even today, however, opium smoking does persist in China, although on nothing like the same scale and with supplies more difficult to obtain. (Hong Kong, on the other hand, now has more opium addicts per head of population than any other part of the world. It is also the most important heroin market-place.) In this next section the China of the turn of the century is evoked by a long-time British resident and novelist, and then the path of the drug and its use are traced around the world to France, America and England.

In the hysteria of foreign public opinion about opium smoking in China at the turn of the century, one voice above all others seems to have remained calm and objective—that of the British novelist and sociologist, *B. L. Putnam Weale* (1860-1923), who lived in Peking. Many of the accusations against the Chinese and their addiction to the drug—and there can be no denying that there was much abuse of it—were being made by people who had never been to the country or seen opium smoking at first hand. The British, those rigid Victorians, were particularly quick to condemn and it is therefore gratifying to find one author at least who was un-biased in his writings. He saw the evils as well as the pleasures and presented his findings in an excellent work, *The Forbidden Boundary,* which was published in 1908. Putnam Weale spent a large part of his life in China as an export official and writer and had experienced much that he wrote about. 'It is my belief,' he wrote at the turn of the century, 'that a man may continue to use opium as we use wine and the lower classes use beer in this country [England], without ever being inclined to use it to excess. I have known men who have told me that they have smoked opium all their lives and were perfectly competent to do the duties of their position.' From his studies, Putnam Weale observed that a moderate user of opium at this time would take about an ounce per day, this allowing for between six to ten pipes. He himself smoked opium on occasions with Chinese friends and knew several of the high-class opium salons where the local officials and the senior foreign residents and businessmen went. He also knew the other side of the coin: the agony of an addict unable to get his regular supplies. This evocative story, 'Drugs and the Man', resulted from a visit Putnam Weale made with a Chinese government official to a notorious Peking salon, and is based on a real incident.

*

I have seen in the case of many Chinese, and in fact have experienced it myself, that if you smoke a single pipe of opium once or twice, it has very little effect on you. But if you smoke for three or four days steadily, a pipe or two a day, it begins to affect you. If you continue with still more pipes it will not be long before you cannot raise your energy sufficiently to go about your daily work without having to take a quantity of opium, a pipe or two.

Letter, 1908

Drugs and the Man
B. L. PUTNAM WEALE

I

The street was long and very narrow, and from a thousand houses hung a multitude of enormous sign-boards, adorned with wondrous characters gaily painted in gold and red, and swinging so far out over the roadway as to make the open street seem even narrower than it really was. The thousand houses were all curious and ill-assorted. Some towered three stories high—three stories of gay little verandahs with much painted woodwork and much open space between the latticed doors and windows. It was just as if theatres had purposely been constructed to look out on to the gay street, and as if only as an afterthought they had been turned into ordinary houses of entertainment, where in the heat and excitement of the evening great crowds might noisily enjoy themselves after their usual wont. There was nothing quite like these houses in any other part of the world.

Side by side with these high structures of mere framework were other little houses of brick and cement, entirely different of aspect, with oblong holes in the walls for doors, in and out of which women were continually running as soon as the tedious and well-slept morning had given place to the waking noon. Far down the street, where it debouched on the broad sweep of road facing the slowly flowing ochre-coloured river, there were European houses, ill-kept and sullen with the hideous sordidness of old age. There was something dispiriting in the mere sight of those buildings; they were a funeral service said in brick and stone. But such houses were few in number and of no importance. They were just the introduction to the real street, which only began with the high theatrical tea-houses and the swinging sign-boards and the little houses with holes in the walls for doors, in and out of which ran women in the trousers and short jackets of indecency.

All the morning there was nothing to be seen except a few sleepy people slowly waking to the spending day; and in the sweetmeat shops, where red sweets and green sweets and yellow sweets stood stacked in red-brown wicker baskets, and most of all in the fashionable shops, where rich robes of wondrous silks and satins were perpetually displayed, and round which cunning touts clustered in the business hours of night, it was hard to see more than a man or two. In the morning the roadway was bare in all truth; and it might have seemed even lonely had it not been for the groups of sweating water-carriers, carrying their ugly wooden buckets and chanting in suppressed half-tones that trembled and quavered under the weight, as they brought their heavy burdens endlessly from the river and poured the cool water into the brown earthenware *kang* placed in the corner of each house. As the fresh morning breezes swept down the street, the thick Eastern smells which had collected during the previous night's carouse were gradually dissipated; and the atmosphere, stripped of its characteristic odours, seemed curiously dead. Marauding dogs, squat-shaped and covered with long discoloured hair— with the streets to themselves, save for these water-carriers and a few yawning shop apprentices,—wandered slowly up and down and scavenged far and wide, sometimes even fighting lazily among themselves. They fought like cowards when they fought—six or seven banding against the weakest and savaging him on the ground. There was no one save the water-carriers to kick them away. It was morning; and therefore the waking hours had not yet arrived.

As the day wore on, however, and the sun, passing the meridian, slowly sank, the scene gradually changed. The street, though narrow, was a 'horse road,' and carriages might pass here without let or hindrance; and so, from adjacent streets and from the street itself came patrons of European carriages, at last alive to the fact that another day had really dawned. Dressed in the extreme of fashion, they yawningly drove out, waving their fans and puffing their Manila cigars in each other's faces. By four or five in the afternoon, with more and more people coming out, business had fairly begun. The women had ceased running in and out from their little houses in much the same disordered clothes as those in which they had slept. All were busy painting and rouging, and combing and oiling their hair with thick evil-smelling pomades—some sitting nonchalantly at their doors and performing their toilets in full view. Cunning tradesmen, adepts in that peculiar Chinese massage and joint-twisting which eases all aches and reposes the exhausted body, were being pestered by the calls of little painted slave-girls, sent out by their mistresses to fetch such precious men, and were exclaiming that it was vain to suppose they could serve the whole town at once. In the high theatre-like teahouses instruments were even being tuned; whilst the cheap-jacks with their packs of cloth on their backs, crowding in all together from the dense city beyond because they knew that the hour had arrived, joined their growing choruses to those of the shop-touts of the street itself.

It was not until the first lights had been lighted, however, that the great life really began. The afternoon was mere preparation, just as the decaying European houses at the river end of the street served as a careless introduction to the street itself. The afternoon crowds were mainly inexperienced people wandering aimlessly to and fro. They were *wai-hang-ti*—not of the business, not *habitués;* indeed, as often as not, they were just country bumpkins and country cousins clothed in common blue cloth and not in silks—men who gazed almost awfully at this renowned promenade of pleasure, and perhaps dreamed wonderful dreams about the lily-footed women who had made the Fourth Horse Road something of a household name from the borders of Mongolia even into the Red River, which is very far. Who indeed does not know the Fourth Horse Road?

But with the first lights all that was changed. No sooner was the first glow of electricity seen, or the first flare of gas or smoking oil-lamp, than in a moment, as if by some well-understood signal, thrice ten thousand lights sprang up and blotted out the fading day. How gay it became! It was a street of lights and nothing else—a street lighted as if to proclaim the belief that all men and women were merely moths and needed only the sight of lamps to crush forward and lose themselves in a hundred pleasures. Far up the sides of the three-storied houses, until the very roofs were reached, these lights now blazed—electricity, gas, and mineral oils sharing their favours with gaudily painted oil-paper lanterns, in which sputtered thick native candles of grease, perpetually smoking and stenching. Every landlord vied with his neighbours in such lighting effects; and as from the neighbouring European quarter all modern conveniences were obtainable, it was not rare to find a dozen electric bulbs, coloured in pink or lemon, shining tranquilly side by side with ancient horn lanterns—the very new and the very old meeting and yet never coalescing. Far beyond the town on dark nights you could see the glare lighting the skies. Country people as they went home to bed muttered to themselves with envy in their hearts as they looked and saw—'It is the Fourth Horse Road!' Oh yes, everybody knew it.

With myriad lights blazing down the long, narrow street the world was at last awake, and a growing clamour greeted one's ears. The tea-houses and the restaurants filled up; tottering old men and vigorous young men, mainly robed in deliciously coloured silks, walked slowly with the left-to-right Chinese paunch-swing of elegance and refinement into their favourite haunts; and, warming to the attractions of the hour by the infectious gaiety around, they called loudly for heated wine and appetite-givers, whilst they invited bedizened courtesans to amuse them with the gossip of the day. The tea-house drawers, hurrying obsequiously to and fro, called down their orders ever faster and faster to the cook-shops below; and the sweating kitchen-men, stripped to the waist and with pigtails tightly rolled about their heads, soon had scarce time to think, much less to talk. Outside in the street the crowds grew thicker and thicker and noisier and noisier, and such carriages as still ventured through had perforce to proceed at a walk, with all cursing them for trespassing on a roadway which had now become—by a custom stronger than law—the walker's very own.

Little sedan-chairs, beautifully finished in silks and as light as feathers on the shoulders of their sturdy bearers, hurried along, each containing a precious flower whose presence had been hurriedly requisitioned by some admirer, and who, for three thousand *cash*, would shrilly sing a song or two accompanied by her own twanging *pi-pa*, and then hurry away to her next appointment. Smaller girls, mere children in fact, but robed as women the better to attract, and covered with seed pearls worked into their hair and dress, were swiftly borne along the street on the shoulders of serving-men, who shouted to the people to make way so that they might the more quickly reach their patrons. These were *chang-san*—singing-girls of the first class. They sat primly and quite unconcernedly on the right shoulders of their bearers; they were accustomed to it. Other girls dressed as boys, with only a single ear-ring in their left ears to show their real sex—this by order of the unpoetical European police,—walked demurely along on their tiny feet to show this latest fashion. They, too, were quite impassive before the inquisitive looks and remarks that followed their every movement; they were tickled only by the grossest comments.

The silk-shop touts shouted louder and louder, and reduced their prices with every breath. The clang of native guitars and the clatter of native castanettes added to the hubbub. The thick smells grew again and hung on the air; laughter and ribald jests broke out in a perpetual undertone; and in out of the doors, which were mere holes in the wall, men and women now hurried unconcernedly together with the coarseness of matter-of-fact vice. The Fourth Horse Road was alive, joyous, humming. For it was night, and the business of the day was in full swing.

II

The old man came out into the glare of this gay scene from a side-street where the booksellers are—that quiet, clean side-street where each shop is full of neatly arranged books placed in glass cases, each book having a long tag of white rice paper attached to it, so that at a glance, without having to open the clumsy Chinese fastening, purchasers can find what they seek. All the good books were there, in costly editions of many volumes each; and each series was fitted into the same sober blue-cloth cases, so as to make a compact bundle in the hand. You could have philosophers as old as Mencius, or Buddhist texts done into the stiff classical language which is now so very hard for the ordinary man that the ordinary man has given up reading it. They were all there. You could have very modern books, with gaudy paper covers modelled after those made in modern Japan, covers ugly enough in their newness to make any old scholar angry. There were also the lewdest publications, such as the *Ching Ping Mei*, which endlessly compares women's backs to the whitest ivory, and their lips to the lush of scented wines. There you could also find the more innocent *Dream of the Red Chamber*, and the historical romances which teach the Chinese so much of their mythical history; and also those other classics which have been read by thirty generations and still sell.

The old man knew them all and, therefore, loved those shops. How many years had he not spent in the literary delight of those who are born for the study of books! How many years indeed! And now as he came blinking and shambling into the joyous Fourth Horse Road, he had to confess to himself that finished were those days when he could sit for quiet hours in the cool of long afternoons, poring over texts through his great horn spectacles, and reflecting on the perfect times of the great Yao and Shun. Yes, such days were finished, completely finished; for now he could dream and think only in the coughing, biting fumes of the drug, the great drug! As he lighted pipe after pipe, slowly and with the skill of the practised smoker, his life would come back to him and it seemed good to live. His brain leapt back, became young, was joyous, alive and alert, and the miseries of real life quickly disappeared. He could forget the harshness of his relatives, who, willing and anxious to fawn on him and compliment him on his many virtues whilst he was rich, now begrudged him a few miserable strings of *cash* a month because he had become poor. Dogs indeed were his relatives; and all those shrill-voiced women, packed into the family house and disputing all day and even half the night about each other's affairs and the affairs of every one else, made of his life a veritable nightmare—when he was not away lying down on the cushioned benches where he could dream.

He thought of all these things wrathfully as he shambled forward in his faded pantaloons of green silk and his seedy coat of plum colour, pinching in his left hand a half-burnt cigarette of the foreign factories. The joyous crowds bumped and jostled him as they sauntered along; and from the great theatre-like tea-houses came the shrill songs of the singing-girls and the clash of cymbals and the rippling notes of reed-pipes. The great volume of sound seemed almost harsh and discordant. Yet all these things he loved and liked. Here were people who knew what life was; here were people who had no vain regrets and no oppressors. And as the singing-girls paused and quavered on impossibly high notes and slid their voices up and down in queer intervals, the joy of life almost returned to him even without the aid of drugs. Who would not love such things? No wonder people were remarking that the street was fast being so overrun and spoilt month after month by mere coolie crowds, attracted in ever greater streams, that in the end such men as he—who knew and understood such things as they should be known and understood—would be outnumbered ten to one.

Pausing in his shamble again and again to greet such acquaintances as were willing to remember him, the old man slowly progressed up the Fourth Horse Road until he had almost reached the end, where there were only, save for a few three-storied buildings, those low-lying brick and cement houses with little holes in the wall for doors, and many women always scuttling in and out for sole tenants. There he stopped and quavered a good-day. He had reached the end of his walk.

III

'It is old Pang,' said the chief drawer of the main tea-room (which was on the ground floor) with a coarse laugh, full of Chinese disrespect, as the old man shambled in. 'It is old Pang,' echoed the second drawer and the cub apprentices with the same derision, because they loved to fawn on their head-man and also loved to jest and sneer. 'Have you the money, old Pang?' continued the chief drawer with such veiled insolence in his tone that everybody laughed delightedly so as to egg him on. 'We hope you have the money, because your account is very old, and perhaps you may not even smoke in the back-room below.' That is what the chief drawer said.

The old man paused with rage, and even more terror, in his heart, and moved his lips to inarticulate sounds as the crowd of customers seated at the square wooden tables sneered and laughed. There was no pity in them. The back-room below—was it really meant in earnest? He hated even to think of it, for one had little enough enjoyment in the secondary rooms where Patna is mixed with two-thirds of native drug, and where it takes five pipes to do the work of three on the topmost floor. Ah, for the topmost floor where Malwa, pure Malwa, with just a pinch of the native cake added thereto so as to give a little more profit to the keepers, was to be had! Delicious Malwa, strong and violent in its action—the heavenly drug straight from the plains of Hindustan! Yet such a thing was not to be thought of. For weeks and months he had been forced into the secondary rooms where they mix for sheer profit and nothing else, because his wretched relatives would pay but half the account. And now they taunted him, and perhaps even threatened him with the back-rooms—the back-rooms where there was but the re-smoke to have—ashes that taste hideous in the mouth except in the case of the coarsest men—ashes soldered over with the Szechuen cake to make it brown and to allow it to burn. It would be gall and wormwood to him.

As he stood there blinking and hesitating, with the roar of the joyous street still sweeping in through the wide-open doors and windows, the drawers made as if they would bar his way upstairs. Then a flood of customers, raw men from the country, carrying their jackets in their hands and showing their bare brown backs to their betters with the utmost unconcern, broke like a wave between him and his tormentors; and, being temporarily forgotten, the old man crept upstairs to the secondary rooms, where, pushing a quarter-string of *cash* into an attendant's hands, he begged quickly for a pipe and a couch. The attendant counted slowly and obeyed.

But he had hardly settled down, lying on his left side and rolling the cake into small balls on the tray of the tiny lamp, when there was an angry voice, and the master of the establishment entered and cuffed the whining attendant.

'Out of it!' he cried; 'out of it, old Pang! We told you that we would give you until to-day to make a half-account settlement. Nothing has been paid, not a *cash*. So out of it, out of it!' The master shouted angrily—he had enough of this; he would not lose more money.

In a quavering voice the old man pleaded for mercy, as he slipped one little ball of opium cunningly into his sleeve; but the master of the establishment was irate, and in the end it was only out of charity that he pushed the old man into the lower back-rooms and let him smoke there if he willed. That was the master's decree, and his decrees were law, for he was very rich.

The dread back-rooms, where mere common coolies, stripped to the waist, lie stenching in their malodorous fumes—had he come to this? The old man climbed on to a settle with rage in his heart, but with the drug habit forcing him to obey. There were four other men already on this bare bamboo settle—two already asleep, with wide-open mouths and whistling breathing; two still working with their pipes and inhaling deep and strong with the powerful lungs of those who 'sell strength' and are mere muscle-bound coolies. These last two looked for a moment with vacant eyes at the late-comer who crowded them so. Yet they did not object. Did they not belong to a common brotherhood—were they not votaries at the same shrine?

Old Pang pushed for himself bare lying-room on the bamboo settle, muttering incoherently to himself the while, and thankful indeed that he had one little ball in his sleeve to commence with. Five on a single couch—what an end indeed after having had a rich Canton blackwood settle all to himself! He did not mind the lack of cushions, nor yet the lack of privacy, so much as the lack of refinement. To lie down in this fashion, thick together, like so many roped pigs in a sampan going to market, seemed to him the worst. He chuckled a little to himself in open derision, as he gazed feebly round and saw how many more there were in this dark room lying so quiet. There were dozens of silent men. The murky atmosphere was lighted by a single oil lantern swinging from the ceiling. Spiders spun their webs in peace everywhere; and the soot and grime of ages lay undisturbed. The old man, nodding and muttering to himself, rolled his little ball tightly into the tiny bowl of the metal pipe, lighted it, and inhaled deeply. He had begun.

IV

It was no use—absolutely no use. Slowly, as his brain awoke to the fact, he became alarmed, and a feeble terror gripped his heart. For listen what had happened. He had slowly smoked his first little ball with that double inhalation—the lung and stomach movement—which only the oldest smokers can properly make. Deep into his frail body the narcotic had at first seemed to be wafted, sending pleasant waves and thrills through his brain and his whole nervous system. Then, just as he was beginning to get relief, the little ball had smoked out, and he had sucked a hot taste of fire which cut like a knife into his throat. That comes in the end when one is over-greedy.

He paused some time before attempting the measure of ashes, caked over with the coarse native-grown stuff, which was set at his side. He did not like the idea of fouling his mouth with such filth after his pipe of secondary mixture. Yet soon, fearful that he would lose what he had already gained in his brain, if he delayed too long, he began rolling once more; and then, as if he were plunging into cold water, he quickly in-sucked.

Yet it had been no use—entirely no use. Sixteen pipes he had tried, which made seventeen in all with that first good pipe; and yet for sole result he had but a dizziness and an uneasiness which were quite new to him. Never before had he been so dizzy, or so uneasy—never, never, never. He tasted, too, an acrid taste in his mouth as of real gall and wormwood; whilst his system, left for years only partially nourished and merely buoyed up temporarily by his smoker's debauches, now seemed to shrink within him. He looked around feebly in the dimly-lighted and evil-smelling back-room; the stale, rank smell of the drug aroused in him a burning desire such as he had never felt before—even on those evil days when his relatives had carried him away, and kept him, by force, from smoking. He now lusted after the drug with an animal craving which gripped him from his head to his feet, and angrily he spurned the remains of the third-class stuff from him. He was being deprived of his rights. He was so violent that one of the four men alongside him half woke and incoherently moved his lips. The old man quavered an apology, and then carefully, with infinite cunning so as to still the creaking of the coarse bamboo settee, he crawled to his feet, stealthily, as a thief does in the night. Though he was very decrepit and very weak, he made his way to the door, and opened it bit by bit with the craft of the murderer and crept outside. He had made up his mind. He was going to risk it.

V

The stairs, like the stairs of all such houses, in spite of their gay street frontage, mounted to the next floor in a mean and humiliating way. The steps were high and narrow, greasy and dirty, and pushed upwards slinkingly; it was as if an afterthought had alone caused them to be added when the rest of the building was complete. Also it was as much as a man could do to squeeze past another on the way; and as old Pang, with a last crafty look around him, risked it, the horrible thought entered his head that if he encountered any one belonging to the house he would be flung down again cruelly, as they did with the dogs. He paused for a moment in doubt. But the hour was already late, and both inside and outside the gay, hot clamour of voices, which he loved and knew so well, was gradually dying down. It was lucky for him, very lucky, he thought; for those drawers were coarse fellows, only too anxious to curry favour with their master by blindly obeying his behests and following whatever lead he might give them. So old Pang crept upstairs quickly and quietly, with an immense relief in his heart at the growing stillness. It would be all right now.

On the first floor he stopped and almost gave way to his immense longing for the speedy taste of the drug. He knew every inch of this first floor—where the smokers lay, where the cake was stored, and where the attendants slumbered. It would be so easy for him to slip into these rooms—with every one deep in their dreams, immovable, log-like on their couches—and to steal from the cupboards a two-man allowance. It would be easier here than on the other floor. But he at last conquered his first inclination, after he had stood awhile wrestling with himself in the deep shadows; and then, slowly and even more carefully than before, he edged towards the second flight of steps which lead to the top floor where Malwa—delicious Malwa—Malwa that was quite pure save for the middleman's slight adulteration—was always smoked. He would have Malwa to-night or nothing.

The second flight was easier to climb than the first; for the staircase was broader and more elegant, as if it were an avenue leading to the Nirvana of all good men. There was even the Red Cloth of Happiness on the hand-rail to prevent one from soiling one's hands. On the top floor he knew that there were only smokers of elegance, lying in pairs, on those broad black-wood couches which he used to know so well. It would be much quieter up there, old Pang reflected, because rich men demanded their ease and quiet even in this land of noise, and because the attendants were very obsequious. It would be more dangerous. Here the attendants hardly slept; if they did, it was with one eye open so as to be always ready for their patrons' calls. He would have to be very cautious.

Old Pang gained the level of the top floor with his wind softly whistling through his teeth, for he was now really faint and weary, and the craving had become terrible. He listened with his ears wide open, as they had never been opened before. They seemed to be stretched to the top of his head; and he picked up every sound as a burglar picks up signs of life in a sleeping house. The craving had made him very crafty. But all was well—he understood that at once. Deep breathing came from every direction, with only an occasional scraping of a foot on the uncarpeted floors. He knew even what that last sound meant. It was the attendants three-quarters asleep in their chairs, fidgeting a little in their dreams. But that was no danger; they were really asleep, although their legs were awake so that they might be ready to move if there were calls. He understood all such things very well, for he was a man of learning, a man who could watch and pick up all manner of things, a man who could reason and explain.

He waited a little, and then moved gently forward; and, standing on tip-toe, carefully and slowly he turned down a lamp so that it might be dark—very dark. Then, satisfied that the game was in his hands, he pushed his loose sleeves quickly far up his shrivelled arms, bound his thin wisp of a pigtail tightly round his head, and crept forward. Like a mere shade he entered a big room on the right, passed two sleeping men on a couch, then two more men on another couch, then the attendant; and at length reached the cupboard where were stored the tiny scales and the neat tins of the drug. His fingers twitched with greed as he pushed open the cupboard and felt in the semi-dark. Ah! he had found a tin; he had opened it; he had a cake in his hands without a single sound, when to his horror he heard a thick Chinese whisper in the direction of the nodding attendant. 'I have followed up old Pang in the dark—where has he gone? where has he gone?' the thick whisper said; and he heard the attendant stir, and try to seize the meaning as sleeping men do. It was awful. Old Pang crept behind a chair, shrivelled himself up and waited. He knew that they would not dare to turn up the lights for fear of waking and offending the four sleeping patrons lying here in pairs; for opium-smokers understand no excuses when they are disturbed. He knew this, and so still hoped that he was safe.

The whispers continued for a while and then ceased, after some moving of feet. Old Pang knew that the attendant must have sworn that he had been awake and that no one could possibly have passed in; for the moving feet were now going in the direction of the other rooms; and from those rooms soon came cautious whispers. They were debating amongst themselves what to do. Now was his chance.

With his head and neck pushed out far in front of him like a vulture, the old man crept back; came out on the bare landing; saw that there was no one there; and now, with the slink of a beaten dog, he made for the staircase. A few seconds and it would be all right. A few seconds——

He woke to the fact that he had been gripped from behind, as a man awakes to the fact that he has been stabbed. His mouth remained open trying to frame articulate prayers and beseechings, yet he could say nothing but *'Ah! Ah!'* in a faint whispering screech. They had trapped him; they had caught him, and his chance was lost. He would not have his Malwa, his blessed Malwa for which he craved; and in an agony of fear he clutched his cake tightly in his hand. The men pulled him roughly but quietly across the landing to the little balcony overlooking the flaring street. Here it was light enough to see plainly; and so, calling him dog's droppings and other obscene names in raucous whispers, they felt him over and over to see what he had taken.

They could find nothing, absolutely nothing. His belt was empty of every *cash;* he had no watch, no valuables, not a thing with which to bribe their silence; and, as the little knot of drawers and attendants realised that they were dealing with a wholly broken and beggared man, who could not even pay a squeeze, they became rougher and rougher. One pinched him; the other pulled him; they called him endless names. Then they slid their arms up their sleeves to see that he had not cunningly taken advantage of them; and once more finding nothing, they pulled at his hands.

It was the drawer who had followed him upstairs who first saw his clenched left hand and bade him open it. Whiningly old Pang protested that he had nothing. But that made no difference; oh no, in a country of lies the denial is the confession, and so they demanded to see. There was nothing, he protested—nothing—nothing—nothing. Suddenly they became angry as they realised that he must have a stolen cake in his palm, and that they would be charged with the theft. Now they understood him.

'All right,' muttered the drawer. 'You will not open?—then we will see'; and whilst he roughly held old Pang's shrivelled ears in his hands, he whispered something to his comrades. When his ears were released, the old man heard with dismay that they were all chuckling, chuckling grossly with an immense pleasure. They were like the dogs on the street preparing to savage, after their custom, the weakest one.

'There is nothing?' asked the drawer for the last time.

'There is nothing,' answered old Pang in a piteous whine.

'All right, all right,' said the drawer. *'Yi shih,* all together,' he exclaimed to the others, and with one accord they seized old Pang more tightly and forced him back until he lay in their arms with his face upwards. As he realised what they were going to do, he tried to shriek; but there was a hand on his gullet and another over his mouth. With quick cunning they forced his own left hand to his mouth, and with a fierce jerk that nearly tore his fingers away, they pressed it open against his teeth. There they held it tight, whilst they swung him backwards choking and coughing. They pressed in his stomach and lungs as hard as devils, and then, suddenly releasing, they slammed him down on the ground. They knew that he would gulp for breath —they knew it—they knew it; and as the wretched man sank faintly to the ground, a dark trickle of saliva came from his lips. He had swallowed.

With a last effort he raised himself, and fell against the crazy balcony rail trying to call aloud the crime. As his cracked voice filled the air the men became nervous. 'Finish, finish,' said one. They banged him down; he tried to escape them; the rail cracked—the devil of a drawer added a push, and with a despairing, smothered cry, old Pang fell headlong on to the street below.

'He ate and then jumped,' they explained casually to the curious people in the street, whilst one hauled out a piece of matting and threw it over him. 'Perhaps he was mad,' they further added. In a few hours an official would come and see all for himself—till then the corpse must not be moved. They almost begrudged the matting. There were four witnesses, and old Pang owed much money. It was quite plain. A few exhausted women came yawningly out of the street brothels and gazed for a little. The lights in the gay street were fading out, and you could even hear the wooden buckets of the water-carriers being bumped together as the toilers prepared to toil. Back in the opium-house an angry voice demanded where the devil every one had gone; and the drawers, as they answered in their hoarse voices, savagely kicked a sniffing yellow dog who was creeping up. It would soon be day, and then they might sleep.

11

The French, as was shown in the previous section, had been experimenting with drugs and their relationship to creative inspiration ever since the pioneer work of Doctor Moreau and the bizarre *Club des Hachischins*. In the early years of the twentieth century, the name of one writer was particularly prominent in this area: *Claude Farrère* (1876-1949). Farrère was the pseudonym of Charles Bargonne, a French naval officer who travelled extensively and experienced life fully. He was regarded as a disciple of Pierre Loti, the romantic novelist, who had experimented with opium and hashish in several parts of the world. Farrère, too, was to experiment on his voyages, especially in the Far East, a part of the world which he came to love and which he portrayed in several of his best works. In 1903 he wrote that he had become a secret smoker and described several of the salons he had visited in Shanghai, 'the opium rendezvous of the whole of the Yangtze—a Deauville, Biarritz and Monte Carlo all in one'. His description of the preparation of the drug, from the same chronicle, is also vivid and dramatic: 'The attendant dips the needle into the little jug filled with sticky opium. Then over the lamp, he proceeds to cook the pearly drop. The drop swells, grows yellow and buds. The man kneads and works it against the bowl of the pipe; he rolls and stretches it, makes it supple—and finally glues it, with a blunt pressure, to the centre of the bowl, against the orifice of the slender stem. As for me, all that I have to do is suck in, with long-drawn breath, the stale and tepid smoke, while he holds above the flame the black pill, which crackles, diminishes, and then evaporates.' From his experiences with opium—the 'kindly drug' as he called it—Farrère wrote *Fumées d'Opium* (1904) which immediately marked him as an original and adventurous novelist. Later works such as *L'Homme qui Assassina* (1907), *La Maison des Morts Vivants* (1911) and *Les Condamnés a Mort* (1921) all reflected his interest in and knowledge of opium. Pierre Louys, the famous French novelist and one of the first enthusiasts of *Fumées d'Opium,* said Farrère possessed the literary skill to 'prolong indefinitely an hour of ecstasy and dream'. When he returned from the Far East he was naturally anxious to discover if similar experiences were to be found in France. He did not have to wait long, as 'The House in Boulevard Thiers' dramatically reveals.

*

Formerly, I believed that Asiatics were separated from my own race by a wide gulf. And, in truth, what a bottomless precipice there is between us! We are children, and they are old men. There is not so much difference between the infant in arms and the centenarian, hastening to his grave, as there is between them and us. But I know, today, that opium is able, in a marvellous manner, to scale that precipice. Opium is a magician which transforms, and works a metamorphosis. The European, the Asiatic are equal—reduced to a level—in the presence of its all-powerful spell. Races, physiologies, psychologies, all are effaced: and other strange new beings are born into the world —the Smokers, who, properly speaking, have ceased to be men.

Fumées d'Opium, 1904

The House in Boulevard Thiers
Claude Farrere

What happened in the house in the Boulevard Thiers, I shall not try to explain. And if I here set down what happened, it is with regrets. For so-called reasonable individuals will jest at it, while others, of whom I am one, will find nothing in the narrative to cure them of their madness.

I shall relate it, nevertheless, for the reason that it is true. It happened the first of May, last year, in a city which I shall not name, —out of prudence. It happened on the fourth floor of a house that is neither old nor mystery-haunted, but newly built, ugly and unpretentious. This house had been erected quite recently, upon the rubbish of a disreputable section of the city. A wide boulevard overlooking the river, today replaces the hovels with closed shutters which formerly clung to the slopes of the cliff. The new quarter has an air of respectability; but it was the old stones, grown vicious from all the vice they had witnessed, which served as foundation for the new buildings. The Boulevard Thiers is, certainly, impregnated with the odour of lurking vice.

The house bears the number seven. It is a house given over to furnished lodgings. We occupied one whole floor, with eight or ten friends. I never was sure who the other tenants were. We had a smoking-den there, with rooms round about it. But no one slept in the rooms, for the reason that all preferred to smoke and talk until dawn, stretched out upon the rice-mats. For opium frees its followers from the yoke of sleep. On certain days, we amused ourselves with table-turning, finding sport in questioning the unknown force which exteriorized itself in our fingers, in order to lift the four legs, one after another. There was among us a singular chap, very young, quite beardless, with long flowing black hair. He was in the habit of dressing in the smoking-room, in a blue and yellow clown's costume, which he pretended was particularly suited to spirit-world experiences. As a matter of fact, he was a very middling sort of magician. The table turned readily enough under our hands, but nothing extraordinary ever happened as a result of it all.

Women frequently would visit us, eager for a taste of the kindly drug, eager also for caresses. For the sensitivity of women is so well padded and lined, during their black drunkenness, that a rude contact with men appears to them as delicate and docile a thing as contact with an androgyne. On the evening of which I am speaking, a girl of twenty had come in. We called her Ether on account of her passion; she needed each evening a full flask of sulphuric ether. That did not prevent her from smoking her fifteen pipes afterwards. On this evening, she was doubly drunk, and was sleeping nude. Some one caressed her lips. The wan lamp filled the den with half-shadows, as the rest of us talked, I no longer know of what.

How it was the fancy suddenly should have seized us to play at turning the table, it is impossible for me to recall. Hartus,—Hartus, the blue and yellow clown, with woman's hair,—was the first to rise, calling me over to assist him in carrying the table into one of the rooms;—for the table cannot turn in the presence of opium. Since I was slow in rising from the mats, he took the table and carried it himself. I can still see his bisected profile, as he bent over with the table resting against his stomach. For a minute, I remained stretched out, sulky at having to leave the gentle torpor of my sixth pipe. At my right, the unconscious Ether, intoxication heavy upon her head, was supporting with her two hands a complacent mouth upon her body. I rose and followed Hartus.

In the damp, almost viscous room, he had lighted a solitary candle, the flame of which was dancing a saraband. Through the tulle curtains of the window panes, the moon was sifting a hoar-frost over the walls. Seated opposite one another, our hands brushing the surface of the wooden table-top, we remained silent for some time. But something had gone wrong, for the table remained motionless. It did not even creak,—you know, those weird dry creaking sounds which precede the exteriorization of movement. No, something had gone wrong. We had already smoked, smoked rather well. That may have been the cause of it.

Finally, tired of the sport, I arose; and, the moon tempting me, I opened the window and leaned out on my elbow. I beheld the serenity of the night, the roofs drowned in whiteness, the river starred with reflection. It was very charming. A gentle breeze half-opened my pajamas and toyed with my bosom. In the absolute silence of that moment, I could hear the blue and yellow clown behind me blowing out the candle. And it was then that an inexplicable thing began to happen.

The breeze playing over my flesh seemed to me, suddenly, cold, very cold, as though the thermometer had dropped a dozen degrees. The table fell noisily and leaped up again. In the darkness, I fancied that Hartus had bumped against it and overturned it. But from the interior of the room, he immediately cried out to me not to make so much noise. I did not say anything; but I knew very well that I had not touched the table.

I was sufficiently frightened to contract my fingers over the window-ledge. Then, collecting my nerves by an effort of will, I turned back a step and stood facing the inexplicable phenomenon. The table was motionless, and Hartus was on his way to the smoking-room. I made a detour of the table, without daring to touch it, and followed him.

In the smoking-room, everything had remained in the state in which it was. Upon the mat, Ether continued to press her lover's lips against her flesh. The heavy curtains excluded the light of the moon. Only the solitary lamp was yellowing the ceiling of the room.

As I entered, Ether removed the man's mouth and nimbly arose. This surprised me greatly, for the moment before, ether and opium had held her completely paralyzed. *But she was no longer drunk now.* I could see her clear eyes, as she leaned against the partition, her hands at her throat. Her slender nudity impressed me as having grown and changed. Not in detail: I could recognize the round shoulders, the small rigid breasts, the narrow, feverish head. But the harmony of the whole was different. It was like coming upon a strange woman, chaste and haughty, with noble blood in her veins and rare thoughts in her brain,—no longer Ether, the courtezan, a washerwoman's illiterate daughter.—As I gazed upon her intently, I fell into a stupor. Her lover called to her, and she replied, in a slow-cadenced voice:

'*Mundi amorem noxium horresco.*'[1]

She did not know how to read. She spoke only French,—a passable

---

[1] Guilty love makes me shudder.

sort of French, sullied with Breton idioms.

She continued, without interruption, in the same austere tone of voice,—the voice of a nun or an abbess:

'*Jejuniis carnem domans, dulcique mentem pabulo nutriens orationis, Coegli gaudiis potiar.*' [2]

The smokers were not in the least astonished. To their dematerialized intellects, no doubt, that which I looked upon as extraordinary appeared as perfectly natural. The blue and yellow clown, alone, arched his eyebrows and glanced at the woman. Then, he remarked to her, with more politeness than was our custom:

'Don't remain standing; you must be tired.'

'*Fiat voluntas Dei! Iter arduum peregi, et affligit me lassitudo. Sed Dominus est praesidium.*' [3]

He questioned her, curiously:

'Where are you from?'

She replied:

'*A terra Britannica. Ibi sacrifico sacrificium justitiae, quia nimis peccavi, cogitatione, verbo et opere. Mea maxima culpa.*' [4]

The clown persisted in his questioning:

'What was your sin?'

'*Cogitatione, verbo et opere. De viro ex me filius natus est.*' [5]

I distinctly saw her white face turn red.

She went on, speaking always Latin, a mediaeval Latin, a Latin of the convent and of the missal, which I understood only by snatches,—the smell of opium assisting my memories of the catechism.—I was near the lamp, and in the intervals between words, could hear the crackling of the drug on the ends of the needles. That was the only thing which tempered my fear,—a muffled fear, which parched my throat, and of which I was unable to rid myself, despite the artlessness of the entire scene. Hartus, emboldened by the pipes he had smoked and complete master of his nerves, continued speaking without any show of doubt. I looked at him, I looked at her, and the picture I have of the two of them is so deeply inlaid upon my retina that no other image ever shall be able to efface it.—I can see them now. He, the blue and yellow man, crouched upon the mats, one hand upon the floor, as the lamp at times turned his flowing black hair to blond. She,

[2] It is by conquering my flesh through fastings, and nourishing my soul on the gentle food of prayer, that I shall finally attain to the joys of Heaven.
[3] May God's will be done! I have travelled a hard path, and I am very tired. But God is my refuge and my strength.
[4] I come from the land of Britain. There I offer just sacrifices, for the reason that I have sinned much, in thought, word and deed. The great fault is mine.
[5] In thought, in word and in deed. By man, of me, a son is born.

the strange woman,—and surely, she was strange!—nude, her back to the wall, her elbows crosswise, her fingers interlaced under her throat. Words came and went between them with a lively see-saw verve, as the room became more and more impregnated with the atmosphere of the beyond. . . . That strange voice preserved the monastic timbre it had had in the beginning, but there was now greater strength behind it,—as though it were drawing nearer. Mere phrases at first, desultory and brief,—phrases uttered in haste, the phrases of a traveller who is in a hurry, who has no time to talk,— expanding now into more plenteous periods, swollen with incidents and flowering with rhetoric. I understood no more, being a poor scholar and too much beside myself.—Later, I questioned Hartus, who has a knowledge of the tongue from seminary days. But he did not answer. He does not like to speak again of those things.

I have preserved only the memory of that voice, that Latinizing voice, gravely intoning what sounded like liturgical responses. I caught certain words on the fly, the names of men or of countries, or ecclesiastical terms, storing them confusedly in my memory, without attributing to them then the sense which I today discover in them, —wrongly discover, it may be.—*Astrolabius, Athanasius, Sens, Argenteuil, excommunitio, concilium, monasterium.*—The voice grew animated and louder. It was like a disputation, an oratorical conflict. Two words, out of all the drift of phrases, remained floating upon the surface, two words ten times repeated, with vehemence and with fury at first, afterwards in a tone of grief and contrition:— *panem supersubstantialem.* And then, suddenly, the voice paused, saddened, infinitely saddened.

I then could hear the blue and yellow clown speaking, and although I knew nothing of what had been said up to then, this voice and question, alike, gave me the feeling of a hoax:

'Sin of lust? What was God's punishment?'

The white face grew violently red, this time, and the voice dropped an octave. There was a solemn whispering, such as is heard in a confessional, and a few words barely reached my ears, with strange and repellant accents. I understood—*modo bestiarum*—*copulatione*— *membris asinorum erectis;* and violently uttered, as though vomited forth in disgust, was the word *castratus.* Having become calm once again, the voice slackened, to such an extent that the wording of the last phrase fixed itself in my memory:

'*Fuit ille sacerdos et pontifex, et beatificus post mortem. Nunc Angelorum Chorus illi obsequantem concinit laudem celebresque palmas. Gloria Patri per omne saeculum.* [6]

[6] He was priest and pontiff, and blessed after his death. The Angelic Choir is now singing his praises with psalms. Glory be to the Father forever.

'And you?' said Hartus.

'*Dominus Omnipotens et Misericors Deus debita mea remisit. Virgo ego fatua. Sed dimissis peccatis meis, nunc ego sum nihil.*'[7]

She repeated, three times, the word: '*nihil.*' And it seemed as though, of a sudden, she were speaking from a long way off. The last '*nihil*' was no more than a breath of sound.

The blue and yellow clown strode up to her, closely enough to reach out and touch her; and then, fastening his gaze upon those unflinching eyes, he called her 'Heloise'. The eyes closed in affirmation.

Then, he took her breasts in his hands and blew some opium into her face. She was motionless. But gradually, her muscles relaxed, and I could see tremors appearing upon her pallid face. A minute more, and the eyes opened and capsized, the head and shoulders drooped, and upon the mats there remained now only a flaccid, lifeless form.

Then, her body slowly stirred, and from her mouth, that same mouth, there came another stammering voice, drowning in drunkenness.

'My Gawd! but it's cold! Hand me a pipe, will you? And now, my petticoat! I'm dying.'

It is true, it was cold, cold as a cellar.

One of the smokers thrust into a pipe-bowl the little brown ball which clung to his needle and extended the pipe to the one who had asked for it. It is possible that he, like myself, had heard. But no doubt the opium had shown him other and still more marvellous visions.

---

[7] The Almighty and Merciful God has forgiven my sins. I was a foolish virgin. But now, my sins have been forgiven, and I am as nothing.

Among the writers and artists who took opium either for experimental reasons or needed it to combat pain and thereby became addicts, there were several who tried with great determination to conceal the fact during their lifetimes. Among literary names that spring to mind are Robert Southey, George Crabbe, Francis Thompson and Lafcadio Hearn. As they represent a facet of drug taking which we have not so far encountered in this collection—the secret imbiber—this seems a suitable moment at which to study the two men who can qualify for inclusion as they turned their experiences into short-story form—albeit not obviously so—Francis Thompson and the extraordinary American, *Lafcadio Hearn* (1850-1904).

Hearn was a writer of bizarre stories and essays, a lover of eccentricity and a seeker of gruesome subjects. Despite the quality of his writing—in particular his American essays and the ghost and horror stories he later wrote when living in Japan—Hearn was little known during his lifetime and has only recently begun to attract any substantial critical attention. For much of his life he was a journalist and newspaper reporter, and it was his fascination with the weird (among the topics he delighted in were murder, grave-robbing, blood drinking, cremation and strange smells!) that first brought him into contact with opium when he was a young man working in Cincinnati in 1875. In search of a story, he went with two local policemen to a Chinese laundry where opium was smoked and there tried the drug himself. He was shown how to prepare the pipe and then smoke it for the best possible effect. Hearn was undoubtedly impressed by the experience and began to smoke regularly, initially in the cause of research, but afterwards because he found the stimulation 'exciting beyond my imagining' (posthumously discovered note). Both in Cincinnati and New Orleans, where he next moved, he continued to write and take opium (probably in the form of laudanum) and there are several essays still extant which describe what he calls 'strict observer's impressions', including 'Opium and Morphia' (March 1875), 'The Opium Habit' (January 1876), 'Opium Eating' (September 1878) and 'Opium Dens' (October 1880). Despite his own involvement, Hearn denied this fact to his friends and even lent his name to some of the first campaigns attempting to suppress the drug in America.

His enquiries into opium had also taken him into the realms of literature, and he became a devoted admirer of the French *Club des Hachischins*—Gautier, Baudelaire and Gérard de Nerval. He subsequently translated much of Gautier's work and said that the Frenchman had 'an imagination wildly luxuriant and highly cultivated'. Perhaps Baudelaire attracted him more than any of the others, for two major reasons. Like the great Frenchman, Hearn was drawn to coloured women and similarly had a pretty mulatto mistress, Althea Foley, to whom he was devoted; furthermore, he admired Baudelaire's 'poetic prose' and deliberately set out to emulate him with a series of essays he called 'Fantastics'. While in New Orleans, Hearn was forced to work exceptionally long hours and this, coupled with the climate which he hated and his enforced separation from Althea Foley, caused him to indulge in opium to a larger degree than at any other period of his life. His life-style also began unconsciously to mirror that of the French writers he admired; apart from his colourful clothes he sported 'a white-handled razor in his stockings and carried a large and deadly telescope'! (He even went so far as to take the pen-name of 'Ozias Midwinter' from Wilkie Collins's laudanum novel, *Armadale*.) It would appear that Hearn got his opium unobtrusively from the Chinese colony and took it while alone in the archipelago of the Gulf. From these experiences came some of his most impressive poems (see 'Spanish Moss') and the essay-story here, 'Torn Letters'. This haunting study of the Gulf coastline and a girl that Hearn sees there has been called a 'masterpiece of prose poetry'; it undoubtedly won many new admirers for the author when it appeared in *Harper's Magazine* in 1888. In the story, which has all the obsessive traits of an opium experience, Hearn believes he is face to face with a woman from the Tertiary period, some 30,000 years ago. The student of Hearn will also see in it his unconscious pining for his absent mistress.

*

The great dreaminess of this land makes itself master of thought and speech—mesmerizes you—caresses with tender treachery—soothes with irresistible languor — woos with unutterable sweetness.... And afterward when you have returned into the vast metropolis, into the dust and turmoil and the roar of traffic and the smoke of industry and the iron cares of life—that mesmerism will not have utterly passed away, nor the perfume of that poppied land wholly evaporated from the brain.

'New Orleans', 1883

Torn Letters
Lafcadio Hearn

I

... Beyond the pale and pitted undulations of the dunes,—forming a billowy cemetery for countless dead and drifted things,—ponderous tides compress the sand to the solidity of pavement, and lick the brown slope till it shimmers. When the southeast wind piles back the waters of the Gulf, the great waves flock to shore with magnificent tumultuousness, in infinite green herds, to be shorn of their fleece of foam. But in those summer days when soft warm breezes blow off shore, the sea dozes in oily silence,—there is scarcely a whispering of ripples,—huge crabs crawl out from beneath the creamy ribbon of spume,—opaline fins wrinkle the surface within a few feet of the shore. And when night opens all her violet immensities, the foam takes flame,—the ripples have luminous bursts,—a shell flung into the sea kindles circles of fire,—and the crabs toddling out of the warm flood, shine like infernal spiders. ...

II

Sometimes when winds are variable and breakers run at long angles to the foam-line, strange sights are to be seen. Unknown perils of the abyss, mysterious panics, drive whole nations of fish to flee from the profundities, and infinite multitudes rush to the shallows,—even to the shore itself—followed by enemies in legion. Then begins the gigantic massacre of an entire population,—the destruction of an innumerable race. Pursuers and pursued spring high into the daylight;—millions of iridescent creatures, mad with fear, leap far out upon the sand,—while behind them the armies of porpoises and of sharks slaughter savagely and silently. And above where the sea is most thickly seamed with those sharp fins that sailors fear,—above the churning and the foaming and the prodigious quivering of terror, triumphantly ride the murderous bands of air,—squadrons of shrieking gulls, and wheeling eagles, and fish-hawks, and frigate birds, hideous of foot and huge of wing. Keen-eyed gulls drop swift as lightning from the storm-cloud of beating wings, and dive, and seize, and tear, and soar again to devour some palpitating silver life between sun and sea,—while pirate birds, seeking to snatch the hard-earned meal, pursue them through the great blaze of blue light. Soon along the beach is spread so mighty a feast that the birds may sicken themselves with luxuries;—they feed upon the eyes only, and only devour one eye of most victims, not seeking even to overturn the flat body in order to tear out the other. Enormous slaughter!—appalling cruelty! —destruction symbolizing grimly the great contests of human life in which the fiercest and strongest and swiftest survive to exemplify Nature's mystic and merciless law,—symbolizing, too, the stranding of countless lives upon the sands of Illusion,—symbolizing, likewise, the loss of unnumbered precious things desperately won only to be wrested brutally from the winner by superior strength and cunning and ferocity in that eternal Battle of Success which is also a tearing-out of hearts. . . .

III

. . . Acres upon acres of silvered corpses with eyes plucked out;—overshadowing stratus-cloud of wings and claws and shrieking feathered throats! . . . The breezes grow heavy with odors of carnage. Yet how small a glimpse is this of Nature's universal aceldama,—of those forces by which are accomplished the infinite evolutions of form! The tender worm hardens its skin against beak and tooth, cases itself in armor, and becomes a warrior crustacean;—self-trained by a million centuries of fear to leap beyond its element, the lithe fish develops wings at last to become itself a destroyer. Marvelous indeed the results, yet atrocious the causes producing them,—producing the man, the woman of the nineteenth century. What myriad cycles of agony, of slaughter, of carnivorous rage, of cannibalism, perhaps, developed the humanity of to-day,—not only the brain that reasons, the knowledge that soars to the stars, but also the beauty that intoxicates, the grace that magnetizes, the unutterable charm of woman,— even the charm I now feel as the old Frenchman's daughter passes by, so lithe, and slender, and tall.

IV

. . . *Papa, voila le monsieur qui arrive!* Her voice is clear and sweet as an altar bell. What a mesmerism is hers!—What artless comeliness, from the lustrous curls of her forehead to the nude feet that seem wrought of mellowed ivory! . . . Visitors to this remote fishing-station seldom call at the weather-beaten cottage which,—with its single vast and deck-like room, its rows of berths, its suspended nets and tackle, its marine clock ticking above the great compass stowed away upon a corner shelf,—suggests a stranded ship rather than a house and home. Therefore uncommon courtesies are shown me. But my attempt at conversation is only partially successful;—the ideas come with effort,—vapidly and vaguely. . . . I am thinking of the grace of the young girl, as she glides hither and thither,—bringing glasses, fetching water, relieving the small round table of its little burden of pious books,—one of which is printed, I observe, in Hebrew characters. The sunlight lingers a moment on the roundness of her cheek, the golden glossiness of her throat:—the beauty of such flesh makes the sunlight seem more beautiful. And the tones of her voice, deeply argentine, seemed to vibrate in every corpuscle of my veins, as I hear her speaking to her father in a strange and fantastic tongue that I cannot recognize.

V

... My venerable friend has had a singular career: first as an ecclesiastical student, then as a soldier in some Algerian legion, then as a colonial trader at Blidah,—Blidah, 'the Little-Rose City',—once destroyed by an earthquake in answer to the prayers of some holy marabout, scandalized by the luxurious sins of its inhabitants. There the retired soldier made and lost a little fortune in trading with those famous M'zabites, who are the fairest-skinned and shrewdest of the tribes, and are believed by many to be the descendants of Moors expelled from Spain. From between the pages of a huge family Bible, the old man plucks out a mysterious and yellow sheet of paper, and offers it to me in witness of the truth. It is a promissory note in Arabic and in French, dated *Bazaar of the Divan, 15 Septembre, 1845,* and bearing the signature of Mohammed ben Moustafa, in characters curved like scimitar-blades. ... And, mounted on the swift Camel of fancy, I follow the veteran over the vast plain of Mitidja and beyond the Mountains of Atlas and far, far southward into the region of vanished seas,—into desolations weirder than the Moon. ...

The sun dips his rim behind the sea-line, the steel blue light changes to lemon-gold, and the gold again deepens to furnace vermilion,—flushing the clouds, reddening the dunes,—and the stars blossom in the darkening azure, and still my aged host continues to tell me of the immeasurable desert and of its swarthy Men of Prey, and the bone-tracked paths of the caravans, and the burning solitudes whose only shadows are cast by the wings of vultures. Even while he speaks the pinkening billows of the dunes seem to me the undulations of Sahara; and the wrecks of embedded drift are the dry ribs of camels; and in the eyes of the soldier's daughter I try to find the gaze of the Arabian maiden,—the eyes of the desert beauty, the eyes of the gazelle. ... But her eyes are gray, like an eagle's.

VI

Not French! ... The strangeness of her beauty is the type of a forgotten people,—that savage and elastic grace an inheritance bequeathed through epochs whose story is written only in Nature's chronicles of stone,—on the hidden tablets of the hills,—in the epitaphs of the strata. Ancient her people were ere the race to which I belong had being: theirs the strange tongue in which I had heard her converse,— the speech of a prehistoric race,— the language of primitive humanity. Continents have vanished, oceans have been conjoined, since men first strove to win such beauty as hers. And in the daintiness of her pretty head,— the strong keen outlines of her face,— the long fine curves of her firm figure,— I can discern a vague and elegant Something that irresistibly recalls to me one of the most singular chapters in the romance of science,— the osteology of the primitive race. . . .

She is a Basque. . . .

VII

. . . The foam breaks with silver sparklings and flashings: waves, malachite-basked and huge, charge up the slope in endless echelon under the enormous day. Those brown Creole boys playing in the surf are her brothers. Their bodies make one think of statues of bright metal partly darkened by long exposure to rain and dew,— so tanned their faces and shoulders and backs have been by this Southern sun; — their limbs seem supple as the bodies of eels;— they turn somersaults on the sand, roll in the surf, leap in the spray, dive, swim in Spanish fashion—hand over hand—scream, laugh. Graceful little fellows!— they wrestle like veritable ephebi. Her children would be beautiful and vigorous like these. . . .

The Basques are Catholics. That is why she has a saint's name, a commonplace name. Marie is melodious; but I should have liked to hear a name more ancient, more pagan,— a primitive name whereof the meaning is forgotten, and the etymology undiscoverable,— a name transmitted from generation to generation through two hundred thousand years. . . .

VIII

. . . Poor little dead birds!— moisture of pain oozing from the tiny lids that will never open to view the sun again,— blood spattering the downy breast, the dainty wing! Destroyed in the fraction of a moment, that beauty slowly formed through years as numerous as the stars of heaven! . . . Marie's brother,— the one with great gray eyes like her own,— has killed them. I buy them from him only because he is her brother; and I wish to be agreeable to him. He strides away with his old-fashioned shotgun,— promising to kill more; and I do not even attempt to dissuade him from such useless slaughter. Moral cowardice, perhaps. . . .

And all the long way home, great flies, metallically green, circle with keen whizzings about the dead birds,—furious to begin their part in the work of dissolution.

IX

... 'Spirit and wind,—ghost and breath,' the father tells me, are the same in the ancient tongue of Scripture; and the dead language seems to live again on his lips as he recalls his collegiate studies, to repeat the original text:—*'Darkness was upon the face of the great deep; and the Spirit of God moved over the waters'* ... It is a wild day;—under a northeast wind the waves take a deep and sinister tint of green. And looking out upon the immensity of waters and winds,—the Visible shifting its colors, moving with multiple thunders in obedience to the voluminous Invisible,—the antique words come to me with new and awful expansion of meaning, with unutterable sublimity and vastness....

Such men as he may readily cast off the constraints of city life, may easily forsake its monotonous pleasures, may boldly free themselves from its pains;—they may find splendor in waste places;—desolation to them makes visible the eternal, because they feel the Infinite. And I, too, love the inspiring calm of great solitudes,—the pure rude joy of living close to nature,—delight of keen sea-winds,—glories of sunrise and sunset,—the thunder-song of long waves,—the light of living waters. If one could but live here always,—in this great blue light,—in this immaculate air. But....

X

... *'Maiteya'*, sweetheart; *'ene maiteya'*, my beloved: these are the only words of the Basque tongue which I know,—which I shall always know, because her own lips first taught me to pronounce them.

... The wind lifts her long loose hair across my face,—as inviting me to inhale its perfume. Exquisite and indescribable perfume of youth! what flower-ghost prisoned in crystal owneth so delicate a magic as thou? Unnumbered the songs which celebrate the breath of blossoms, the scent of gardens,—yet what blossom-soul, what flower-witchery might charm the sense like the odor of a woman's hair, the natural perfume of beauty, the fresh and delicious fragrance of youth?...

... Only the great slow slopping of the sea under the stars,—to break a hush like the silence of Revelations. Something that Nature wishes to say swells at my heart,—flames in my veins,—struggles at my lips,—tugs fiercely at the slender, straining tether of Will that holds it back. Yet she seems to wait ... even the stars seem to wait, and the waves, and the winds that play with her hair! And tomorrow will be too late. But I may never say it!

XI

... And this was my dream:—

I stood upon a low land washed by a vast sea, whose waters had no voice; and the light was gray, for the sun was a phantom sun that only made a gloaming; and I also seemed to be a phantom. And Marie was there, seated upon the drifted trunk of some mighty tree; and I strove to speak to her, but found myself also voiceless like that spectral surge. Then I would have kissed her, but that a Shape—a woman's Shape, came between, all suddenly and noiselessly, I knew not from whence. And the face was the face of one long dead, yet I knew that face!— the eyes were hollows of darkness only, yet I knew those eyes!—the smile was the smile of that sphinx whose secrets are never betrayed, whose mysteries are never revealed — the smile that seems an eternal mockery of love and hate, of hope and despair, of faith and doubt,— the universal smile death wears when the mask of the flesh hath fallen ... and yet I knew the smile! And I looked at the bones of the face that smiled; and I felt the bones of the thin dead hands drawing me, dragging me away from the dim light, into vast and moonless darknesses beyond,—so that I feared with unutterable fear, and strove to call the name of Marie, and strove in vain. And Marie seemed to know it not; — her great gray eyes, steadily gazing over that shadowy sea, seemed as the eyes of one who knoweth neither hate nor pity. ...

XII

... Still I can see her beauty outlined against the great disk of gold— 'a Woman standing in the sun,'—as she watches our white ship receding, diminishing, melting into the West. Even so will I behold her again in dream, haloed with the glory of morning, framed in the light of sunrise,—many, many times; and memory will waft to me again the perfume of her hair,—and slumber will vouchsafe to me shadowy caress of lips that I may never kiss, the charm of eyes whose gaze will never again meet mine.... Now vanished the many-angled roofs, the thin bright edge of green, all the long island line with its white fringe of surges!—there is only sky and sea and the sun that may kiss that golden throat of hers, the dear sun that revealed to me her beauty,—the sun that shines upon us both even at this moment— that will illumine each of us when seas shall roll between,—that will pour his gold upon our graves when all our pains and hopes and loves and memories shall have become as though they had never been....

O blessed blue light! O pure sweet air! O living winds and leaping waters, how dear ye are, how divine ye seem at parting! Were it even possible to forget. . . . But there will be long, long nights, when I must hear a voice of ghostly winds, and see the shimmering of fancied waters, and follow in vision the curves of a smooth low shore to meet One standing in the light of dreams, against that weird sun that giveth no warmth, that casteth no shadow;—and I must awake to find about me darkness and silence only,—to wrestle with mocking and invincible memories,—to be vanquished by regrets as irrepressible, as hopeless, as tears for the dead, as prayer for pardon at a tomb. . . .

The second 'secret imbiber', *Francis Thompson* (1859-1907), shared with Lafcadio Hearn an admiration for an early group of addict-writers, in his case the Englishmen, Samuel Coleridge and Thomas De Quincey. On first impressions, it might be easy to accuse Thompson of hypocrisy for he frequently spoke harshly of others who indulged in opium while secretly taking quite considerable quantities himself. Yet the beauty of his verse and the strength of his prose, plus the abject sadness of much of his life, make him a sympathetic character it is not too hard to forgive. Biographers have noted the similarity between much of Thompson's life and that of his idol, De Quincey, and J. C. Reid in his *Francis Thompson: Man and Poet* has summarized this admirably: 'Both were dreamers as children, lonely and unhappy at school, became opium addicts, and moved to London to be befriended in their poverty by good-natured prostitutes.' Thompson's early years were a complete contrast to the despair that was to follow: born in Preston, Lancashire, he was brought up a devout Catholic and for a time studied for the priesthood. However, his temperament proved unsuitable and he decided instead to try medicine, but was unable to graduate. In his desolation he turned to opium and was taking about six ounces a day when, at the age of twenty-six, he arrived in London. His naturally dreamy nature, combined with his increasing dependence on opium, made him unable to keep a job and he slowly descended into destitution, often sleeping rough and begging money to pay for his drugs.

In 1888 he was briefly rescued from his dissolution, but unable to resist the pull of opium, sank back again to the streets and this time was only saved from starvation by a prostitute who took him home on the nights when she had no clients. All this while Thompson had been writing poetry; one of his poems, painstakingly written on a sheet of soiled, torn paper, was finally accepted and published by *Merry England,* the literary magazine run by Wilfred and Alice Meynell. These two were so impressed by Thompson's writing that they determined to find the author, and after months of fruitless effort traced him to a squalid London doss-house. This was to prove the turning point of his life; nursed back to health partly by the Meynells and partly at a monastery in Sussex, he began writing poems and prose again and 'work poured from him like a rich floodtide' to quote Wilfred Meynell. Although he was to live quietly writing for the rest of his life, Thompson could not break the secret hold that opium had on him. He also began to translate into writing his obsession and identification with De Quincey, and J. C. Reid comments that 'his poetry became a species of "confession" as De Quincey's prose was'. He wrote several essays on both De Quincey and Samuel Coleridge and while he praised De Quincey for his 'severe struggle with opium, which he ultimately reduced to within limited compass' he chided Coleridge because 'if he had had half De Quincey's grit he might have left us a less piteously wasted record'. Thompson's own work contained only the merest hints of his addiction and perhaps only his poem 'Dream Tryst' and the short story 'Finis Coronat Opus', reprinted here, bear the unmistakable marks of opium vision. Wilfred Meynell, who not only befriended Thompson, but also became his literary executor and first biographer, thought this story 'a fantasia which might appropriately have been produced in competition with Mary Shelley'. J. C. Reid finds it 'stamped with opium-heightened hallucinations'. There can be no doubt that it reflects much of what was in the troubled mind of the author, at one of the worst periods of his addiction—or that it displays the influence of Edgar Allen Poe whom Thompson also admired. It might further be seen as a presentiment of his final agonies when he lay dying, whispering over and over again, 'My withered dreams, my withered dreams. . . .'

*

They had exchanged, as it were, stores of human lifeblood for strange and artistic vibrations, fashioned from those poisoned dreams, masterpieces of form, permanent manifestations of what they had purchased from art at the expense of life. . . . Yet none could ever have regretted their strange barter.

Essay on the addict poets, 1903

Finis Coronat Opus
Francis Thompson

In a city of the future, among a people bearing a name I know not, lived Florentian the poet, whose place was high in the retinue of Fortune. Young, noble, popular, influential, he had succeeded to a rich inheritance, and possessed the natural gifts which gain the love of women. But the seductions which Florentian followed were darker and more baleful than the seductions of women; for they were the seductions of knowledge and intellectual pride. In very early years he had passed from the pursuit of natural to the pursuit of unlawful science; he had conquered power where conquest is disaster, and power servitude.

But the ambition thus gratified had elsewhere suffered check. It was the custom of this people that among their poets he who by universal acclaim outsoared all competitors should be crowned with laurel in public ceremony. Now between Florentian and this distinction there stood a rival. Seraphin was a spirit of higher reach than Florentian, and the time was nearing fast when even the slow eyes of the people must be opened to a supremacy which Florentian himself acknowledged in his own heart. Hence arose in his lawless soul an insane passion; so that all which he had seemed to him as nothing beside that which he had not, and the compassing of this barred achievement became to him the one worthy object of existence. Repeated essay only proved to him the inadequacy of his native genius, and he turned for aid to the power which he served. Nor was the power of evil slow to respond. It promised him assistance that should procure him his heart's desire, but demanded in return a crime before which even the unscrupulous selfishness of Florentian paled. For he had sought and won the hand of Aster, daughter to the Lady Urania, and the sacrifice demanded from him was no other than the sacrifice of his betrothed, the playmate of his childhood. The horror of such a suggestion prevailed for a time over his unslacked ambition. But he, who believed himself a strong worker of ill, was in reality a weak follower of it; he believed himself a Vathek, he was but a Faust: continuous pressure and gradual familiarization could warp him to any sin. Moreover his love for Aster had been gradually and unconsciously sapped by the habitual practice of evil. So God smote Florentian, that his antidote became to him his poison, and love the regenerator love the destroyer. A strong man, he might have been saved by love: a weak man, he was damned by it.

The palace of Florentian was isolated in the environs of the city;

and on the night before his marriage he stood in the room known to his domestics as the Chamber of Statues. Both its appearance, and the sounds which (his servants averred) sometimes issued from it, contributed to secure for him the seclusion that he desired whenever he sought this room. It was a chamber in many ways strongly characteristic of its owner, a chamber 'like his desires lift upwards and exalt,' but neither wide nor far-penetrating; while its furnishing revealed his fantastic and somewhat childish fancy. At the extremity which faced the door there stood, beneath a crucifix, a small marble altar, on which burned a fire of that strange greenish tinge communicated by certain salts. Except at this extremity, the walls were draped with deep violet curtains bordered by tawny gold, only half displayed by the partial illumination of the place. The light was furnished from lamps of coloured glass, sparsely hung along the length of the room, but numerously clustered about the altar: lamps of diverse tints, amber, peacock-blue, and changefully mingled harmonies of green like the scales on a beetle's back. Above them were coiled thinnest serpentinings of suspended crystal, hued like the tongues in a wintry hearth, flame-colour, violet, and green; so that, as in the heated current from the lamps the snakes twirled and flickered, and their bright shadows twirled upon the wall, they seemed at length to undulate their twines, and the whole altar became surrounded with a fiery fantasy of sinuous stains.

On the right hand side of the chamber there rose—appearing almost animated in the half lustre—three statues of colossal height, painted to resemble life; for in this matter Florentian followed the taste of the ancient Greeks. They were statues of three poets, and, not insignificantly, of three pagan poets. The first two, Homer and Aeschylus, presented no singularity beyond their Titanic proportions; but it was altogether otherwise with the third statue, which was unusual in conception. It was the figure of Virgil; not the Virgil whom we know, but the Virgil of mediaeval legend, Virgil, magician and poet. It bent forwards and downwards towards the spectator; its head was uncircled by any laurel, but on the flowing locks was an impression as of where the wreath had rested; its lowered left hand proffered the magician's rod, its outstretched right poised between light finger-tips the wreath of gilded metal whose impress seemed to linger on its hair: the action was as though it were about to place the laurel on the head of someone beneath. This was the carved embodiment of Florentian's fanatical ambition, a perpetual memento of the double end at which his life was aimed. On the necromancer's rod he could lay his hand, but the laurel of poetic supremacy hung yet beyond his reach. The opposite side of the chamber had but one object to arrest attention: a curious head upon a pedestal, a head of copper with a silver beard, the features not unlike those of a Pan, and the tongue protruded as in derision. This, with a large antique clock, completed the noticeable garniture of the room.

Up and down this apartment Florentian paced for long, his countenance expressive of inward struggle, till his gaze fell upon the figure of Virgil. His face grew hard; with an air of sudden decision he began to act. Taking from its place the crucifix he threw it on the ground; taking from its pedestal the head he set it on the altar, and it seemed to Florentian as if he reared therewith a demon on the altar of his heart, round which also coiled burning serpents. He sprinkled, in the flame which burned before the head, some drops from a vial; he wounded his arm, and moistened from the wound the idol's tongue, and, stepping back, he set his foot upon the prostrate cross.

A darkness rose like a fountain from the altar, and curled downward through the room as wine through water, until every light was obliterated. Then from out of the darkness grew gradually the visage of the idol, soaked with fire; its face was as the planet Mars, its beard as white-hot wire that seethed and crept with heat; and there issued from the lips a voice that threw Florentian on the ground: 'Whom seekest thou?' Twice was the question repeated; and then, as if the display of power were sufficient, the gloom gathered up its edges like a mantle and swept inwards towards the altar; where it settled in a cloud so dense as to eclipse even the visage of fire. A voice came forth again; but a voice that sounded not the same; a voice that seemed to have withered in crossing the confines of existence, and to traverse illimitable remotenesses beyond the imagining of man; a voice melancholy with a boundless calm, the calm not of a crystalline peace but of a marmoreal despair, 'Knowest thou me; what I am?'

Vanity of man! He who had fallen prostrate before this power now rose to his feet with the haughty answer, 'My deity and my slave!'

The unmoved voice held on its way:

'Scarce high enough for thy deity, too high for thy slave, I am pain exceeding great; and the desolation that is at the heart of things, in the barren heath and the barren soul. I am terror without beauty, and force without strength, and sin without delight. I beat my wings against the cope of Eternity, as thou thine against the window of Time. Thou knowest me not, but I know thee, Florentian, what thou art and what thou wouldst. Thou wouldst have and wouldst not give, thou wouldst not render, yet wouldst receive. This cannot be with me. Thou art but half baptized with my baptism, yet wouldst have thy supreme desire. In thine own blood thou wast baptized, and I gave my power to serve thee; thou wouldst have my spirit to inspire thee — thou must be baptized in blood not thine own!'

'Any way but one way!' said Florentian, shuddering.

'One way: no other way. Knowest thou not that in wedding thee to her thou givest me a rival? Thinkest thou my spirit can dwell beside her spirit? Thou must renounce her or me: aye, thou wilt lose not only all thou dreadest to sin for, but all thou hast already sinned for. Render me her body for my temple, and I render thee my spirit to inhabit it. This supreme price thou must pay for thy supreme wish. I ask not her soul. Give that to the God Whom she serves, give her body to me whom thou servest. Why hesitate? It is too late to hesitate, for the time is at hand to act. Choose, before this cloud dissolve which is now dissolving. But remember: thine ambition thou mightest have had; love thou art too deep damned to have.'

The cloud turned from black to grey. 'I consent!' cried Florentian, impetuously.

Three years—what years! since I planted in the grave the laurel which will soon now reach its height; and the fatal memory is heavy upon me, the shadow of my laurel is as the shadow of funeral yew. If confession indeed give ease, I, who am deprived of all other confession, may yet find some appeasement in confessing to this paper. I am not penitent; yet I will do fiercest penance. With the scourge of inexorable recollection I will tear open my scars. With the cuts of a pitiless analysis I make the post-mortem examen of my crime.

Even now can I feel the passions of that moment when (since the forefated hour was not till midnight), leaving her under the influence of the merciful potion which should save *her* from the agony of knowledge and *me* from the agony of knowing that she knew, I sought, in the air of night and in hurrying swiftness, the resolution of which she had deprived me. The glow-worm lamps went out as I sped by, the stars in rainy pools leaped up and went out, too, as if both worm and star were quenched by the shadow of my passing, until I stopped exhausted on the bridge, and looked down into the river. How dark it ran, how deep, how pauseless; how unruffled by a memory of its ancestral hills! Wisely unruffled, perchance. When it first danced down from its native source, did it not predestine all the issues of its current, every darkness through which it should flow, every bough which it should break, every leaf which it should whirl down in its way? Could it, if it would, revoke its waters, and run upward to the holy hills? No; the first step includes all sequent steps; when I did my first evil, I did also this evil; years ago had this shaft been launched, though it was but now curving to its mark; years ago had I smitten her, though she was but now staggering to her fall. Yet I hesitated to act who had already acted, I ruffled my current which I could not draw in. When at length, after long wandering, I retraced my steps, I had not resolved, I had recognized that I could resolve no longer.

She only cried three times. Three times, O my God!—no, not *my* God.

It was close on midnight, and I felt her only, (she was not visible,) as she lay at the feet of Virgil, magician and poet. The lamp had fallen from my hand, and I dared not relume it. I even placed myself between her and the light of the altar though the salt-green fire was but a spectre of a flame. I reared my arm; I shook; I faltered. At that moment, with a deadly voice, the accomplice-hour gave forth its sinister command.

I swear I struck not the first blow. Some violence seized my hand, and drove the poniard down. Whereat she cried; and I, frenzied, dreading detection, dreading, above all, her wakening,—I struck again, and again she cried; and yet again, and yet again she cried. Then—her eyes opened. I *saw* them open, through the gloom I saw them; through the gloom they were revealed to me, that I might see them to my hour of death. An awful recognition, an unspeakable consciousness grew slowly into them. Motionless with horror they were fixed on mine, motionless with horror mine were fixed on them, as she wakened into death.

How long had I seen them? I saw them still. There was a buzzing in my brain as if a bell had ceased to toll. How long had it ceased to toll? I know not. Has any bell been tolling? I know not. All my senses are resolved into one sense, and that is frozen to those eyes. Silence now, at least; abysmal silence; except the sound (or is the sound in me?), the sound of dripping blood; except that the flame upon the altar sputters, and hisses, and bickers, as if it licked its jaws. Yes, there is another sound—hush, hark!—It is the throbbing of my heart. Not—no, nevermore the throbbing of her heart! The loud pulse dies slowly away, as I hope my life is dying; and again I hear the licking of the flame.

A mirror hung opposite to me, and for a second, in some mysterious manner, without ever ceasing to behold the eyes, I beheld also the mirrored flame. The hideous, green, writhing tongue was streaked and flaked with *red!* I swooned, if swoon it can be called; swooned to the mirror, swooned to all about me, swooned to myself, but swooned not to those eyes.

Strange, that no one has taken me, me for such long hours shackled in a gaze! It is night again, is it not? Nay, I remember, I have swooned; what now stirs me from my stupor? Light; the guilty gloom is shuddering at the first sick rays of day. Light? not that, not that; anything but that. Ah! the horrible traitorous light, that will denounce me to myself, that will unshroud to me my dead, that will show me all the monstrous fact. I swooned indeed.

When I recovered consciousness, It was risen from the ground, and kissed me with the kisses of Its mouth.

They told me during the day that the great bell of the cathedral, though no man rang it, had sounded thrice at midnight. It was not a fancy, therefore, that I heard a bell toll *there,* where—when she cried three times. And they asked me jestingly if marriage was ageing me already. I took a mirror to find what they meant. On my forehead were graven three deep wrinkles; and in the locks which fell over my right shoulder I beheld, long and prominent, three white hairs. I carry those marks to this hour. They and a dark stain on the floor at the feet of Virgil are the sole witnesses to that night.

It is three years, I have said, since then; and how have I prospered? Has Tartarus fulfilled its terms of contract, as I faithfully and frightfully fulfilled mine? Yes. In the course which I have driven through every obstacle and every scruple, I have followed at least no phantom-lure. I have risen to the heights of my aspiration, I have overtopped my sole rival. True, it is a tinsel renown; true, Seraphin is still the light-bearer, I but a dragon vomiting infernal fire and smoke which sets the crowd a-gaping. But it is your nature to gape, my good friend of the crowd, and I would have you gape at me. If you prefer to Jove Jove's imitator, what use to be Jove? 'Gods,' you cry; 'what a clatter of swift-footed steeds, and clangour of rapid rolling brazen wheels, and vibrating glare of lamps! Surely, the thunder-maned horses of heaven, the chariot of Olympus; and you must be the mighty Thunderer himself, with the flashing of his awful bolts!' Not so, my short-sighted friend: very laughably otherwise. It is but vain old Salmoneus, gone mad in Elis. I know you, and I know myself. I have what I would have. I work for the present: let Seraphin have the moonshine future, if he lust after it. Present renown means present power; it suffices me that I am supreme in the eyes of my fellowmen. A year since was the laurel decreed to me, and a day ordained for the ceremony: it was only postponed to the present year because of what they thought my calamity. They accounted it calamity, and knew not that it was deliverance. For, my ambition achieved, the compact by which I had achieved it ended, and the demon who had inspired forsook me. Discovery was impossible. A death sudden but natural: how could men know that it was death of the Two-years-dead? I drew breath at length in freedom. For two years It had spoken to me with her lips, used her gestures, smiled her smile:—ingenuity of hell! for two years the breathing Murder wrought before me, and tortured me in a hundred ways with the living desecration of her form.

Now, relief unspeakable! that vindictive sleuth-hound of my sin has at last lagged from the trail; I have had a year of respite, of

9 Charles Baudelaire, 'the playboy of Paris'.

10 A drawing by Baudelaire, executed under the influence of hashish.

11 'The Nights of Monsieur Baudelaire'; a caricature by Durandeau.

12 'The Death of Gérard de Nerval'; an interpretation by Gustave Doré.

release from all torments but those native to my breast; in four days I shall receive the solemn gift of what I already virtually hold; and now, surely, I exult in fruition. If the approach of possession brought not also the approach of recollection, if—Rest, O rest, sad ghost! Is thy grave not deep enough, or the world wide enough, that thou must needs walk the haunted precincts of my heart? Are not spectres there too many, without thee?

Later in the same day. A strange thing has happened to me—if I ought not rather to write a strange nothing. After laying down my pen, I rose and went to the window. I felt the need of some distraction, of escaping from myself. The day, a day in the late autumn, a day of keen winds but bright sunshine, tempted me out: so, putting on cap and mantle, I sallied into the country, where winter pitched his tent on fields yet reddened with the rout of summer. I chose a sheltered lane, whose hedge-rows, little visited by the gust, still retained much verdure; and I walked along, gazing with a sense of physical refreshment at the now rare green. As my eyes so wandered, while the mind for a time let slip its care, they were casually caught by the somewhat peculiar trace which a leaf-eating caterpillar had left on one of the leaves. I carelessly outstretched my hand, plucked from the hedge the leaf, and examined it as I strolled. The marking—a large marking which traversed the greater part of the surface—took the shape of a rude but distinct figure, the figure 3. Such a circumstance, thought I, might by a superstitious man be given a personal application; and I fell idly to speculating how it might be applied to myself.

Curious!—I stirred uneasily; I felt my cheek pale, and a chill which was not from the weather creep through me. Three years since *that;* three strokes—three cries—three tolls of the bell—three lines on my brow—three white hairs in my head! I laughed: but the laugh rang false. Then I said, 'Childishness,' threw the leaf away, walked on, hesitated, walked back, picked it up, walked on again, looked at it again. Then, finding I could not laugh myself out of the fancy, I began to reason myself out of it. Even were a supernatural warning probable, a warning refers not to the past but to the future. This referred only to the past, it told me only what I knew already. *Could* it refer to the future? To the bestowal of the laurel? No; that was four days hence, and on the same day was the anniversary of what I feared to name, even in thought. Suddenly I stood still, stabbed to the heart by an idea. I was wrong. The enlaurelling had been postponed to a year from the day on which my supposed affliction was discovered. Now this, although it took place on the day of terrible anniversary, was not known till the day ensuing. Consequently, though it wanted four days to the bestowal of the laurel, it lacked but three days to the date of my crime. The chain of coincidence was complete. I dropped the leaf as if it had death in it, and strove to evade, by rapid motion and thinking of other things, the idea which appalled me. But, as a man walking in a mist circles continually to the point from which he started, so, in whatever direction I turned the footsteps of my mind, they wandered back to that unabandonable thought. I returned trembling to the house.

Of course it is nothing; a mere coincidence, that is all. Yes; a mere coincidence, perhaps, if it had been *one* coincidence. But when it is seven coincidences! Three stabs, three cries, three tolls, three lines, three hairs, three years, three days; and on the very date when these coincidences meet, the key to them is put into my hands by the casual work of an insect on a casual leaf, casually plucked. This day alone of all days in my life the scattered rays converge; they are instantly focussed and flashed on my mind by a leaf! It may be a coincidence, only a coincidence; but it is a coincidence at which my marrow sets. I will write no further till the day comes. If by that time anything has happened to confirm my dread, I will record what has chanced.

One thing broods over me with the oppression of certainty. If this incident be indeed a warning that but three days stand as barriers between me and nearing justice, then doom will come upon me at the unforgettable minute when it came on her.

The third day.—It is an hour before midnight, and I sit in my room of statues. I dare not sleep if I could sleep; and I write, because the rushing thoughts move slower through the turnstile of expression. I have chosen this place to make what may be my last vigil and last notes, partly from obedience to an inexplicable yet comprehensible fascination, partly from a deliberate resolve. I would face the lightning of vengeance on the very spot where I most tempt its stroke, that if it strike not I may cease to fear its striking. Here then I sit to tease with final questioning the Sibyl of my destiny. With *final* questioning; for never since the first shock have I ceased to question her, nor she to return me riddling answers. She unrolls her volume till my sight and heart ache at it together. I have been struck by innumerable deaths; I have perished under a fresh doom every day, every hour—in these last hours, every minute. I write in black thought; and tear, as soon as written, guess after guess at fate till the floor of my brain is littered with them.

That the deed has been discovered—that seems to me most probable, that is the conjecture which oftenest recurs. Appallingly probable! Yet how improbable, could I only reason it. Aye, but I cannot reason it. What reason will be left me, if I survive this hour? What, indeed, have I to do with reason, or has reason to do with this, where all is beyond reason, where the very foundation of my dread is unassailable simply because it is unreasonable? What crime can be interred so cunningly, but it will toss in its grave, and tumble the sleeked earth above it? Or some hidden witness may have beheld me, or the prudently-kept imprudence of this writing may have encountered some unsuspected eye. In any case the issue is the same; the hour which struck down her, will also strike down me: I shall perish on the scaffold or at the stake, unaided by my occult powers; for I serve a master who is the prince of cowards, and can fight only from ambush. Be it by these ways, or by any of the countless intricacies that my restless mind has unravelled, the vengeance will come: its occasion may be an accident of the instant, a wandering mote of chance; but the vengeance is pre-ordained and inevitable. When the Alpine avalanche is poised for descent, the most trivial cause—a casual shout—will suffice to start the loosened ruin on its way; and so the mere echoes of the clock that beats out midnight will disintegrate upon me the precipitant wrath.

Repent? Nay, nay, it could not have been otherwise than it was; the defile was close behind me, I could but go forward, forward. If I was merciless to her, was I not more merciless to myself; could I hesitate to sacrifice her life, who did not hesitate to sacrifice my soul? I do not repent, I cannot repent; it is a thing for inconsequent weaklings. To repent your purposes is comprehensible, to repent your deeds most futile. To shake the tree, and then not gather the fruit— a fool's act! Aye, but if the fruit be not worth the gathering? If this fame was not worth the sinning for—this fame, with the multitude's clapping hands half-drowned by the growl of winds that comes in gusts through the unbarred gate of hell? If I am miserable with it, and might have been happy without it? With her, without ambition— yes, it might have been. Wife and child! I have more in my heart than I have hitherto written. I have an intermittent pang of loss. Yes, I, murderer, worse than murderer, have still passions that are not deadly, but tender.

I met a child to-day; a child with great candour of eyes. They who talk of children's instincts are at fault: she knew not that hell was in my soul, she knew only that softness was in my gaze. She had been gathering wild flowers, and offered them to me. To me, to *me!* I was inexpressibly touched and pleased, curiously touched and pleased. I spoke to her gently, and with open confidence she began to talk. Heaven knows it was little enough she talked of! Commonest common things, pettiest childish things, fondest foolish things. Of her school, her toys, the strawberries in her garden, her little brothers and sisters—nothing, surely, to interest any man. Yet I listened enchanted. How simple it all was; how strange, how wonderful, how sweet! And she knew not that my eyes were anhungered of her, she knew not that my ears were gluttonous of her speech, she could not have understood it had I told her; none could, none. For all this exquisiteness is among the commonplaces of life to other men, like the raiment they indue at rising, like the bread they weary of eating, like the daisies they trample under blind feet; knowing not what raiment is to him who has felt the ravening wind, knowing not what bread is to him who has lacked all bread, knowing not what daisies are to him whose feet have wandered in grime. How can these elves be to such men what they are to me, who am damned to the eternal loss of them? Why was I never told that the laurel could soothe no hunger, that the laurel could staunch no pang, that the laurel could return no kiss? But needed I to be told it, did I not know it? Yes, my brain knew it, my heart knew it not. And now——

At half-past eleven.

O lente, lente currite, noctis equi!

Just! they are the words of that other trafficker in his own soul.[1] Me, like him, the time tracks swiftly down; I can fly no farther, I fall exhausted, the fanged hour fastens on my throat: they will break into the room, my guilt will burst its grave and point at me; I shall be seized, I shall be condemned, I shall be executed; I shall be no longer I, but a nameless lump on which they pasture worms. Or perhaps the hour will herald some yet worser thing, some sudden death, some undreamable, ghastly surprise—ah! what is that at the door there, that, that with *her* eyes? Nothing: the door is shut. Surely, surely, I am not to die now? Destiny steals upon a man asleep or off his guard, not when he is awake, as I am awake, at watch, as I am at watch, wide-eyed, vigilant, alert. Oh, miserable hope! Watch the eaves of your house, to bar the melting of the snow; or guard the gateways of the clouds, to bar the forthgoing of the lightning; or guard the four quarters of the heavens, to bar the way of the winds: but what prescient hand can close the Hecatompyloi of fate, what might arrest the hurrying retributions whose multitudinous tramplings converge upon me in a hundred presages, in a hundred shrivelling menaces, down all the echoing avenues of doom? It is but a question of which shall arrive the fleetest and the first. I cease to think. I am all a waiting and a fear. *Twelve!*

[1] Faustus, in the last scene of Marlowe's play.

At half-past two. Midnight is stricken, and I am unstricken. Guilt, indeed, makes babies of the wisest. Nothing happened; absolutely nothing. For two hours I watched with lessening expectance: still nothing. I laughed aloud between sudden light-heartedness and scorn. Ineffable fool that I was, I had conjured up death, judgement, doom—heaven knows what, all because a caterpillar had crawled along a leaf! And then, as I might have done before had not terror vitiated my reason, I made essay whether I still retained my power. I retain it. Let me set down for my own enhardiment what the oracle replied to my questioning.

'Have I not promised and kept my promise, shall I not promise and keep? You would be crowned and you shall be crowned. Does your way to achievement lie through misery?—is not that the way to all worth the achieving? Are not half the mill-wheels of the world turned by waters of pain? Mountain summit that would rise into the clouds, can you not suffer the eternal snows? If your heart fail you, turn; I chain you not. I will restore you your oath. I will cancel your bond. Go to the God Who has tenderness for such weaklings: *my* service requires the strong.'

What a slave of my fancy was I! Excellent fool, what! pay the forfeit of my sin and forgo the recompense, recoil from the very gates of conquest? I fear no longer: the crisis is past, the day of promise has begun, I go forward to my destiny; I triumph.

Florentian laid down his pen, and passed into dreams. He saw the crowd, the throne, the waiting laurel, the sunshine, the flashing of rich robes; he heard the universal shout of acclaim, he felt the flush of intoxicating pride. He rose, his form dilating with exultation, and passed, lamp in hand, to the foot of the third statue. The colossal figure leaned above him with its outstretched laurel, its proffered wand, its melancholy face and flowing hair; so lifelike was it that in the wavering flame of the lamp the laurel seemed to move. 'At length, Virgil,' said Florentian, 'at length I am equal with you; Virgil, magician and poet, your crown shall descend on me!'

One. . Two. . Three! The strokes of the great clock shook the chamber, shook the statues; and after the strokes had ceased, the echoes were still prolonged. Was it only an echo?

Boom!

Or—*was it the cathedral bell?*

Boom!

It *was* the cathedral bell. Yet a third time, sombre, surly, ominous as the bay of a nearing bloodhound, the sound came down the wind.

Boom!

Horror clutched his heart. He looked up at the statue. He turned to fly. But a few hairs, tangled round the lowered wand, for a single instant held him like a cord. He knew, without seeing, that they were the three white hairs.

When, later in the day, a deputation of officials came to escort Florentian to the place fixed for his coronation, they were informed that he had been all night in his Chamber of Statues, nor had he yet made his appearance. They waited while the servant left to fetch him. The man was away some time, and they talked gaily as they waited: a bird beat its wings at the window; through the open door came in a stream of sunlight, and the fragmentary song of a young girl passing:

> Oh, syne she tripped, and syne she ran
> (The water-lily's a lightsome flower),
> All for joy and sunshine weather
> The lily and Marjorie danced together,
> As he came down from Langley Tower.
>
> There's a blackbird sits on Langley Tower,
> And a throstle on Glenlindy's tree;
> The throstle sings 'Robin, my heart's love!'
> And the blackbird, 'Bonnie, sweet Marjorie!'

The man came running back at last, with a blanched face and a hushed voice. 'Come,' he said, 'and see!'

They went and saw.

At the feet of Virgil's statue Florentian lay dead. A dark pool almost hid that dark stain on the ground, the three lines on his forehead were etched in blood, and across the shattered brow lay a ponderous gilded wreath; while over the extinguished altar-fire the idol seemed to quiver its derisive tongue.

'He is already laurelled,' said one, breaking at length the silence; 'we come too late.'

Too late. The crown of Virgil, magician and poet, had descended on him.

If one can fairly describe Francis Thompson's life as having many common features with that of Thomas De Quincey, a similar parallel can be drawn between Edgar Allan Poe and the final contributor to this section, *James Thomson* (1834-1882), the writer and poet widely known as 'B.V.'. Thomson, not to be confused with the eighteenth-century Scottish poet of the same name, was for much of his life a lonely, tortured soul, addicted to alcohol, tobacco and opium, and writing verse and prose full of the weirdest images and situations. Like Poe, he was brought up in an orphanage, found his restless and erratic nature a constant impediment to regular employment, and declined into an early and lonely death brought on by dissipation and exhaustion.

James Thomson was born in Glasgow, the son of a sea captain and an emotional and highly imaginative Englishwoman. Unhappily the captain suffered a paralysing stroke while on one of his voyages and, unable to support his family, had to have the boy placed in an orphan asylum for his education. His mother died not long after this, and James developed the gloomy and introspective nature which gripped him for the rest of his life. In 1855 he joined the army and became an instructor, but in his self-imposed isolation from others took to drinking heavily. He made use of this depressive state, however, to write poetry of a style and brilliance that led to almost immediate publication. Leaving the army he was 'adopted' by Charles Bradlaugh and his family and became a contributor—under various pen-names, including 'B.V.'—to the *National Reformer* from 1860 to 1875. His work consisted chiefly of prose-fantasies and poems which were 'so profoundly gloomy in tone and so intensely pessimistic in doctrine, that one can see how he was wracked by insomnia (from which he suffered throughout his life) and how the sad streets of London and the wretched souls therein affected him,' to quote his biographer H. S. Salt. When he did manage to escape the grip of London for a short period, first as a mining clerk in America, then as a war correspondent for the *New York World* in Spain covering the Carlist insurrection in 1873, he did enjoy a temporary relief from suffering. However, his failure to succeed at either job (he was even refused his wages by the newspaper for filing only three reports during the entire time he was in Spain) threw him into even greater despair and he sought relief in alcohol and opium. From all this sadness came his masterwork, the lengthy poem, 'The City of Dreadful Night' (1874), which was undoubtedly inspired by his use of opium and was greeted with great critical acclaim. But Thomson was little affected by this success and indeed wrote virtually no poetry during the next seven years. His attitude was perhaps summed up in a diary entry which reads, 'Verse by an unknown man is always a drug on the market, and when it is atheistic it is a virulently poisonous drug with which publishers would rather have nothing to do.' Instead, to stave off penury, Thomson turned to writing hack journalism for a variety of publications, including *Cope's Tobacco Plant,* which no doubt contributed to his continuing dependence on stimulants by the nature of the work called for. In 1880 'The City of Dreadful Night' was finally published in book form, and he also laboriously compiled some volumes of his short essays and fantasies while all the time working against the debilitating effects of an excess of drink and drugs. His death, at University College Hospital in London, in June 1882, followed directly on his being found in a state of collapse and suffering from internal bleeding.

Apart from his essays, Thomson is remembered for several of his fantasies (including the notable novella *A Lady of Sorrow* which clearly shows his admiration for De Quincey's dream figures) and the magnificent poem, 'Insomnia', according to Salt, 'the very darkest and most terrible of all his writings, with its marked resemblance to Coleridge's "Ode to Dejection" '. Of his short stories, several of which show similarities to Poe's *Tales of the Grotesque and Arabesque,* I think the one most suited to this collection is this visionary episode of a flight to the stars, clearly inspired by an opium 'high'.

*

> From wandering through many a solemn scene,
> Of opium visions, with a heart serene,
> And intellect miraculously bright :
> I wake from daydreams to this real night.
>
> *The City of Dreadful Night, 1874*

A Walk Abroad
James Thomson

It was the night of Saint Sylvester. I had been spending some golden hours with a friend philosophic and genial, drinking punch of a certain Irish whisky many years in the sherry-wood, a whisky that makes Fenianism preposterous, and the wrongs of Ireland incomprehensible; except, indeed, the brutal Sassenachs drink so much of it that the natives cannot get a fair share. In the words of the rhymer,

> It is amber as the western skies
> When the sunset glows serenest;
> It is mellow as the mild moonrise
> When the shamrock-leaves fold greenest.

With this we had been smoking a certain tobacco, tobacco of before the American War, 'a weed of glorious feature,' golden-leaved, honey-dew Virginian; surely the very weed whereof the sage Spenser sagely sang,

> And whether it divine tobacco were,
> Or panacea, or polygony—

Of this my friend had given me half a dozen noble cakes, each about a quarter of a pound, as I left him with 'Peace be upon this house!' and verily if he that giveth a cup of cold water to one of the little ones shall not go without his reward, can any reward be rich enough for him who to one of the little ones giveth, not a cup of cold water, but several glasses of hot punch, and thereto much tobacco exquisite as hasheesh?

The night was clear, still, and cold; the freshness of the air was delicious, and I resolved to take a ramble before going home. In my elevated spiritualised condition I managed quite easily and naturally to stray off this little earth of ours; and finding that the gas lamps of London had disappeared, I was attracted by those other lights, the 'street lamps of the City of God.' I may note for the benefit of any future wayfarers who take the same route, that the clouds are apt to put out one's pipe, and that a full flask in the pocket is desirable as medicine against their dampness; but when one has passed through the low cloud-strata and the few miles of earth-atmosphere, he enters into an aether wonderfully calm, pure, and exhilarating, wherein the pipe burns clearly yet not too quickly, and the respiration in itself is better than drinking from any flask. The following are my brief notes of what I saw and heard at the spots where I paused in my ramblings.

A wide marshy moor, black scarred with yellow and brown. The time seemed afternoon. No sun was visible, it was raining heavily; cobweb clouds were brushing fast over the dirty white-washed ceiling of sky. Across the moor lay a canal all livid from the long and violent lashing of the rain. A dingy barge came creeping down, drawn by the skeleton of Apocalyptic Death's white horse; and at the tiller of the barge sat a thin young man in shabby-genteel black frock-coat and other gear such as decent men wear in cities, on his head an old-fashioned cylindrical hat!—Ho! gallant sailor, what country is this? —This is *Mercury,* my lord. Could your lordship vouchsafe me a pipe of tobacco and a couple of lights?—Most assuredly, your grace. Rather dull, eh?—Dull! I got this position by special favour. This is the best boat, the fastest horse, on the canal. We are all very honest and poor here, my lord; and the most of us are somewhat sluggish and dreamy. But I am of daring and adventurous spirit; I rejoice in this rapid motion, I love the swift variations of the landscape, I have even a stern pleasure in confronting the perils of the locks! My mother and father weep for me, but the heroic impulse drives me on.—What cargo?—Only ballast this return trip; the barge that follows me has a freight of wood in barter for the freight of peat I delivered, and will take back my ballast when it returns to its own place.—Truly an admirable arrangement, my friend! yet with so much skill and enterprise you are not wealthy?—Oh, I am better off than most, your worship; we are a poor people, very poor, but at any rate we are all honest and truthful.—I gave him a piece of tobacco, and having several silver coins in my pocket (a fact far more astounding than my presence in *Mercury*), I gave him eke half-a-crown. He was calling down the most beautiful benedictions upon my head as I strolled away.

I next came to a rocky realm dim in twilight, where was heard all around and about a tumult as of the rushing and roaring of seas. I discerned a large number of lean little fellows all very busily employed, dressed in ragged quaker costume; but that sleekness of sensual spiritualism well-to-do in the world, which is the common expression of quakers in our time, was absent from these faces, and in its stead gaunt earnestness. They were ploughing the rocky ground with painful industry, the men tugging, the women driving; their ploughs were rough broken branches, the shares were rude blades awkwardly attached with strips of bark. From my inmost soul I compassionated them.—O man of red *Mars,* do you reap fat harvests from these fields?—Alack, no, your honour; we are sore beset with famine, yet this is one of our richest districts. Fortunately we are a tranquil folk, and when we can't get food, just lie down and perish placidly.—Will you have some tobacco, my friend?—We account it wicked to smoke, sire; but if your majesty could spare a few pence to buy a poor man a little bread?—I gave him a half-a-crown, and went off feeling less jolly.

I next called at an immense village of miserable huts and hovels, a village in four-mooned *Jupiter*. I saw great gaps of charred ruins where fire had raged, and saw many of the hovels marked with great red crosses; all about me was very still. Then a murmur and a rattling came, and I saw a large body of tall men, very gaunt and livid, with a number of low donkey-trucks. The men entered the hovels that bore the stigma, and emerged carrying corpses more livid than themselves, dark blue corpses of the plague-smitten; and side by side on each donkey-truck stretched a pair, and went on toward some burial-pit. I spoke to the last of them. How many has the plague killed, my poor friend?—Nearly one in six already, my lord; and it is to be hoped that it will kill at least half of us, for better to die quickly of pest than slowly of hunger.—I am burning a sacred incense of disinfection: will you have some? He went down on his knees in reverential rapture.—Most gracious Sovereign, I will give it to my wife that she may bury me!—I gave him some tobacco and half-a-crown, and went away feeling still less jolly.

I then arrived at *Saturn,* of whose belts and moons I shall say nothing, in mercy to the astronomers: why should they be deprived of the dear pleasure of speculating and guessing a few centuries more? I came plumb upon a channel of the sea, wherein I might have been drowned had not the natural antipathy of good whisky to overmuch water kept the very soles of my feet unwet. I saw two ranks of large rough boats, in each of which was one enormous naked man, in each of whom was one enormous eye. They were engaged in barter, the one set having things edible in wicker baskets, the other set things drinkable in gourds. They all looked very healthy, very strong, thoroughly good tempered and perfectly stupid. I held up half-a-crown and asked who would have it; every big eye regarded me with cunning senile disdain. I held up a piece of tobacco and asked who would have it; big noses came surging against my hand and snored with deep delight, then the creatures all roared together like good-natured thunder, Me, me, me! So I organised a race for it on the sublime principles of true donkey racing; every one to shift into another's boat, and the owner (not the paddler) of the last boat to win. After about an hour of eloquent and lucid exposition, I succeeded in persuading them that they comprehended the plan. Then I cried Start! but no one moved; every one was watching his own boat to make sure that it did not get ahead, and feeling very triumphant as he saw that it did not even stir. About another hour of demonstration, exhortation, execration, winding up with a modest but very effective threat to thwack them all round if they did not row as hard as ever they could; then I cried Start again. Row hard they did, and every one dashed to cannon against his own boat in order to put it out of the running and thus secure its victory. The result was a general smash and upset; and they all swam about grinning and snorting and shouting, every one claiming 'the nice stuff to flavour sweet drink.' I placed the piece on the round back of the nearest boat; a grand scrambling swimming match ensued; and I departed feeling much more jolly.

I next stopped at *Uranus,* which was almost termed Georgium Sidus: the poor Olympians must lament the lost honour of a Guelph King of England among them! *Moi, je l'aurais plutôt nommé Pluton,* a friend suggests, seeing that it is associated with Saturn, and Jupiter, and Neptune; but my profound knowledge of science and its history enables me to inform him sternly that Neptune was not born or even thought of in the astronomic womb, when the big last baby Uranus needed christening. I found myself in a realm like the China pictured on porcelain, whereof the poet saith, 'In this realm nature and man cannot look each other in the face without laughing. They do not laugh out loud, both are too polished and civilised, but holding in the laugh they make the queerest grimaces. There one finds neither shadow nor perspective; and upon the houses of a thousand colours rise one above the other roofs, stretched like umbrellas, hung with bells of jingling metal, so that the very wind produces a comical noise and becomes ridiculous in passing over this land.' I saw quaint little men whose pigtail knobs kept bobbing on the ground behind them; I saw quaint little women moving in jerky pitter-patter as puppets move, their oblique eyes flush with the face. All looked withered and poor, yet all were solemnly grimacing. Peeping under verandahs I saw families at dinner, supping messes in which floated snails and beetles and cockroaches, picking daintily the bones (which they afterwards crunched like barley-sugar) of 'rats and mice and such small deer.' The populace themselves swarmed like cockroaches, and their talk was in quick mouselike squeaks. On the table of one family I put half-a-crown and a piece of tobacco; the patriarch extemporised an astonishingly eloquent oration of the most panegyrical character in squeaks now staccato and now slurred by twenties; a wrinkled child cried with rapture, 'We'll have a big dog for dinner to-morrow!' and the whole family fell down and worshipped me as I departed.

And then I came to *Neptune* and saw a vast stretch of brown land heaved up into a cirque of large molehills around a dull lake. Very rough draughts of fair humanity, both male and female, were swimming and diving in the water like so many otters, then came waddling up the shore with fish in their mouths, and burrowed hastily, for the large molehills were their dens. They seemed a very stupid race, with the mind in a permanent state of hibernation; but very soft and mild except to the poor fish. They seemed, too, always hungry, for scarcely had they disappeared into their dens than they emerged again for more fishing. I tendered one of them half-a-crown. He took it as if it were a thing of course, and gazed on it long with stolid attention in his protuberant goggle eyes; at length dawned a certain gleam of thought; he wrapped the coin in a piece of fish-skin, and hung it round his neck, doubtless as a talisman or sacred charm, for he showed pride and exultation. I gave another a bit of tobacco; he threw it at once into his mouth and swallowed it with very little chewing, I hope without bad results. I went away bemused, and hurried homewards.

But I did not like to return without calling at *Venus*. There I found myself in a large, silent city, full of tall gloomy buildings like convents or barracks, all enclosed by high blank walls. I saw a long procession of macerated old virgins, shrouded somewhat like sisters of mercy, defiling through the wicket in the gates into one of these convents. How plain, not to say hideous, the poor creatures were! They were all muttering in unmusical dolorous monotony a litany for deliverance from the world, the flesh, and the devil: their world they might well wish to be delivered from, the flesh they were almost delivered from already, and the devil is too busy with the pretty girls to meddle with such withered old maidens. The dark serge cloaks in which they were muffled had each a hood or head-bag hanging behind. Into that of the last I dropt half-a-crown and a piece of tobacco, and whispered, Where are the men?—The men, O bold stranger, are in their own city on the other side of the river.—Why don't you mingle with them?—Can it be that you know not we are Malthusians? It was found that we were outgrowing the food of our world. Only one-half our people are permitted to marry, and but one child is permitted to each family; such families, however, as are childless may give or sell their right of production to others, and we have heard of one terrible pair who have used up a large fortune in purchasing the privilege of having twenty-three children besides their first.—I departed in a state of mind not to be described.

My last visit I paid to the *Moon*, not to the side of it turned toward us, for I have ever felt a remarkable interest in the other which we never see. It happened to be deep night there, and I saw many people squatted around fires of forest wood, while others were continually coming in with fresh fuel. The teeth were chattering, the bodies cowering, and the catlike eyes glared green phosphorescence in the darkness. A careworn man, bilious and nervous, an ardent mind in a frozen body, took me aside mysteriously and descanted on the wretched condition of himself and his compatriots. He said that the forests were nearly used up, that brushwood was getting scarce, that they had frightful alternations of intense cold and intense heat, that they were always half-starved. But the moral injustice of their doom was what hurt them most. Was it fair that one side of the moon should be always turned away from the earth, and the other always turned toward it? He had heard that a benevolent earth-lord wanted to give both sides turn and turn, but the other astronomical earth-lords wouldn't agree. Would I present his petition and advocate his claims of justice and equality? Look at the monstrous monopolies of the other side! It is to the earth as the whole moon, it is honoured with beautiful names, and sacred to the proudest goddesses; it enjoys an immense revenue of odes and sonnets and songs, has a magnificent royalty in all eloquence of similes and metaphors, a tender interest and delicious part in all love-affairs.—I was afflicted by his complaint, and promised to use my great influence on the right side.— Truly unjust is your treatment, O other-side-of-the-moon-man, I said; and I have noticed many other cases of injustice in my visits during this night, for I am not an official inspector. What inequalities in the distances of the planets from the sun and by consequence in their orbits and periods of revolution; what flagrant inequalities of size and mass among them; what an unequal distribution of moons throughout the solar system! What right has Saturn to his monopoly of the belts? Why are the stars so irregularly scattered in space? Even on our earth, which is your mother-country, we suffer similar wrongs. Heat and light, palm-trees and elephants, whales and walrusses, mountains and rivers, islands and lakes, land and water, white and black and tawny complexions, and many other things, are most unequally distributed throughout it; its very axis is iniquitously oblique. And even among ourselves, among us the earth-lords, the same lawless law obtains. Large limbs and broad backs, aquiline noses and brilliant eyes, clear brains and warm hearts, are shamefully confined to a few. But cheer up, let us both cheer up, O other-side-of-the-moon-man, this state of things cannot last much longer. For we have now societies numerous and powerful for the extinction of all wrongs, real and imaginary: Missionary Societies, Bible Societies, Religious Tract Societies; Societies for the Prorogation of the Gospel, the Confusion of Useful Knowledge, the Perversion of the Jews; a Temperance League, a Reform League, a National Secular Society, an International Society: and the least of these stupendous and glorious associations intends to accomplish things much more difficult than this slight alteration in your mode of revolution which you have done me the honour to put under my especial patronage. Courage, then, my friend. Here is half-a-crown, and there is a piece of tobacco; employ yourself in getting up a monster petition, and don't let any one sign it more than twenty times, and if you can keep the fictitious names in the minority do so. Couldn't you make a demonstration from our side of the moon? A sudden irruption might put it in your possession for one night? Let your cry be, Jellinger Symons to the rescue!—So I departed fervent with lofty zeal, as he pronounced me Lord of the Lord-earth most enlightened and illustrious!

I found myself in London, not far from my habitation. It was considerably past midnight. We were in the new year. A poor woman offered me a box of matches; as I didn't want any, she begged a penny, which I gave. A girl well dressed asked for sixpence or a drop of gin, as she was perished with cold, &c. I gave her sixpence, but told her that in my humble opinion such hours and habits were scarcely conducive to health and morality. A whining man asked for twopence to get a bed, and a penny to get a roll; I gave him threepence. A ragged boy, thin-faced and large-eyed, asked for twopence to get some coffee and toke; I gave the twopence. A cabby asked me to get in; I gave him a polite refusal.

When I got home I fell into a profound and melancholy musing over my pipe and a glass of grog. I found that I had but four shillings and tenpence and a cake of the tobacco left. How veritable, I thought, are the words of the great poet (is it Shakespeare or Mr Tupper, is it Shelley or Dr Isaac Watts?)

> Whene'er I take my walks abroad,
> How many poor I see!

But never before in my walks abroad did I see so many poor as I have seen in my walk abroad to-night. Indigence everywhere, and I have nearly emptied my pockets without relieving the millionth part of a millionth part of it. When all the planets hold out their hands in beggary, what can a man do with a pound and a quarter of tobacco and about as much in loose silver? And then our poor old earth! Cattle disease, cholera, Overend and Gurney, flourishing banks through which flowed rivers of wealth, the London, Chatham, and Dover, Austria, the Pope, the dear little German Kingikins, Turkey, the Reform Bill, and the Liberal Ministry! The solar system is clearly insolvent, and I suppose the rest of the universe is in like case. I shouldn't wonder if it turns out that the sun has been blazing away out of his capital for the last few hundred years. Is the end of the world really at hand? The only resource I can think of is that the great private firm which owns and works it should sell the whole concern at about three times its value, and the goodwill for about double what it would be worth were the business immensely profitable; and dissolve into a Limited Liability Company. And I do not know that they could get a more active and able managing director than their old rival Satan. He is the fellow to keep its shares from falling into the 'realms of gloomy Dis.,' for he always keeps himself out of them in spite of doom and predestination, and goes up and down on the earth like a roaring Joint Stock Company seeking whom he may devour. And his interest in the world is so much larger than any one else's, that he would do his best to keep it going. Anyhow, something decisive must be done, and that very soon. And I fell asleep into wild dreams, murmuring those words of the illustrious poet (*is* it Shelley or Mr Tupper, *is* it Shakespeare or Dr Isaac Watts?)

> Whene'er I take my walks abroad,
> How many poor I see!

IV

Behind the door, beyond the light
Who is it waits there in the night?
When he has entered he will stand,
Imposing with his silent hand
Some silent thing upon the night.

Behold the image of my fear.
O rise not, move not, come not near!
That moment, when you turned your face
A demon seemed to leap through space;
His gesture strangled me with fear.

And yet I am the lord of all,
And this brave world magnificent,
Veiled in so variable a mist
It may be rose or amethyst,
Demands me for the lord of all!

Who said the world is but a mood
In the eternal thought of God?
I know, real though it seems
The phantom of a hachisch dream
In that insomnia which is God.

ARTHUR SYMONS
(1865-1945)

Just as the bohemians of Paris had found inspiration for their *Club des Hachischins* and drug experimentation in general from the Anglo-Saxon writers, Coleridge, De Quincey and Poe, so were they in turn to infuse enthusiasm for experimentation among the English 'decadents' of the turn of the century. There, in London, the bright young artists and writers—'The Tragic Generation' as W. B. Yeats called them—were beginning to look for new avenues of awareness and experience with drugs and they added a new chapter to 'visionary' literature. Initially these young men, led, figuratively speaking, by the poet Arthur Symons, were a pale imitation of the French; they drank laudanum, smoked opium, and ate hashish—particularly in the universities and the favourite cafés and dives of the period. Among their ranks were many familiar names, Oscar Wilde, Aubrey Beardsley, Richard Le Gallienne, Ernest Dowson and Selwyn Image. These men, with their flamboyant dress and extravagant and dissipated lifestyle, took the drugs more in a spirit of bravura, than of actual experimentation (although Symons himself was careful to record his experiences under both opium and hashish in two striking poems) and it was not until the very last years of the century that someone took the enquiry a stage further. This man was Havelock Ellis, now world-renowned for his studies of the psychology of sex, who undertook the pioneer research into the drug mescaline, and thereby began a new era of investigation into the hallucinogens which is still continuing today. Ellis quickly found a devoted following among the younger generation, and the findings of this group were to inspire others to voyage into yet more distant areas of drug stimulation.

The man who inspired the new direction for drug experimentation at the turn of the century—although the fact was very little realized at the time and has not even now become widely known—was *Henry Havelock Ellis* (1859-1939). Although Ellis's fame is as a pioneer sexologist and the author of a seven volume masterwork, *Studies in the Psychology of Sex* (1897-1928), one of his enduring interests was in the relationship between dreams, visions and drugs.

Born the son of a sea-captain in the London suburb of Croydon, he took up the study of medicine as a young man at St Thomas's Hospital in the City. He had already begun to take notes of his own dreams when, in the course of his studies, he came across references to the Mexican Indian drug, mescaline. The accounts he read of its effect on the mind tempted him to experiment, and in 1896, when he was living in London at Temple Court, he began to administer doses of the drug to himself. In the spring of 1898 he published his findings in a remarkable article, 'Mescal: A New Artificial Paradise' in *The Contemporary Review*. The essay, which I have reprinted below, caused a sensation. It aroused heated controversy and discussion and Ellis suddenly found himself the new idol of the young. Older people, however, were incensed at the insinuations of the piece and actually believed that the author was 'offering a short cut to the Grace of Vision', to quote one correspondent. During the course of his research, Ellis had tried the drug on several subjects, and continued to do so with a number of interested people. The eventual results of his work were to be published along with his theories on dreams in *The World of Dreams* in 1911. In this work the public learned that, for comparison, Ellis had also indulged himself in other drugs, but found mescaline by far the most satisfactory. 'The mescalin drinker remains calm and collected under the sensory turmoil around him,' he wrote, 'and the inner visions are of the utmost clarity and persuasion.' Ellis's work in this field was to be totally vindicated in subsequent years and he can be credited with first awakening measures of tolerance and understanding of drugs among many people, where before had been only prejudice and bigotry. (Ellis's article also, of course, pre-dates by nearly a quarter of a century Aldous Huxley's remarkable and personally-experienced work, 'The Doors of Perception', which is often erroneously held to be the first work by a Western writer on consciousness-expanding drugs).

*

Many of the words and verses of writers and poets cannot be appreciated in their full significance, I am tempted to say, by one who has never been under the influence of Mescal.

The World of Dreams, 1911

A New Artificial Paradise
HAVELOCK ELLIS

It has been known for some years that the Kiowa Indians of New Mexico are accustomed to eat, in their religious ceremonies, a certain cactus called Anhalonium Lewinii, or mescal button. Mescal—which must not be confounded with the intoxicating drink of the same name made from an agave—is found in the Mexican valley of the Rio Grande, the ancestral home of the Kiowa Indians, as well as in Texas, and is a brown and brittle substance, nauseous and bitter to the taste, composed mainly of the blunt dried leaves of the plant. Yet, as we shall see, it has every claim to rank with haschisch and the other famous drugs which have procured for men the joys of an artificial paradise. Upon the Kiowa Indians, who first discovered its rare and potent virtues, it has had so strong a fascination that the missionaries among these Indians, finding here a rival to Christianity not yielding to moral suasion, have appealed to the secular arm, and the buying and selling of the drug has been prohibited by Government under severe penalties. Yet the use of mescal prevails among the Kiowas to this day.

It has indeed spread, and the mescal rite may be said to be today the chief religion of all the tribes of the Southern plains of the United States. The rite usually takes place on Saturday night; the men then sit in a circle within the tent round a large camp-fire, which is kept burning brightly all the time. After prayer the leader hands each man four buttons, which are slowly chewed and swallowed, and altogether about ten or twelve buttons are consumed by each man between sundown and daybreak. Throughout the night the men sit quietly round the fire in a state of reverie—amid continual singing and the beating of drums by attendants—absorbed in the colour visions and other manifestations of mescal intoxication, and about noon on the following day, when the effects have passed off, they get up and go about their business, without any depression or other unpleasant after-effect.

There are five or six allied species of cacti which the Indians also use and treat with great reverence. Thus Mr Carl Lumholtz has found that the Tarahumari, a tribe of Mexican Indians, worship various cacti as gods, only to be approached with uncovered heads. When they wish to obtain these cacti, the Tarahumari cense themselves with copal incense, and with profound respect dig up the god, careful lest they should hurt him, while women and children are warned from the spot. Even Christian Indians regard Hikori, the cactus god, as co-equal with their own divinity, and make the sign of the cross in its presence. At all great festivals, Hikori is made into a drink and consumed by the medicine man, or certain selected Indians, who sing as they partake of it, invoking Hikori to grant a 'beautiful intoxication;' at the same time a rasping noise is made with sticks, and men and women dance a fantastic and picturesque dance—the women by themselves in white petticoats and tunics—before those who are under the influence of the God.

In 1891 Mr James Mooney, of the United States Bureau of Ethnology, having frequently observed the mescal rites of the Kiowa Indians and assisted at them, called the attention of the Anthropological Society at Washington to the subject, and three years later he brought to Washington a supply of mescal, which was handed over for examination to Drs Prentiss and Morgan. These investigators experimented on several young men, and demonstrated, for the first time, the precise character of mescal intoxication and the remarkable visions to which it gives rise. A little later Dr Weir Mitchell, who, in addition to his eminence as a physician, is a man of marked aesthetic temperament, experimented on himself, and published a very interesting record of the brilliant visions by which he was visited under the influence of the plant. In the spring of the past year I was able to obtain a small sample of mescal in London, and as my first experiment with mescal was also, apparently, the first attempt to investigate its vision-producing properties outside America,[1] I will describe it in

---

[1] Lewin, of Berlin, indeed, experimented with Anhalonium Lewinii, to which he gave its name, as early as 1888, and as he found that even a small portion produced dangerous symptoms, he classed it amongst the extremely poisonous drugs, like strychnia. He failed to discover its vision-producing properties, and it seems, in fact, highly probable that he was really experimenting with a different cactus from that now known by the same name.

some detail, in preference to drawing on the previously published descriptions of the American observers.

On Good Friday I found myself entirely alone in the quiet rooms in the Temple which I occupy when in London, and judged the occasion a fitting one for a personal experiment. I made a decoction (a different method from that adopted in America) of three buttons, the full physiological dose, and drank this at intervals between 2.30 and 4.30 p.m. The first symptom observed during the afternoon was a certain consciousness of energy and intellectual power.[2] This passed off, and about an hour after the final dose I felt faint and unsteady; the pulse was low, and I found it pleasanter to lie down. I was still able to read, and I noticed that a pale violet shadow floated over the page around the point at which my eyes were fixed. I had already noticed that objects not in the direct line of vision, such as my hands holding the book, showed a tendency to look obtrusive, heightened in colour, almost monstrous, while, on closing my eyes, after-images were vivid and prolonged. The appearance of visions with closed eyes was very gradual. At first there was merely a vague play of light and shade, which suggested pictures, but never made them. Then the pictures became more definite, but too confused and crowded to be described, beyond saying that they were of the same character as the images of the kaleidoscope, symmetrical groupings of spiked objects. Then, in the course of the evening, they became distinct, but still indescribable —mostly a vast field of golden jewels, studded with red and green stones, ever changing. This moment was, perhaps, the most delightful of the experience, for at the same time the air around me seemed to be flushed with vague perfume—producing with the visions a delicious effect—and all discomfort had vanished, except a slight faintness and tremor of the hands, which, later on, made it almost impossible to guide a pen as I made notes of the experiment; it was, however, with an effort, always possible to write with a pencil. The visions never resembled familiar objects; they were extremely definite, but yet always novel; they were constantly approaching, and yet constantly eluding, the semblance of known things. I would see thick glorious fields of jewels, solitary or clustered, sometimes brilliant and sparkling, sometimes with a dull rich glow. Then they would spring up into flower-like shapes beneath my gaze, and then seem to turn into gorgeous butterfly forms or endless folds of glistening, iridescent, fibrous wings of wonderful insects; while sometimes I seemed to be gazing into a vast hollow revolving vessel, on whose polished concave

---

[2] I pass lightly over the purely physiological symptoms which I have described in some detail in a paper on 'The Phenomena of Mescal Intoxication' (*Lancet,* June 5, 1897), which, however, contains no description of the visions.

mother-of-pearl surface the hues were swiftly changing. I was surprised, not only by the enormous profusion of the imagery presented to my gaze, but still more by its variety. Perpetually some totally new kind of effect would appear in the field of vision; sometimes there was swift movement, sometimes dull, sombre richness of colour, sometimes glitter and sparkle, once a startling rain of gold, which seemed to approach me. Most usually there was a combination of rich sober colour, with jewel-like points of brilliant hue. Every colour and tone conceivable to me appeared at some time or another. Sometimes all the different varieties of one colour, as of red—with scarlets, crimsons, pinks—would spring up together, or in quick succession. But in spite of this immense profusion, there was always a certain parsimony and aesthetic value in the colours presented. They were usually associated with form, and never appeared in large masses, or, if so, the tone was very delicate. I was further impressed, not only by the brilliance, delicacy, and variety of the colours, but even more by their lovely and various texture—fibrous, woven, polished, glowing, dull, veined, semi-transparent—the glowing effects, as of jewels, and the fibrous, as of insects' wings, being perhaps the most prevalent. Although the effects were novel, it frequently happened, as I have already mentioned, that they vaguely recalled known objects. Thus, once the objects presented to me seemed to be made of exquisite porcelain, again they were like elaborate sweetmeats, again of a somewhat Maori style of architecture, and the background of the pictures frequently recalled, both in form and tone, the delicate architectural effects, as of lace carved in wood, which we associate with the *mouchrabieh* work of Cairo. But always the visions grew and changed without any reference to the characteristics of those real objects of which they vaguely reminded me, and when I tried to influence their course it was with very little success. On the whole, I should say that the images were most usually what might be called living arabesques. There was often a certain incomplete tendency to symmetry, as though the underlying mechanism was associated with a large number of polished facets. The same image was in this way frequently repeated over a large part of the field; but this refers more to form than to colour, in respect to which there would still be all sorts of delightful varieties, so that if, with a certain uniformity, jewel-like flowers were springing up and expanding all over the field of vision, they would still show every variety of delicate tone and tint.

Weir Mitchell found that he could only see the visions with closed eyes and in a perfectly dark room. I could see them in the dark with almost equal facility, though they were not of equal brilliancy, when my eyes were wide open. I saw them best, however, when my eyes were closed, in a room lighted only by flickering firelight. This evidently accords with the experience of the Indians, who keep a fire burning brightly throughout their mescal rites.

The visions continued with undiminished brilliance for many hours, and, as I felt somewhat faint and muscularly weak, I went to bed, as I undressed being greatly impressed by the red, scaly, bronzed, and pigmented appearance of my limbs whenever I was not directly gazing at them. I had not the faintest desire for sleep; there was a general hyperæsthesia of all the senses as well as muscular irritability, and every slightest sound seemed magnified to startling dimensions. I may also have been kept awake by a vague alarm at the novelty of my condition, and the possibility of further developments.

After watching the visions in the dark for some hours I became a little tired of them and turned on the gas. Then I found that I was able to study a new series of visual phenomena, to which previous observers had made no reference. The gas jet (an ordinary flickering burner) seemed to burn with great brilliance, sending out waves of light, which expanded and contracted in an enormously exaggerated manner. I was even more impressed by the shadows, which were in all directions heightened by flushes of red, green, and especially violet. The whole room, with its white-washed but not very white ceiling, thus became vivid and beautiful. The difference between the room as I saw it then and the appearance it usually presents to me was the difference one may often observe between the picture of a room and the actual room. The shadows I saw were the shadows which the artist puts in, but which are not visible in the actual scene under normal conditions of casual inspection. I was reminded of the paintings of Claude Monet, and as I gazed at the scene it occurred to me that mescal perhaps produces exactly the same conditions of visual hyperæsthesia, or rather exhaustion, as may be produced on the artist by the influence of prolonged visual attention. I wished to ascertain how the subdued and steady electric light would influence vision, and passed into the next room; but here the shadows were little marked, although walls and floor seemed tremulous and insubstantial, and the texture of everything was heightened and enriched.

About 3.30 a.m. I felt that the phenomena were distinctly diminishing—though the visions, now chiefly of human figures, fantastic and Chinese in character, still continued—and I was able to settle myself to sleep, which proved peaceful and dreamless. I awoke at the usual hour and experienced no sense of fatigue, nor other unpleasant reminiscence of the experience I had undergone. Only my eyes seemed unusually sensitive to colour, especially to blue and violet; I can, indeed, say that ever since this experience I have been more æsthetically sensitive than I was before to the more delicate phenomena of light and shade and colour.

It occurred to me that it would be interesting to have the experiences of an artist under the influence of mescal, and I induced an artist friend to make a similar experiment. Unfortunately no effects whatever were produced at the first attempt, owing, as I have since discovered, to the fact that the buttons had only been simply infused and their virtues not extracted. To make sure of success the experiment was repeated with four buttons, which proved to be an excessive and unpleasant dose. There were paroxysmal attacks of pain at the heart and a sense of imminent death, which naturally alarmed the subject, while so great was the dread of light and dilation of the pupils that the eyelids had to be kept more or less closed, though it was evident that a certain amount of vision was still possible. The symptoms came on very suddenly, and when I arrived they were already at their height. As the experiences of this subject were in many respects very unlike mine, I will give them in his own words : 'I noticed first that as I happened to turn my eyes away from a blue enamel kettle at which I had been unconsciously looking, and which was standing in the fender of the fireplace, with no fire in it, it seemed to me that I saw a spot of the same blue in the black coals of the grate, and that this spot appeared again, further off, a little brighter in hue. But I was in doubt whether I had not imagined these blue spots. When, however, I lifted my eyes to the mantelpiece, on which were scattered all sorts of odds and ends, all doubt was over. I saw an intensely vivid blue light begin to play around every object. A square cigarette-box, violet in colour, shone like an amethyst. I turned my eyes away, and beheld this time, on the back of a polished chair, a bar of colour glowing like a ruby. Although I was expecting some such manifestation as one of the first symptoms of the intoxication, I was nevertheless somewhat alarmed when this phenomenon took place. Such a silent and sudden illumination of all things around, where a moment before I had seen nothing uncommon, seemed like a kind of madness beginning from outside me, and its strangeness affected me more than its beauty. A desire to escape from it led me to the door, and the act of moving had, I noticed, the effect of dispelling the colours. But a sudden difficulty in breathing and a sensation of numbness at the heart brought me back to the arm-chair from which I had risen. From this moment I had a series of attacks or paroxysms, which I can only describe by saying that I felt as though I were dying. It was impossible to move, and it seemed almost impossible to breathe. My speedy dissolution, I half imagined, was about to take place, and the power of making any resistance to the violent sensations that were arising within was going, I felt, with every second.

'The first paroxysms were the most violent. They would come on with tinglings in the lower limbs, and with the sensation of a nauseous and suffocating gas mounting up into my head. Two or three times this was accompanied by a colour vision of the gas bursting into flame as it passed up my throat. But I seldom had visions during the paroxysms; these would appear in the intervals. They began with a spurting up of colours; once, of a flood of brightly illuminated green water covering the field of vision, and effervescing in parts, just as when fresh water with all the air-bubbles is pumped into a swimming bath. At another time my eye seemed to be turning into a vast drop of dirty water in which millions of minute creatures resembling tadpoles were in motion. But the early visions consisted mostly of a furious succession of coloured arabesques, arising and descending or sliding at every possible angle into the field of view. It would be as difficult as to give a description of the whirl of water at the bottom of a waterfall as to describe the chaos of colour and design which marked this period.

'Now also began another series of extraordinary sensations. They set in with bewildering suddenness and followed one another in rapid succession. These I now record as they occur to my mind at haphazard: (1) My right leg became suddenly heavy and solid; it seemed indeed as if the entire weight of my body had shifted into one part, about the thigh and knee, and that the rest of my body had lost all substantiality. (2) With the suddenness of a neuralgic pang, the back of my head seemed to open and emit streams of bright colour; this was immediately followed by the feeling as of a draught blowing like a gale through the hair in the same region. (3) At one moment the colour, green, acquired a taste in my mouth; it was sweetish and somewhat metallic. Blue, again, would have a taste that seemed to recall phosphorus. These are the only colours that seemed to be connected with taste. (4) A feeling of delightful relief and preternatural lightness about my forehead, succeeded by a growing sensation of contraction. (5) Singing in one of my ears. (6) A sensation of burning heat in the palm of my left hand. (7) Heat about both eyes. The last continued throughout the whole period, except for a moment when I had a sensation of cold upon the eyelids, accompanied with a colour vision of the wrinkled lid, of the skin disappearing from the brow, of dead flesh, and finally of a skull.

'Throughout these sensations and visions my mind remained not only perfectly clear, but enjoyed, I believe, an unusual lucidity. Certainly I was conscious of an odd contrast in hearing myself talk rationally with H. E., who had entered the room a short time before, and experiencing at the same moment the wild and extraordinary pranks that were taking place in my body. My reason appeared to be the sole survivor of my being. At times I felt that this, too, would go, but the sound of my own voice would establish again the communication with the outer world of reality.

'Tremors were more or less constant in my lower limbs. Persistent, also, was the feeling of nausea. This, when attended by a feeling of suffocation and a pain at the heart, was relieved by taking brandy, coffee, or biscuit. For muscular exertion I felt neither the wish nor the power. My hands, however, retained their full strength.

'It was painful for me to keep my eyes open above a few seconds; the light of day seemed to fill the room with a blinding glare. Yet every object, in the brief glimpse I caught, appeared normal in colour and shape. With my eyes closed, most of the visions, after the first chaotic display, represented parts or the whole of my body undergoing a variety of marvellous changes, of metamorphoses or illumination. They were more often than not comic and grotesque in character, though often beautiful in colour. At one time I saw my right leg filling up with a delicate heliotrope; at another the sleeve of my coat changed into a dark green material in which was worked a pattern in red braid, and the whole bordered at the cuff with sable. Scarcely had my new sleeve taken shape than I found myself attired in a complete costume of the same fashion, mediæval in character, but I could not say to what precise period it belonged. I noted that a chance movement—of my hand, for instance—would immediately call up a colour vision of the part exerted, and that this again would pass, by a seemingly natural transition, into another wholly dissimilar. Thus, pressing my fingers accidentally against my temples, the fingertips became elongated, and then grew into the ribs of a vaulting or of a dome-shaped roof. But most of the visions were of a more personal nature. I happened once to lift a spoonful of coffee to my lips, and as I was in the act of raising my arm for that purpose, a vision flashed before my closed (or nearly closed) eyes, in all the hues of the rainbow, of my arm separated from my body, and serving me with coffee from out of dark and indefinite space. On another occasion, as I was seeking to relieve slight nausea by taking a piece of biscuit, passed to me by H. E., it suddenly streamed out into blue flame. For an instant I held the biscuit close to my leg. Immediately my trouser caught alight, and then the whole of the right side of my body, from the foot to the shoulder, was enveloped in waving blue flame. It was a sight of wonderful beauty. But this was not all. As I placed the biscuit in my mouth it burst out again into the same coloured fire and illuminated the interior of my mouth, casting a blue reflection on the roof. The light in the Blue Grotto at Capri, I am able to affirm, is not nearly as blue as seemed for a short space of time the interior of my mouth. There were many visions of which I could not trace the origin. There were spirals and arabesques and flowers, and sometimes objects more trivial and prosaic in character. In one vision I saw a row of small white flowers, one against the other like pearls of a necklace, begin to revolve in the form of a spiral. Every flower, I observed, had the texture of porcelain. It was at a moment when I had the sensation of my cheeks growing hot and feverish that I experienced the strangest of all the colour visions. It began with feeling that the skin of my face was becoming quite thin and of no stouter consistency than tissue paper, and the feeling was suddenly enhanced by a vision of my face, paper-like and semi-transparent and somewhat reddish in colour. To my amazement I saw myself as though I were inside a Chinese lantern, looking *out through my cheek* into the room. Not long after this I became conscious of a change in the visions. Their *tempo* was more moderate, they were less frequent, and they were losing somewhat in distinctness. At the same time the feeling of nausea and of numbness was departing. A short period followed in which I had no visions at all, and experienced merely a sensation of heaviness and torpor. I found that I was able to open my eyes again and keep them fixed on any object in the room without observing the faintest blue halo or prism, or bar of glowing colour, and that, moreover, no visions appeared on closing them. It was now twilight, but beyond the fact of not seeing light or colour either without or within, I had a distinct feeling that the action of the drug was at an end and that my body had become sober, suddenly. I had no more visions, though I was not wholly free from abnormal sensations, and I retired to rest. I lay awake till the morning, and with the exception of the following night, I scarcely slept for the next three days, but I cannot say that I felt any signs of fatigue, unless, perhaps, on one of the days when my eyes, I noticed, became very susceptible to any indications of blue in an object. Of colour visions, or of any approach to colour visions, there was no further trace; but all sorts of odd and grotesque images passed in succession through my mind during part of the first night. They might have been the dreams of a Baudelaire or of an Aubrey Beardsley. I would see figures with prodigious limbs, or strangely dwarfed and curtailed, or impossible combinations such as five or six fish, the colour of canaries, floating about in air in a gold wire cage. But these were purely mental images, like the visions seen in a dream by a distempered brain.

'Of the many sensations of which my body had been the theatre during three hours, not the least strange was the feeling I experienced on coming back into a normal condition. The recovery did not proceed gradually, but the whole outer and inner world of reality came back, as it were, with a bound. And for a moment it seemed strange. It was the sensation—only much intensified—which every one has known on coming out into the light of day from an afternoon performance at a theatre, where one has sat in an artificial light of gas and lamps, the spectator of a fictitious world of action. As one pours out with the crowd into the street, the ordinary world, by force of contrast with the sensational scenes just witnessed, breaks in upon one with almost a sense of unreality. The house, the aspect of the street, even the light of day appear a little foreign for a few moments. During these moments everything strikes the mind as odd and unfamiliar, or at least with a greater degree of objectivity. Such was my feeling with regard to my old and habitual self. During the period of intoxication, the connection between the normal condition of my body and my intelligence had broken—my body had become in a manner a stranger to my reason—so that now on reasserting itself it seemed, with reference to my reason, which had remained perfectly sane and alert, for a moment sufficiently unfamiliar for me to become conscious of its individual and peculiar character. It was as if I had unexpectedly attained an objective knowledge of my own personality. I saw, as it were, my normal state of being with the eyes of a person who sees the street on coming out of the theatre in broad day.

'This sensation also brought out the independence of the mind during the period of intoxication. It alone appeared to have escaped the ravages of the drug; it alone remained sane during a general delirium, vindicating, so it seemed, the majesty of its own impersonal nature. It had reigned for a while, I now felt, as an autocrat, without ministers and their officiousness. Henceforth I should be more or less conscious of the interdependence of body and brain; a slight headache, a touch of indigestion, or what not, would be able to effect what a general intoxication of my senses and nerves could not touch.'

I next made experiments on two poets, whose names are both well known. One is interested in mystical matters, an excellent subject for visions, and very familiar with various vision-producing drugs and processes. His heart, however, is not very strong. While he obtained the visions, he found the effects of mescal on his breathing somewhat unpleasant; he much prefers haschisch, though recognising that its effects are much more difficult to obtain. The other enjoys admirable health, and under the influence of mescal he experienced scarcely the slightest unpleasant reaction, but, on the contrary, a very marked state of well-being and beatitude. He took somewhat less than three buttons, so that the results were rather less marked than in my case, but they were perfectly definite. He writes: 'I have never seen a succession of absolutely pictorial visions with such precision and such unaccountability. It seemed as if a series of dissolving views were carried swiftly before me, all going from right to left, none corresponding with any seen reality. For instance, I saw the most delightful dragons, puffing out their breath straight in front of them like rigid lines of steam, and balancing white balls at the end of their breath!

When I tried to fix my mind on real things, I could generally call them up, but always with some inexplicable change. Thus, I called up a particular monument in Westminster Abbey, but in front of it, to the left, knelt a figure in Florentine costume, like some one out of a picture of Botticelli; and I *could not* see the tomb without also seeing this figure. Late in the evening I went out on the Embankment, and was absolutely fascinated by an advertisement of "Bovril," which went and came in letters of light on the other side of the river; I cannot tell you the intense pleasure this moving light gave me, and how dazzling it seemed to me. Two girls and a man passed me, laughing loudly, and lolling about as they walked. I realised, intellectually, their coarseness, but visually I saw them, as they came under a tree, fall into the lines of a delicate picture; it might have been an Albert Moore. After coming in I played the piano with closed eyes, and got waves and lines of pure colour, almost always without form, though I saw one or two appearances which might have been shields or breastplates—pure gold, studded with small jewels in intricate patterns. All the time I had no unpleasant feelings whatever, except a very slight headache, which came and went. I slept soundly and without dreams.'

The results of music in the case just quoted—together with the habit of the Indians to combine the drum with mescal rites, and my own observation that very slight jarring or stimulation of the scalp would affect the visions—suggested to me to test the influence of music on myself. I therefore once more put myself under the influence of mescal (taking a somewhat smaller dose than on the first occasion), and lay for some hours on a couch with my head more or less in contact with the piano, and with closed eyes directed towards a subdued light, while a friend played, making various tests, of his own devising, which were not explained to me until afterwards. I was to watch the visions in a purely passive manner, without seeking to direct them, nor was I to think about the music, which, so far as possible, was unknown to me. The music stimulated the visions and added greatly to my enjoyment of them. It seemed to harmonise with them, and, as it were, support and bear them up. A certain persistence and monotony of character in the music was required in order to affect the visions, which then seemed to fall into harmony with it, and any sudden change in the character of the music would blur the visions, as though clouds passed between them and me. The chief object of the tests was to ascertain how far a desire on the composer's part to suggest definite imagery would affect my visions. In about half the cases there was no resemblance, in the other half there was a distinct resemblance which was sometimes very remarkable. This was especially the case with Schumann's music, for example with his *Waldscenen* and *Kinder-*

scenen; thus 'The Prophet Bird' called up vividly a sense of atmosphere and of brilliant feathery bird-like forms passing to and fro; 'A Flower Piece' provoked constant and persistent images of vegetation; while 'Scheherazade' produced an effect of floating white raiment, covered by glittering spangles and jewels. In every case my description was, of course, given before I knew the name of the piece. I do not pretend that this single series of experiments proves much, but it would certainly be worth while to follow up this indication and to ascertain if any light is hereby thrown on the power of a composer to suggest definite imagery, or the power of a listener to perceive it.

It would be out of place here to discuss the obscure question as to the underlying mechanism by which mescal exerts its magic powers. It is clear from the foregoing descriptions that mescal intoxication may be described as chiefly a saturnalia of the specific senses, and, above all, an orgy of vision. It reveals an optical fairyland, where all the senses now and again join the play, but the mind itself remains a self-possessed spectator. Mescal intoxication thus differs from the other artificial paradises which drugs procure. Under the influence of alcohol, for instance, as in normal dreaming, the intellect is impaired, although there may be a consciousness of unusual brilliance; haschisch, again, produces an uncontrollable tendency to movement and bathes its victims in a sea of emotion. The mescal drinker remains calm and collected amid the sensory turmoil around him; his judgment is as clear as in the normal state; he falls into no oriental condition of vague and voluptuous reverie. The reason why mescal is of all this class of drugs the most purely intellectual in its appeal is evidently because it affects mainly the most intellectual of the senses. On this ground it is not probable that its use will easily develop into a habit. Moreover, unlike most other intoxicants, it seems to have no special affinity for a disordered and unbalanced nervous system; on the contrary, it demands organic soundness and good health for the complete manifestation of its virtues.[3] Further, unlike the other chief substances to which it may be compared, mescal does not wholly carry us away from the actual world, or plunge us into oblivion; a large part of its charm lies in the halo of beauty which it casts around the simplest and commonest things. It is the most democratic of the plants which lead men to an artificial paradise. If it should ever chance that the consumption of mescal becomes a habit, the favourite poet of the mescal drinker will certainly be Wordsworth. Not only the general attitude of Wordsworth, but many of his most memorable poems and

---

[3] It is true, as many persons do not need to be reminded, that in neurasthenia and states of over-fatigue, symptoms closely resembling the slight and earlier phenomena of mescal intoxication are not uncommon; but in such cases there is rarely any sense of well-being and enjoyment.

phrases cannot—one is almost tempted to say—be appreciated in their full significance by one who has never been under the influence of mescal. On all these grounds it may be claimed that the artificial paradise of mescal, though less seductive, is safe and dignified beyond its peers.

At the same time it must be remembered that at present we are able to speak on a basis of but very small experience, so far as civilised men are concerned. The few observations recorded in America and my own experiments in England do not enable us to say anything regarding the habitual consumption of mescal in large amounts. That such consumption would be gravely injurious I cannot doubt. Its safeguard seems to lie in the fact that a certain degree of robust health is required to obtain any real enjoyment from its visionary gifts. It may at least be claimed that for a healthy person to be once or twice admitted to the rites of mescal is not only an unforgettable delight but an educational influence of no mean value.

13 James Thomson.
14 Lafcadio Hearn.
15 Claude Farrère.
16 Francis Thompson.

17 Ernest Dowson.

18 Havelock Ellis.

19 W. B. Yeats in 1897. Portrait by his father.

20 Algernon Blackwood.

The two poets whom Havelock Ellis invited to 'experiment' with mescaline, are indeed 'both well known' though he chose to conceal their identities in his essay: one was the Irish author and occultist W. B. Yeats and the other the strange, dissolute writer Ernest Dowson. Both, too, were familiar with the effects of drug-taking and had had experiences previously with hashish and opium. The man most impressed by his mescaline experience was undoubtedly *William Butler Yeats* (1865-1939) and it is his account that Ellis reprints verbatim in his report.

Yeats, whose work has been described as 'mysterious wisdom won by toil', was the son of the Irish artist and writer, Jack Yeats, and like him was much concerned with reviving interest in ancient Irish life and culture. Following in his father's footsteps, W. B. Yeats was educated in Ireland and England and became an art student both in London and Paris. At this time he developed an interest in occultism and theosophy. These were to prove focal points for much of his work and to bring him into contact with many of the leading occultists of the turn of the century (including MacGregor Mathers and Madame Blavatsky) and a coterie of brilliant young writers including Bernard Shaw, Arthur Symons, Joseph Conrad and Oscar Wilde—not to mention Havelock Ellis and Ernest Dowson. Through his meeting with Mathers, Yeats was to become a member of the then most important and dedicated occult group, The Hermetic Order of the Golden Dawn, and from his experiences at their bizarre gatherings were to come several essays and works such as *The Secret Rose* and 'Rosa Alchemica'. In common with these writers, he tells us in his autobiography, he found 'a partiality for subjects long forbidden' and a determination to 'explore all that passes before the mind's eye—and merely because it passes'.

Although it would be wrong to think of Yeats as an indulger in drugs, he certainly took hashish on several occasions when he was in Paris, and apart from the experiments with Havelock Ellis, he also had a number of experiences with opium while in London. At the time of the Ellis experiments he was living near him in the Temple chambers; another resident was Arthur Symons from whom he learned about the 'Hashish Club' of Gautier, Baudelaire and Gérard de Nerval, and read its members' visionary prose. From the fact that Yeats completed his work on *The Secret Rose* while living in the Temple in 1896, it has been argued that he put some of his drug-induced visions to effect in the stories that comprise this volume. Certainly several contain scenes of architectural splendour reminiscent of opium visions, while others utilize the space-time discrepancies which mark hashish experiences. They also draw on Yeats's delvings into the occult and were deservedly hailed by George Moore as 'a summer night equal to anything in literature, even in that ancient literature of which Mr Yeats's work seems to be a survival or a renaissance.' If the author had needed any further encouragement to pursue his objective of reviving the ancient culture of Ireland, here it was; and his work from this point—the plays, the poetry, the philosophy and the autobiography—became a constantly ascending monument to his genius. He was awarded the Nobel Prize in 1923 and, following his death in 1939, was finally re-interred in his beloved Ireland in 1948. The story I have selected to represent Yeats here seems to me to contain the flavour of vision; it also deals with the mythology and occultism so close to the author's heart, not to mention Paris where he first experienced drugs.

*

I take hashish with some followers of the 18th-century mystic Saint-Martin. At one in the morning, while we are talking wildly, and some are dancing, there is a tap at the shuttered window; we open it and three ladies enter, the wife of a man of letters who thought to find no one but a confederate, and her husband's two young sisters whom she brought secretly to some disreputable dance. She is very confused at seeing us, but as she looks from one to another understands that we have taken some drug and laughs; caught in our dream we know vaguely that she is scandalous according to our code and to all codes, but smile at her benevolently and laugh.

The Trembling of the Veil, 1926

The Adoration of the Magi
W. B. Yeats

I was sitting reading late into the night when I heard a light knocking on my front door. I found upon the doorstep three very old men with stout sticks in their hands, who said they had been told I should be up and about, and that they were to tell me important things. I brought them into my study, and when the peacock curtains had closed behind us, I set their chairs for them close to the fire, for I saw that the frost was on their great-coats of frieze and upon the long beards that flowed almost to their waists. They took off their great-coats, and leaned over the fire warming their hands, and I saw that their clothes had much of the country of our time, but a little also, as it seemed to me, of the town life of a more courtly time. When they had warmed themselves —and they warmed themselves, I thought, less because of the cold of the night than because of a pleasure in warmth for the sake of warmth —they turned towards me, so that the light of the lamp fell full upon their weather-beaten faces, and told the story I am about to tell. Now one talked and now another, and they often interrupted one another, with a desire, like that of countrymen, when they tell a story, to leave no detail untold. When they had finished they made me take notes of whatever conversation they had quoted, so that I might have the exact words, and got up to go. When I asked them where they were going, and what they were doing, and by what names I should call them, they would tell me nothing, except that they had been commanded to travel over Ireland continually, and upon foot and at night, that they might live close to the stones and the trees and at the hours when the immortals are awake.

I have let some years go by before writing out this story, for I am always in dread of the illusions which come of that inquietude of the veil of the Temple, which M. Mallarmé considers a characteristic of our times; and only write it now because I have grown to believe that there is no dangerous idea which does not become less dangerous when written out in sincere and careful English.

The three old men were three brothers, who had lived in one of the western islands from their early manhood, and had cared all their lives for nothing except for those classical writers and old Gaelic writers who expounded an heroic and simple life; night after night in winter, Gaelic story-tellers would chant old poems to them over the poteen; and night after night in summer, when the Gaelic story-tellers were at work in the fields or away at the fishing, they would read to one another Virgil and Homer, for they would not enjoy in solitude, but as the ancients enjoyed. At last a man, who told them he was Michael Robartes, came to them in a fishing-boat, like St Brandan drawn by some vision and called by some voice; and spoke of the coming again of the gods and the ancient things; and their hearts, which had never endured the body and pressure of our time, but only of distant times, found nothing unlikely in anything he told them, but accepted all simply and were happy. Years passed, and one day, when the oldest of the old men, who travelled in his youth and thought sometimes of other lands, looked out on the grey waters, on which the people see the dim outline of the Islands of the Young—the Happy Islands where the Gaelic heroes live the lives of Homer's Phæacians—a voice came out of the air over the waters and told him of the death of Michael Robartes. They were still mourning when the next oldest of the old men fell asleep while reading out the Fifth Eclogue of Virgil, and a strange voice spoke through him, and bid them set out for Paris, where a woman lay dying, who would reveal to them the secret names of the gods, which can be perfectly spoken only when the mind is steeped in certain colours and certain sounds and certain odours; but at whose perfect speaking the immortals cease to be cries and shadows, and walk and talk with one like men and women.

They left their island, at first much troubled at all they saw in the world, and came to Paris, and there the youngest met a person in a dream, who told him they were to wander about at hazard until those who had been guiding their footsteps had brought them to a street and a house, whose likeness was shown him in the dream. They wandered hither and thither for many days, but one morning they came into some narrow and shabby streets, on the south of the Seine, where women with pale faces and untidy hair looked at them out of the windows; and just as they were about to turn back because Wisdom could not have alighted in so foolish a neighbourhood, they came to the street and the house of the dream. The oldest of the old men, who still remembered some of the modern languages he had known in his youth, went up to the door and knocked, but when he had knocked, the next in age to him said it was not a good house, and could not be the house they were looking for, and urged him to ask for some one that they knew was not there and go away. The door was opened by an old over-dressed woman, who said, 'O you are her three kinsmen from Ireland. She has been expecting you all day.' The old men looked at one another and followed her upstairs, passing doors from which pale and untidy women thrust out their heads, and into a room where a beautiful woman lay asleep in a bed, with another woman sitting by her.

The old woman said: 'Yes, they have come at last; now she will be able to die in peace,' and went out.

'We have been deceived by devils,' said one of the old men, 'for the immortals would not speak through a woman like this.'

'Yes,' said another, 'we have been deceived by devils, and we must go away quickly.'

'Yes,' said the third, 'we have been deceived by devils, but let us kneel down for a little, for we are by the deathbed of one that has been beautiful.' They knelt down, and the woman who sat by the bed, and seemed to be overcome with fear and awe, lowered her head. They watched for a little the face upon the pillow and wondered at its look, as of unquenchable desire, and at the porcelain-refinement of the vessel in which so malevolent a flame had burned.

Suddenly the second oldest of them crowed like a cock, and until the room seemed to shake with the crowing. The woman in the bed still slept on in her death-like sleep, but the woman who sat by her head crossed herself and grew pale, and the youngest of the old men cried out: 'A devil has gone into him, and we must begone or it will go into us also.' Before they could rise from their knees, a resonant chanting voice came from the lips that had crowed and said: 'I am not a devil, but I am Hermes the Shepherd of the Dead, and I run upon the errands of the gods, and you have heard my sign, that has been my sign from the old days. Bow down before her from whose lips the secret names of the immortals, and of the things near their hearts, are about to come, that the immortals may come again into the world. Bow down, and understand that when they are about to overthrow the things that are to-day and bring the things that were yesterday, they have no one to help them, but one whom the things that are to-day have cast out. Bow down and very low, for they have chosen for their priestess this woman in whose heart all follies have gathered, and in whose body all desires have awaked; this woman who has been driven out of Time and has lain upon the bosom of Eternity. After you have bowed down the old things shall be again, and another Argo shall carry heroes over sea, and another Achilles beleaguer another Troy.'

The voice ended with a sigh, and immediately the old man awoke out of sleep, and said: 'Has a voice spoken through me, as it did when I fell asleep over my Virgil, or have I only been asleep?'

The oldest of them said: 'A voice has spoken through you. Where has your soul been while the voice was speaking through you?'

'I do not know where my soul has been, but I dreamed I was under the roof of a manger, and I looked down and I saw an ox and an ass; and I saw a red cock perching on the hayrack; and a woman hugging a child; and three old men, in armour studded with rubies, kneeling with their heads bowed very low in front of the woman and the child. While I was looking the cock crowed and a man with wings on his heels swept up through the air, and as he passed me, cried out: "Foolish old men, you had once all the wisdom of the stars." I do not understand my dream or what it would have us do, but you who have heard the voice out of the wisdom of my sleep know what we have to do.'

Then the oldest of the old men told him they were to take the parchments they had brought with them out of their pockets and spread them on the ground. When they had spread them on the ground, they took out of their pockets their pens, made of three feathers, which had fallen from the wing of the old eagle that is believed to have talked of wisdom with St Patrick.

'He meant, I think,' said the youngest, as he put their ink-bottles by the side of the rolls of parchment, 'that when people are good the world likes them and takes possession of them, and so eternity comes through people who are not good or who have been forgotten. Perhaps Christianity was good and the world liked it, so now it is going away and the immortals are beginning to awake.'

'What you say has no wisdom,' said the oldest, 'because if there are many immortals, there cannot be only one immortal.'

Then the woman in the bed sat up and looked about her with wild eyes; and the oldest of the old men said: 'Lady, we have come to write down the secret names,' and at his words a look of great joy came into her face. Presently she began to speak slowly, and yet eagerly, as though she knew she had but a little while to live, and in the Gaelic of their own country; and she spoke to them many secret powerful names, and of the colours, and odours, and weapons, and instruments of music and instruments of handicraft belonging to the owners of those names; but most about the Sidhe of Ireland and of their love for the Cauldron, and the Whetstone, and the Sword, and the Spear. Then she tossed feebly for a while and moaned, and when she spoke again it was in so faint a murmur that the woman who sat by the bed leaned down to listen, and while she was listening the spirit went out of the body.

Then the oldest of the old men said in French to the woman who was still bending over the bed: 'There must have been yet one name which she had not given us, for she murmured a name while the spirit was going out of the body,' and the woman said, 'She was but murmuring over the name of a symbolist painter she was fond of. He used to go to something he called the Black Mass, and it was he who taught her to see visions and to hear voices. She met him for the first time a few months ago, and we have had no peace from that day because of her talk about visions and about voices. Why! it was only last night that I dreamed I saw a man with a red beard and red hair, and dressed in red, standing by my bedside. He held a rose in one hand,

and tore it in pieces with the other hand, and the petals drifted about the room, and became beautiful people who began to dance slowly. When I woke up I was all in a heat with terror.'

This is all the old men told me, and when I think of their speech and of their silence, of their coming and of their going, I am almost persuaded that had I gone out of the house after they had gone out of it, I should have found no footsteps on the snow. They may, for all I or any man can say, have been themselves immortals: immortal demons, come to put an untrue story into my mind for some purpose I do not understand. Whatever they were, I have turned into a pathway which will lead me from them and from the Order of the Alchemical Rose. I no longer live an elaborate and haughty life, but seek to lose myself among the prayers and the sorrows of the multitude. I pray best in poor chapels, where the frieze coats brush by me as I kneel, and when I pray against the demons I repeat a prayer which was made I know not how many centuries ago to help some poor Gaelic man or woman who had suffered with a suffering like mine.

> *Seacht b-páidreacha fó seacht*
> *Chuir Muire faoi n-a Mac,*
> *Chuir Brighid faoi n-a brat,*
> *Chuir Dia faoi n-a neart,*
> *Eider sinn 'san Sluagh Sidhe.*
> *Eidir sinn 'san Sluagh Gaoith.*

> Seven paters seven times,
> Send Mary by her Son,
> Send Bridget by her mantle,
> Send God by His strength,
> Between us and the faery host,
> Between us and the demons of the air.

Ernest Dowson (1867-1900) was, as I have already mentioned, the second poet whom Havelock Ellis used for his experiments with mescaline. Unlike Yeats, however, Dowson was a man completely used to stimulants, indeed already virtually dominated by them, and this is perhaps why Ellis does not give us a report by him. Ernest Dowson, though only moderately well-known today, was something of a legend in his own lifetime, becoming in the words of his biographers, 'the archetypal young poet who lived in squalor and produced beauty from his wretchedness.'

Born the child of wealthy parents, he spent much of his youth in France where his ailing father was forced to live for his health. He studied at Oxford but achieved little academically, devoting most of his time to riotous living and indulging in alcohol and hashish. On his father's death he inherited a dock in London's East End (then a more fashionable place than it is now) and began to circulate among the young dilettantes and writers of the time. For a while in the early 1890s he cut a striking figure and was always immaculately dressed as he met with Symons, Wilde, Beardsley, Le Gallienne and the others in their favourite pubs and restaurants. He contributed to several of the well-known magazines, including *The Savoy,* and became known as an expert on mysticism which he had studied. Then, suddenly and dramatically, the eccentric and self-destructive traits which Arthur Symons, for one, felt were always inherent in his character, took over. He retreated to the grimy dock he had inherited and lived in a tumbledown house there. He also became totally infatuated with the daughter of the owner of a seedy restaurant he occasionally used— only to see her marry one of the waiters. (The girl was to prove the inspiration of one of his finest and most enduring poems, 'Cynara.')

Dowson was already drinking heavily—mainly absinthe—and taking opium, and even a move to France in late 1896 could not save him. His friends in London could keep little track of him as he moved from one dive to another, first in Paris, then in Dieppe, earning a meagre living by translating and writing the occasional poem. He returned to London in 1899, but his dissolution was now almost complete. He insisted on being left alone and, despite the efforts of his friends, was eventually taken ill and found dying in an old wine cellar. On his death this 'miserable and unkempt' man left only enough poetry to fill a volume, several dozen original essays and some short stories as his sole literary endeavours. Yet his admirers have found a place for him in English letters, and his life-style and writing have earned him frequent comparison to De Quincey, Poe and Baudelaire, all of whom he admired, and the last of whom he translated. Whether it was alcohol or drugs that killed him is still a much debated question. His friend, Arthur Symons, places the major blame on absinthe, but adds, 'As a young man his favourite form of intoxication was hashish.' Francis Gribble is more emphatic, 'Hashish, they say, was Dowson's most formidable enemy.' The truth probably lies somewhere in between these two statements: Dowson was perhaps using drugs in occasional, excessive bouts as he did so many things in his life. Of his prose pieces, two are perhaps worth mentioning here; the first, 'Absinthia Tætra', is a 'sort of "Confessions of an English Absinthe Drinker"' to quote one biographer, Mark Longaker, and reflects his experiences during the closing years of his life. The second, 'The Dying of Francis Donne', which I am reprinting here, is more autobiographical still, as Longaker has remarked. 'No doubt Dowson experienced all the sensations he recorded and more. Anyone who wishes to know the essential voice of Dowson at the time when his dread malady was tightening its grip should reflect on the significance of this record.' Norris Getty is even more emphatic in his summation, 'The feeling of death that Dowson created is far too vividly memorable for comfort. By comparison, "The Turn of the Screw" is material for *Woman's Home Companion*.'

*

The man had known the obscure night of the soul, and lay even now in the valley of humiliation; and the tiger menace of the things to be was red in the skies. But for a little while he had forgotten.

'Absinthia Tætra', 1899

The Dying of Francis Donne
Ernest Dowson

I

He had lived so long in the meditation of death, visited it so often in others, studied it with such persistency, with a sentiment in which horror and fascination mingled; but it had always been, as it were, an objective, alien fact, remote from himself and his own life. So that it was in a sudden flash, quite too stupefying to admit in the first instance of terror, that knowledge of his mortality dawned on him. There was absurdity in the idea too.

'I, Francis Donne, thirty-five and some months old, am going to die,' he said to himself; and fantastically he looked at his image in the glass, and sought, but quite vainly, to find some change in it which should account for this incongruity, just as, searching in his analytical habit into the recesses of his own mind, he could find no such alteration of his inner consciousness as would explain or justify his plain conviction. And quickly, with reason and casuistry, he sought to rebut that conviction.

The quickness of his mind—it had never seemed to him so nimble, so exquisite a mechanism of syllogism and deduction—was contraposed against his blind instinct of the would-be self-deceiver, in a conflict to which the latter brought something of desperation, the fierce, agonized desperation of a hunted animal at bay. But piece by piece the chain of evidence was strengthened. That subtle and agile mind of his, with its special knowledge, cut clean through the shrinking protests of instinct, removing them as surely and as remorslessly, he reflected in the image most natural to him, as the keen blades of his surgical knives had removed malignant ulcers.

'I, Francis Donne, am going to die,' he repeated, and, presently, *I am going to die soon;* in a few months, in six perhaps, certainly in a year.'

Once more, curiously, but this time with a sense of neutrality, as he had often diagnosed a patient, he turned to the mirror. Was it his fancy, or, perhaps, only for the vague light that he seemed to discover a strange grey tone about his face?

But he had always been a man of a very sallow complexion.

There were a great many little lines, like pen-scratches, scarring the parchment-like skin beneath the keen eyes : doubtless, of late, these had multiplied, become more noticeable, even when his face was in repose.

But, of late, what with his growing practice, his lectures, his writing; all the unceasing labour, which his ambitions entailed, might well have aged him somewhat. That dull, immutable pain, which had first directed his attention from his studies, his investigations, his profession, to his corporal self, the actual Francis Donne, that pain which he would so gladly have called inexplicable, but could explain so precisely, had ceased for the moment. Nerves, fancies! How long it was since he had taken any rest! He had often intended to give himself a holiday, but something had always intervened. But he would do so now, yes, almost immediately; a long, long holiday—he would grudge nothing—somewhere quite out of the way, somewhere, where there was fishing; in Wales, or perhaps in Brittany; that would surely set him right.

And even while he promised himself this necessary relaxation in the immediate future, as he started on his afternoon round, in the background of his mind there lurked the knowledge of its futility; rest, relaxation, all that, at this date, was, as it were, some tardy sacrifice, almost hypocritical, which he offered to powers who might not be propitiated.

Once in his neat brougham, the dull pain began again; but by an effort of will he put it away from him. In the brief interval from house to house—he had some dozen visits to make—he occupied himself with a medical paper, glanced at the notes of a lecture he was giving that evening at a certain Institute on the 'Limitations of Medicine'.

He was late, very late for dinner, and his man, Bromgrove, greeted him with a certain reproachfulness, in which he traced, or seemed to trace, a half-patronizing sense of pity. He reminded himself that on more than one occasion, of late, Bromgrove's manner had perplexed him. He was glad to rebuke the man irritably on some pretext, to dismiss him from the room, and he hurried, without appetite, through the cold or overdone food which was the reward of his tardiness.

His lecture over, he drove out to South Kensington, to attend a reception at the house of a great man—great not only in the scientific world, but also in the world of letters. There was some of the excitement of success in his eyes as he made his way, with smiles and bows, in acknowledgement of many compliments, through the crowded rooms. For Francis Donne's lectures—those of them which were not entirely for the initiated—had grown into the importance of a social function. They had almost succeeded in making science fashionable, clothing its dry bones in a garment of so elegantly literary a pattern. But even in the ranks of the profession it was only the envious, the unsuccessful, who ventured to say that Donne had sacrificed doctrine to popularity, that his science was, in their contemptuous parlance, 'mere literature'.

Yes, he had been very successful, as the world counts success, and his consciousness of this fact, and the influence of the lights, the crowd, the voices, was like absinthe on his tired spirit. He had forgotten, or thought he had forgotten, the phantom of the last few days, the phantom which was surely waiting for him at home.

But he was reminded by a certain piece of news which late in the evening fluttered the now diminished assembly: the quite sudden death of an eminent surgeon, expected there that night, an acquaintance of his own, and more or less of each one of the little, intimate group which tarried to discuss it. With sympathy, with a certain awe, they spoke of him, Donne and others; and both the awe and the sympathy were genuine.

But as he drove home, leaning back in his carriage, in a discouragement, in a lethargy, which was only partly due to physical reaction, he saw visibly underneath their regret—theirs and his own—the triumphant assertion of life, the egoism of instinct. They were sorry, but oh, they were glad! royally glad, that it was another, and not they themselves whom something mysterious had of a sudden snatched away from his busy career, his interests, perhaps from all intelligence; at least, from all the pleasant sensuousness of life, the joy of the visible world, into darkness. And honestly dared not to blame it. How many times had not he, Francis Donne himself experienced it, that egoistic assertion of life in the presence of the dead—the poor, irremediable dead? . . . And now, he was only good to give it to others.

Latterly, he had been in the habit of subduing sleeplessness with injections of morphia, indeed in infinitesimal quantities. But to-night, although he was more than usually restless and awake, by a strong effort of reasonableness he resisted his impulse to take out the little syringe. The pain was at him again with the same dull and stupid insistence; in its monotony, losing some of the nature of pain and becoming a mere nervous irritation. But he was aware that it would not continue like that. Daily, almost hourly, it would gather strength and cruelty; the moments of respite from it would become rarer, would cease. From a dull pain it would become an acute pain, and then a torture, and then an agony, and then a madness. And in those last days, what peace might be his would be the peace of morphia, so that it was essential that, for the moment, he should not abuse the drug.

And as he knew that sleep was far away from him, he propped himself up with two pillows, and by the light of a strong reading lamp settled himself to read. He had selected the work of a distinguished German savant upon the cardiac functions, and a short treatise of his own, which was covered with recent annotations, in his crabbed handwriting, upon 'Aneurism of the Heart'. He read avidly, and against his own deductions, once more his instinct raised a vain protest. At last he threw the volumes aside, and lay with his eyes shut, without, however, extinguishing the light. A terrible sense of helplessness overwhelmed him; he was seized with an immense and heartbreaking pity for poor humanity as personified in himself; and, for the first time since he had ceased to be a child, he shed puerile tears.

II

The faces of his acquaintance, the faces of the students at his lectures, the faces of Francis Donne's colleagues at the hospital, were altered; were, at least, sensibly altered to his morbid self-consciousness. In every one whom he encountered, he detected, or fancied that he detected, an attitude of evasion, a hypocritical air of ignoring a fact that was obvious and unpleasant. Was it so obvious, then, the hidden horror which he carried incessantly about him? Was his secret, which he would still guard so jealously, become a by-word and an anecdote in his little world? And a great rage consumed him against the inexorable and inscrutable forces which had made him to destroy him; against himself, because of his proper impotence; and, above all, against the living, the millions who would remain when he was no longer, the living, of whom many would regret him (some of them his personality, and more, his skill), because he could see under all the unconscious hypocrisy of their sorrow, the exultant self-satisfaction of their survival.

And with his burning sense of helplessness, of a certain bitter injustice in things, a sense of shame mingled; all the merely physical dishonour of death shaping itself to his sick and morbid fancy into a violent symbol of what was, as it were, an actual *moral* or intellectual dishonour. Was not death, too, inevitable and natural an operation as it was, essentially a process to undergo apart and hide jealously, as much as other natural and ignoble processes of the body?

And the animal, who steals away to an uttermost place in the forest, who gives up his breath in a solitude and hides his dying like a shameful thing,—might he not offer an example that it would be well for the dignity of poor humanity to follow?

Since Death is coming to me, said Francis Donne to himself, let me meet it, a stranger in a strange land, with only strange faces round me and the kind indifference of strangers, instead of the intolerable pity of friends.

III

On the bleak and wave-tormented coast of Finisterre, somewhere between Quiberon and Fouesnant, he reminded himself of a little fishing-village: a few scattered houses (one of them being an *auberge* at which ten years ago he had spent a night), collected round a poor little grey church. Thither Francis Donne went, without leave-takings or explanation, almost secretly, giving but the vaguest indications of the length or direction of his absence. And there for many days he dwelt, in the cottage which he had hired, with one old Breton woman for his sole attendant, in a state of mind which, after all the years of energy, of ambitious labour, was almost peace.

Bleak and grey it had been, when he had visited it of old, in the late autumn; but now the character, the whole colour of the country was changed. It was brilliant with the promise of summer, and the blue Atlantic, which in winter churned with its long crested waves so boisterously below the little white lighthouse, which warned mariners (alas! so vainly), against the shark-like cruelty of the rocks, now danced and glittered in the sunshine, rippled with feline caresses round the hulls of the fishing-boats whose brown sails floated so idly in the faint air.

Above the village, on a grassy slope, whose green was almost lurid, Francis Donne lay, for many silent hours, looking out at the placid sea, which could yet be so ferocious, at the low violet line of the Island of Groix, which alone interrupted the monotony of sky and ocean.

He had brought many books with him but he read in them rarely; and when physical pain gave him a respite for thought, he thought almost of nothing. His thought was for a long time a lethargy and a blank.

Now and again he spoke with some of the inhabitants. They were a poor and hardy, but a kindly race: fishers and the wives of fishers, whose children would grow up and become fishermen and the wives of fishermen in their turn. Most of them had wrestled with death; it was always so near to them that hardly one of them feared it; they were fatalists, with the grim and resigned fatalism of the poor, of the poor who live with the treachery of the sea.

Francis Donne visited the little cemetery, and counted the innumerable crosses which testified to the havoc which the sea had wrought. Some of the graves were nameless; holding the bodies of strange seamen which the waves had tossed ashore.

'And in a little time I shall lie here,' he said to himself; 'and here as well as elsewhere,' he added with a shrug, assuming, and for once, almost sincerely, the stoicism of his surroundings, 'and as lief to-day as to-morrow.'

On the whole, the days were placid; there were even moments when, as though he had actually drunk in renewed vigour from that salt sea air, the creative force of the sun, he was tempted to doubt his grievous knowledge, to make fresh plans for life. But these were fleeting moments, and the reaction from them was terrible. Each day his hold on life was visibly more slender, and the people of the village saw, and with a rough sympathy, which did not offend him, allowed him to perceive that they saw, the rapid growth and the inevitableness of his end.

IV

But if the days were not without their pleasantness, the nights were always horrible—a torture of the body and an agony of the spirit. Sleep was far away, and the brain, which had been lulled till the evening, would awake, would grow electric with life and take strange and abominable flights into the darkness of the pit, into the black night of the unknowable and the unknown.

And interminably, during those nights which seemed eternity, Francis Donne questioned and examined into the nature of that Thing, which stood, a hooded figure beside his bed, with a menacing hand raised to beckon him so peremptorily from all that lay within his consciousness.

He had been all his life absorbed in science; he had dissected, how many bodies? and in what anatomy had he ever found a soul? Yet if his avocations, his absorbing interest in physical phenomena had made him somewhat a materialist, it had been almost without his consciousness. The sensible, visible world of matter had loomed so large to him, that merely to know that had seemed to him sufficient. All that might conceivably lie outside it, he had, without negation, been content to regard as outside his province.

And now, in his weakness, in the imminence of approaching dissolution, his purely physical knowledge seemed but a vain possession, and he turned with a passionate interest to what had been said and believed from time immemorial by those who had concentrated their intelligence on that strange essence, which might after all be the essence of one's personality, which might be that sublimated consciousness—the Soul—actually surviving the infamy of the grave?

> Animula, vagula, blandula!
> Hospes comesque corporis,
> Quae nunc abibis in loca?
> Pallidula, rigida, nudula.

Ah, the question! It was a harmony, perhaps (as, who had maintained? whom the Platonic Socrates in the 'Phaedo' had not too successfully refuted), a harmony of life, which was dissolved when life was over? Or, perhaps, as how many metaphysicians had held both before and after a sudden great hope, perhaps too generous to be true, had changed and illuminated, to countless millions, the inexorable figure of Death—a principle, indeed, immortal, which came and went, passing through many corporal conditions until it was ultimately resolved into the great mind, pervading all things? Perhaps? . . . But what scanty consolation, in all such theories, to the poor body, racked with pain and craving peace, to the tortured spirit of self-consciousness so achingly anxious not to be lost.

And he turned from these speculations to what was, after all, a possibility like the others; the faith of the simple, of these fishers with whom he lived, which was also the faith of his own childhood, which, indeed, he had never repudiated, whose practices he had simply discarded, as one discards puerile garments when one comes to man's estate. And he remembered, with the vividness with which in moments of great anguish, one remembers things long ago familiar, forgotten though they may have been for years, the triumphant declarations of the Church:

Omnes quidem resurgemus, sed non omnes immutabimur. In momento, in ictu oculi, in novissima tuba: canet enim tuba: et mortui resurgent incorrupti, et nos immutabimur. Oportet enim corruptibile hoc induere immortalitatem. Cum autem mortale hoc induerit immortalitatem tunc fiet sermo qui scriptus est: Absorpta est mors in victoria. Ubi est, mors, victoria tua? Ubi est, mors, stimulus tuus?

Ah, for the certitude of that! of that victorious confutation of the apparent destruction of sense and spirit in a common ruin . . . But it was a possibility like the rest; and had it not more need than the rest to be more than a possibility, if it would be a consolation, in that it promised more? And he gave it up, turning his face to the wall, lay very still, imagining himself already stark and cold, his eyes closed, his jaw closely tied (lest the ignoble changes which had come to him should be too ignoble), while he waited until the narrow boards, within which he should lie, had been nailed together, and the bearers were ready to convey him into the corruption which was to be his part.

And as the window-pane grew light with morning, he sank into a drugged, unrestful sleep, from which he would awake some hours later with eyes more sunken and more haggard cheeks. And that was the pattern of many nights.

V

One day he seemed to wake from a night longer and more troubled than usual, a night which had, perhaps, been many nights and days, perhaps even weeks; a night of an ever-increasing agony, in which he was only dimly conscious at rare intervals of what was happening, or of the figures coming and going around his bed: the doctor from a neighbouring town, who had stayed by him unceasingly, easing his paroxysms with the little merciful syringe; the soft, practised hands of a sister of charity about his pillow; even the face of Bromgrove, for whom doubtless he had sent, when he had foreseen the utter helplessness which was at hand.

He opened his eyes, and seemed to discern a few blurred figures against the darkness of the closed shutters through which one broad ray filtered in; but he could not distinguish their faces, and he closed his eyes once more. An immense and ineffable tiredness had come over him that this—*this* was Death; this was the thing against which he had cried and revolted; the horror from which he would have escaped; this utter luxury of physical exhaustion, this calm, this release.

The corporal capacity of smiling had passed from him, but he would fain have smiled.

And for a few minutes of singular mental lucidity, all his life flashed before him in a new relief; his childhood, his adolescence, the people whom he had known; his mother, who had died when he was a boy, of a malady from which, perhaps, a few years later, his skill had saved her; the friend of his youth who had shot himself for so little reason; the girl whom he had loved, but who had not loved him . . . All that was distorted in life was adjusted and justified in the light of his sudden knowledge. *Beati mortui* . . . and then the great tiredness swept over him once more, and a fainter consciousness, in which he could yet just dimly hear, as in a dream, the sound of Latin prayers, and feel the application of the oils upon all the issues and approaches of his wearied sense; then utter unconsciousness, while pulse and heart gradually grew fainter until both ceased. And that was all.

Aside from the interest in drug experimentation among the young English writers and poets in the early years of this century, there was also an increasing amount of drug usage in the varied occult and mystic groups which were being formed. This enquiry into the mysterious forces of nature—in astrology, astronomy, witchcraft and Black Magic—had again developed from French origins in the previous century, and I have traced its course and its main characters in a previous volume.[1] Some of these groups were no more than thrill seekers and perverts, using ostensibly occult motives as a cover for debauchery, while others sought conscientiously to find answers to the mysteries they were confronted with by the use of hallucinatory drugs. Writers on occult themes in both fact and fiction at this time had a plentiful supply to draw from,[2] but only one of them, *Algernon Blackwood* (1869-1951), seems to have genuinely explored the motivations of the drug takers and experienced what they did.

Blackwood, whose masterly short stories have delighted thousands of readers for years, was an adventurous soul who tramped his way through much of Canada and America as a young man and indulged in many strange pleasures. A mysterious acquaintance of his youth, Dr Huebner, who was a confirmed addict, introduced him to drugs through the pages of De Quincey's 'Confessions' and then urged him to sample the delights of morphine, a derivative of opium, for himself. 'I became so "interesting" after I took this drug and entertained the old doctor so successfully that he found himself able to do without his own dose for a time,' he wrote later in his autobiography. 'But without the stuff in my blood I was gloomy, stupid, dull.' For weeks Blackwood was aware of slipping into the power of the old man and of the morphine, each time taking a stronger dose to counter the after-effects. Then, he says, it dawned on him that the 'balm that assuaged' would deny him the freedom of movement he wanted and he gave it up—unfortunately denying us any details in his biography of how he did this. He was to return again to the subject in London at the

---

[1] *The Magicians,* Peter Owen, 1972.
[2] Perhaps the most notable piece of fiction from this period—although it was faithfully based on fact and years of personal enquiry—was Sax Rohmer's *Dope: A Story of Chinatown and the Drug Traffic* published in

turn of the century when he was moving freely among the occult circles, absorbing the atmosphere and rituals for his writing. This time he took hashish and wrote an account of the experience for a national newspaper. 'It was not taken for indulgence, nor to bring a false, temporary happiness into a life I loathed,' he said afterwards. 'I did it to earn a little money!' By this, of course, Blackwood meant that he took it to get the material for his report—but he also took it several times more, *for the experience,* and utilized what happened for the story 'A Psychical Invasion'. This story is one of the adventures that went to make up his book, *John Silence, Physician Extraordinary,* a study on various psychic themes published in 1910. It deals with consciousness-expanding drugs in a way which must have been outspoken at the time when it was first published and which is still applicable today.

*

Such intensification, I well knew, could be produced by better, if more difficult ways, ways that caused no reaction, ways that constructed instead of destroyed ... and the first pleasure I derived from my experience, the interest that first stirred flashingly and at once through my cleared mind, was the absolute conviction that the teachings and theories in my books were true....

Episodes Before Thirty, 1923

1919. Rohmer himself had some slight knowledge of the effects of drugs, having smoked hashish in Egypt and taken opium once (it made him sick though), and claimed that the whole story was based on real people and incidents. *Dope* deals with the experiences of a thrill-seeking young girl who is introduced to the 'ultra-smart and vicious set' in London, who illicitly smoke opium, and charts her downward path to suffering and degradation. In the course of the book, Rohmer gives a revealing insight into drug-taking at the turn of the century: 'The prevalence of the drug habit in society—especially in London society—is a secret which has remained hidden so long from the general public: drug takers, indeed, form a kind of brotherhood, and outside the charmed circle they are as secretive as members of the Mafia. The stage is made the scapegoat whenever the voice of scandal breathes the word "dope", but we rarely hear the names of the worst offenders even whispered. I have thought for a long time that the authorities must know the names of the receivers and distributors of cocaine, veronal, opium, and the other drugs, huge quantities of which find their way regularly to the West End of London. Pharmacists sometimes experience the greatest difficulty in obtaining the drugs which they legitimately require and the prices have increased extraordinarily. Cocaine, for instance, has gone up from five and sixpence an ounce to eighty-seven shillings, and heroin from three and sixpence to over forty shillings, whilst opium that was once about twenty shillings a pound is now eight times the price.' No comment is necessary, I think, on the cheapness of these prices by today's standards!

A Psychical Invasion

ALGERNON BLACKWOOD

'And what is it makes you think I could be of use in this particular case?' asked Dr John Silence, looking across somewhat sceptically at the Swedish lady in the chair facing him.

'Your sympathetic heart and your knowledge of occultism—'

'Oh, please—that dreadful word!' he interrupted, holding up a finger with a gesture of impatience.

'Well, then,' she laughed, 'your wonderful clairvoyant gift and your trained psychic knowledge of the processes by which a personality may be disintegrated and destroyed—these strange studies you've been experimenting with all these years—'

'If it's only a case of multiple personality I must really cry off,' interrupted the doctor again hastily, a bored expression in his eyes.

'It's not that; now, please, be serious, for I want your help,' she said; 'and if I choose my words poorly you must be patient with my ignorance. The case I know will interest you, and no one else could deal with it so well. In fact, no ordinary professional man could deal with it at all, for I know of no treatment or medicine that can restore a lost sense of humour!'

'You begin to interest me with your "case,"' he replied, and made himself comfortable to listen.

Mrs Sivendson drew a sigh of contentment as she watched him go to the tube and heard him tell the servant he was not to be disturbed.

'I believe you have read my thoughts already,' she said; 'your intuitive knowledge of what goes on in other people's minds is positively uncanny.'

Her friend shook his head and smiled as he drew his chair up to a convenient position and prepared to listen attentively to what she had to say. He closed his eyes, as he always did when he wished to absorb the real meaning of a recital that might be inadequately expressed, for by this method he found it easier to set himself in tune with the living thoughts that lay behind the broken words.

By his friends John Silence was regarded as an eccentric, because he was rich by accident, and by choice—a doctor. That a man of independent means should devote his time to doctoring, chiefly doctoring folk who could not pay, passed their comprehension entirely. The native nobility of a soul whose first desire was to help those who could not help themselves, puzzled them. After that, it irritated them, and, greatly to his own satisfaction, they left him to his own devices.

Dr Silence was a free-lance, though, among doctors, having neither consulting room, bookkeeper, nor professional manner. He took no fees, being at heart a genuine philanthropist, yet at the same time did no harm to his fellow-practitioners, because he only accepted unremunerative cases, and cases that interested him for some very special reason. He argued that the rich could pay, and the very poor could avail themselves of organized charity, but that a very large class of ill-paid, self-respecting workers, often followers of the arts, could not afford the price of a week's comforts merely to be told to travel. And it was these he desired to help: cases often requiring special and patient study—things no doctor can give for a guinea, and that no one would dream of expecting him to give.

But there was another side to his personality and practice, and one with which we are now more directly concerned; for the cases that especially appealed to him were of no ordinary kind, but rather of that intangible, elusive, and difficult nature best described as psychical afflictions; and, though he would have been the last person himself to approve of the title, it was beyond question that he was known more or less generally as the 'Psychic Doctor.'

In order to grapple with cases of this peculiar kind, he had submitted himself to a long and severe training, at once physical, mental, and spiritual. What precisely this training had been, or where undergone, no one seemed to know—for he never spoke of it, as, indeed, he betrayed no single other characteristic of the charlatan—but the fact that it had involved a total disappearance from the world for five years, and that after he returned and began his singular practice no one ever dreamed of applying to him the so-easily acquired epithet of quack, spoke much for the seriousness of his strange quest and also for the genuineness of his attainments.

For the modern psychical researcher he felt the calm tolerance of the 'man who knows'. There was a trace of pity in his voice—contempt he never showed—when he spoke of their methods.

'This classification of results is uninspired work at best,' he said once to me, when I had been his confidential assistant for some years. 'It leads nowhere, and after a hundred years will lead nowhere. It is playing with the wrong end of a rather dangerous toy. Far better, it would be, to examine the causes, and then the results would so easily slip into place and explain themselves. For the sources are accessible, and open to all who have the courage to lead the life that alone makes practical investigation safe and possible.'

And towards the question of clairvoyance, too, his attitude was significantly sane, for he knew how extremely rare the genuine power was, and that what is commonly called clairvoyance is nothing more than a keen power of visualizing.

'It connotes a slightly increased sensibility, nothing more,' he would say. 'The true clairvoyant deplores his power, recognizing that it adds a new horror to life, and is in the nature of an affliction. And you will find this always to be the real test.'

Thus it was that John Silence, this singularly developed doctor, was able to select his cases with a clear knowledge of the difference between mere hysterical delusion and the kind of psychical affliction that claimed his special powers. It was never necessary for him to resort to the cheap mysteries of divination; for, as I have heard him observe, after the solution of some peculiarly intricate problem :

'Systems of divination, from geomancy down to reading by tea-leaves, are merely so many methods of obscuring the outer vision, in order that the inner vision may become open. Once the method is mastered, no system is necessary at all.'

And the words were significant of the methods of this remarkable man, the keynote of whose power lay, perhaps, more than anything else, in the knowledge, first, that thought can act at a distance, and, secondly, that thought is dynamic and can accomplish material results.

'Learn how to *think*,' he would have expressed it, 'and you have learned to tap power at its source.'

To look at—he was now past forty—he was sparely built, with speaking brown eyes in which shone the light of knowledge and self-confidence, while at the same time they made one think of that wondrous gentleness seen most often in the eyes of animals. A close beard concealed the mouth without disguising the grim determination of lips and jaw, and the face somehow conveyed an impression of transparency, almost of light, so delicately were the features refined away. On the fine forehead was that indefinable touch of peace that comes from identifying the mind with what is permanent in the soul, and letting the impermanent slip by without power to wound or distress; while, from his manner—so gentle, quiet, sympathetic—few could have guessed the strength of purpose that burned within like a great flame.

'I think I should describe it as a psychical case,' continued the Swedish lady, obviously trying to explain herself very intelligently, 'and just the kind you like. I mean a case where the cause is hidden deep down in some spiritual distress, and—'

'But the symptoms first, please, my dear Mrs Sivendson,' he interrupted, with a strangely compelling seriousness of manner, 'and your deductions afterwards.'

She turned round sharply on the edge of her chair and looked him in the face, lowering her voice to prevent her emotion betraying itself too obviously.

'In my opinion there's only one symptom,' she half whispered, as though telling something disagreeable: 'fear—simply fear.'

'Physical fear?'

'I think not; though how can I say? I think it's a horror in the psychical region. It's no ordinary delusion; the man is quite sane: but he lives in mortal terror of something—'

'I don't know what you mean by his "psychical region,"' said the doctor, with a smile; 'though I suppose you wish me to understand that his spiritual, and not his mental, processes are affected. Anyhow, try and tell me briefly and pointedly what you know about the man, his symptoms, his need for help, *my* peculiar help, that is, and all that seems vital in the case. I promise to listen devotedly.'

'I am trying,' she continued earnestly, 'but must do so in my own words and trust to your intelligence to disentangle as I go along. He is a young author, and lives in a tiny house off Putney Heath somewhere. He writes humorous stories—quite a genre of his own: Pender —you must have heard the name—Felix Pender? Oh, the man had a great gift, and married on the strength of it; his future seemed assured. I say "had," for quite suddenly his talent utterly failed him. Worse, it became transformed into its opposite. He can no longer write a line in the old way that was bringing him success—'

Dr Silence opened his eyes for a second and looked at her. 'He still writes, then? The force has not gone?' he asked briefly, and then closed his eyes again to listen.

'He works like a fury,' she went on, 'but produces nothing'—she hesitated a moment—'nothing that he can use or sell. His earnings have practically ceased, and he makes a precarious living by book-reviewing and odd jobs—very odd, some of them. Yet, I am certain his talent has not really deserted him finally, but is merely—'

Again Mrs Sivendson hesitated for the appropriate word.

'In abeyance,' he suggested, without opening his eyes.

'Obliterated,' she went on, after a moment to weight the word, 'merely obliterated by something else—'

'By some *one* else?'

'I wish I knew. All I can say is that he is haunted, and temporarily his sense of humour is shrouded—gone—replaced by something dreadful that writes other things. Unless something competent is is done, he will simply starve to death. Yet he is afraid to go to a doctor for fear of being pronounced insane; and anyhow, a man can hardly ask a doctor to take a guinea to restore a vanished sense of humour, can he?'

'Has he tried any one at all?'

'Not doctors yet. He tried some clergymen and religious people; but they *know* so little and have so little intelligent sympathy. And most of them are so busy balancing on their own little pedestals—'

John Silence stopped her tirade with a gesture. 'And how is it that you know so much about him?' he asked gently.

'I know Mrs Pender well—I knew her before she married him—'

'And is she a cause, perhaps?'

'Not in the least. She is devoted; a woman very well educated, though without being really intelligent, and with so little sense of humour herself that she always laughs at the wrong places. But she has nothing to do with the cause of his distress; and indeed, has chiefly guessed it from observing him, rather than from what little he has told her. And he, you know, is a really lovable fellow, hard-working, patient—altogether worth saving.'

Dr Silence opened his eyes and went over to ring for tea. He did not know very much more about the case of the humorist than when he first sat down to listen; but he realized that no amount of words from his Swedish friend would help to reveal the real facts. A personal interview with the author himself could alone do that.

'All humorists are worth saving,' he said with a smile, as she poured out tea. 'We can't afford to lose a single one in these strenuous days. I will go and see your friend at the first opportunity.'

She thanked him elaborately, effusively, with many words, and he, with much difficulty, kept the conversation thenceforward strictly to to the teapot.

And, as a result of this conversation, and a little more he had gathered by means best known to himself and his secretary, he was whizzing in his motor-car one afternoon a few days later up the Putney Hill to have his first interview with Felix Pender the humour writer who was the victim of some mysterious malady in his 'psychical region' that had obliterated his sense of the comic and threatened to wreck his life and destroy his talent. And his desire to help was probably of equal strength with his desire to know and to investigate.

The motor stopped with a deep purring sound, as though a great black panther lay concealed within its hood, and the doctor—the 'psychic doctor,' as he was sometimes called—stepped out through the gathering fog, and walked across the tiny garden that held a blackened fir tree and a stunted laurel shrubbery. The house was very small, and it was some time before any one answered the bell. Then, suddenly, a light appeared in the hall, and he saw a pretty little woman standing on the top step begging him to come in. She was dressed in gray, and the gaslight fell on a mass of deliberately brushed light hair. Stuffed, dusty birds, and a shabby array of African spears, hung on the wall behind her. A hatrack, with a bronze plate full of very large cards, led his eye swiftly to a dark staircase beyond. Mrs Pender had round eyes like a child's, and she greeted him with an effusiveness that barely concealed her emotion, yet strove to appear naturally cordial. Evidently she had been looking out for his arrival, and had outrun the servant girl. She was a little breathless.

'I hope you've not been kept waiting—I think it's *most* good of you to come—' she began, and then stopped sharp when she saw his face in the gaslight. There was something in Dr Silence's look that did not encourage mere talk. He was in earnest now, if ever man was.

'Good evening, Mrs Pender,' he said, with a quiet smile that won confidence, yet deprecated unnecessary words, 'the fog delayed me a little. I am glad to see you.'

They went into a dingy sitting-room at the back of the house, neatly furnished but depressing. Books stood in a row upon the mantelpiece. The fire had evidently just been lit. It smoked in great puffs into the room.

'Mrs Sivendson said she thought you might be able to come,' ventured the little woman again, looking up engagingly into his face and betraying anxiety and eagerness in every gesture. 'But I hardly dared to believe it. I think it is really too good of you. My husband's case is so peculiar that — well, you know, I am quite sure any *ordinary* doctor would say at once the asylum—'

'Isn't he in, then?' asked Dr Silence gently.

'In the asylum?' she gasped. 'Oh dear, no—not yet!'

'In the house, I meant,' he laughed.

She gave a great sigh. 'He'll be back any minute now,' she replied, obviously relieved to see him laugh; 'but the fact is, we didn't expect you so early—I mean, my husband hardly thought you would come at all.'

'I am always delighted to come—when I am really wanted, and can be of help,' he said quickly; 'and, perhaps, it's all for the best that your husband is out, for now that we are alone you can tell me something about his difficulties. So far, you know, I have heard very little.'

Her voice trembled as she thanked him, and when he came and took a chair close beside her she actually had difficulty in finding words with which to begin.

'In the first place,' she began timidly, and then continuing with a nervous incoherent rush of words, 'he will be simply delighted that you've really come, because he said you were the only person he would consent to see at all—the only doctor, I mean. But, of course, he doesn't know how frightened I am, or how much I have noticed. He pretends with me that it's just a nervous breakdown, and I'm sure he doesn't realize all the odd things I've noticed him doing. But the main thing, I suppose—'

'Yes, the main thing, Mrs Pender,' he said encouragingly, noticing her hesitation.

'— is that he thinks we are not alone in the house. That's the chief thing.'

'Tell me more facts—just facts.'

'It began last summer when I came back from Ireland; he had been here alone for six weeks, and I thought him looking tired and queer— ragged and scattered about the face, if you know what I mean, and his manner worn out. He said he had been writing hard, but his inspiration had somehow failed him, and he was dissatisfied with his work. His sense of humour was leaving him, or changing into something else, he said. There was something in the house, he declared, that'—she emphasized the words—'prevented his feeling funny.'

'Something in the house that prevented his feeling funny,' repeated the doctor. 'Ah, now we're getting to the heart of it!'

'Yes,' she resumed vaguely, 'that's what he kept saying.'

'And what was it he did that you thought strange?' he asked sympathetically. 'Be brief, or he may be here before you finish.'

'Very small things, but significant it seemed to me. He changed his workroom from the library, as we call it, to the sitting-room. He said all his characters became wrong and terrible in the library; they altered, so that he felt like writing tragedies—vile, debased tragedies, the tragedies of broken souls. But now he says the same of the smoking-room, and he's gone back to the library.'

'Ah!'

'You see, there's so little I can tell you,' she went on, with increasing speed and countless gestures. 'I mean it's only very small things he does and says that are queer. What frightens me is that he assumes there is someone else in the house all the time—someone I never see. He does not actually say so, but on the stairs I've seen him standing aside to let someone pass; I've seen him open a door to let someone in or out; and often in our bedroom he puts chairs about as though for someone else to sit in. Oh—oh yes, and once or twice,' she cried— 'once or twice—'

She paused, and looked about her with a startled air.

'Yes?'

'Once or twice,' she resumed hurriedly, as though she heard a sound that alarmed her, 'I've heard him running—coming in and out of the rooms breathless as if something were after him—'

The door opened while she was still speaking, cutting her words off in the middle, and a man came into the room. He was dark and cleanshaven, sallow rather, with the eyes of imagination, and dark hair growing scantily about the temples. He was dressed in a shabby tweed suit, and wore an untidy flannel collar at the neck. The dominant expression of his face was startled—hunted; an expression that might any moment leap into the dreadful stare of terror and announce a total loss of self-control.

The moment he saw his visitor, a smile spread over his worn features, and he advanced to shake hands.

'I hoped you would come; Mrs Sivendson said you might be able to find time,' he said simply. His voice was thin and reedy. 'I am very glad to see you, Dr Silence. It is "Doctor," is it not?'

'Well, I am entitled to the description,' laughed the other, 'but I rarely get it. You know, I do not practice as a regular thing; that is, I only take cases that specially interest me, or—'

He did not finish the sentence, for the men exchanged a glance of sympathy that rendered it unnecessary.

'I have heard of your great kindness.'

'It's my hobby,' said the other quickly, 'and my privilege.'

'I trust you will still think so when you have heard what I have to tell you,' continued the author, a little wearily. He led the way across the hall into the little smoking-room where they could talk freely and undisturbed.

In the smoking-room, the door shut and privacy about them, Pender's attitude changed somewhat, and his manner became very grave. The doctor sat opposite, where he could watch his face. Already, he saw, it looked more haggard. Evidently it cost him much to refer to his trouble at all.

'What I have is, in my belief, a profound spiritual affliction,' he began quite bluntly, looking straight into the other's eyes.

'I saw that at once,' Dr Silence said.

'Yes, you saw that, of course; my atmosphere must convey that much to any one with psychic perceptions. Besides which, I feel sure from all I've heard, that you are really a soul-doctor, are you not, more than a healer merely of the body?'

'You think of me too highly,' returned the other; 'though I prefer cases, as you know, in which the spirit is disturbed first, the body afterwards.'

'I understand, yes. Well, I have experienced a curious disturbance in—*not* in my physical region primarily. I mean my nerves are all right, and my body is all right. I have no delusions exactly, but my spirit is tortured by a calamitous fear which first came upon me in a strange manner.'

John Silence leaned forward a moment and took the speaker's hand and held it in his own for a few brief seconds, closing his eyes as he did so. He was not feeling his pulse, or doing any of the things that doctors ordinarily do; he was merely absorbing into himself the main note of the man's mental condition, so as to get completely his own point of view, and thus be able to treat his case with true sympathy. A very close observer might perhaps have noticed that a slight tremor ran through his frame after he had held the hand for a few seconds.

'Tell me quite frankly, Mr Pender,' he said soothingly, releasing the hand, and with deep attention in his manner, 'tell me all the steps that led to the beginning of this invasion. I mean tell me what the particular drug was, and why you took it, and how it affected you—'

'Then you know it began with a drug!' cried the author, with undisguised astonishment.

'I only know from what I observe in you, and in its effect upon myself. You are in a surprising psychical condition. Certain portions of your atmosphere are vibrating at a far greater rate than others. This is the effect of a drug, but of no ordinary drug. Allow me to finish, please. If the higher rate of vibrations spreads all over, you will become, of course, permanently cognisant of a much larger world than the one you know normally. If, on the other hand, the rapid portion sinks back to the usual rate, you will lose these occasional increased perceptions you now have.'

'You amaze me!' exclaimed the author; 'for your words exactly describe what I have been feeling—'

'I mention this only in passing, and to give you confidence before you approach the account of your real affliction,' continued the doctor. 'All perception, as you know, is the result of vibrations; and clairvoyance simply means becoming sensitive to an increased scale of vibrations. The awakening of the inner senses we hear so much about means no more than that. Your partial clairvoyance is easily explained. The only thing that puzzles me is how you managed to procure the drug, for it is not easy to get in pure form, and no adulterated tincture could have given you the terrific impetus I see you have acquired. But, please, proceed now and tell me your story in your own way.'

'This *Cannabis indica*,' the author went on, 'came into my possession last autumn while my wife was away. I need not explain how I got it, for that has no importance; but it was the genuine fluid extract, and I could not resist the temptation to make an experiment. One of its effects, as you know, is to induce torrential laughter—'

'Yes, sometimes.'

'—I am a writer of humorous tales, and I wished to increase my own sense of laughter—to see the ludicrous from an abnormal point of view. I wished to study it a bit, if possible, and—'

'Tell me!'

'I took an experimental dose. I starved for six hours to hasten the effect, locked myself in this room, and gave orders not to be disturbed. Then I swallowed the stuff and waited.'

'And the effect?'

'I waited one hour, two, three, four, five hours. Nothing happened.

No laughter came, but only a great weariness instead. Nothing in the room or in my thoughts came within a hundred miles of a humorous aspect.'

'Always a most uncertain drug,' interrupted the doctor. 'We make very small use of it on that account.'

'At two o'clock in the morning I felt so hungry and tired that I decided to give up the experiment and wait no longer. I drank some milk and went upstairs to bed. I felt flat and disappointed. I fell asleep at once and must have slept for about an hour, when I awoke suddenly with a great noise in my ears. It was the noise of my own laughter! I was simply shaking with merriment. At first I was bewildered and thought I had been laughing in dreams, but a moment later I remembered the drug, and was delighted to think that after all I had got an effect. It had been working all along, only I had miscalculated the time. The only unpleasant thing *then* was an odd feeling that I had not waked naturally, but had been wakened by someone else—deliberately. This came to me as a certainty in the middle of my noisy laughter and distressed me.'

'Any impression who it could have been?' asked the doctor, now listening with close attention to every word, very much on the alert.

Pender hesitated and tried to smile. He brushed his hair from his forehead with a nervous gesture.

'You must tell me all your impressions, even your fancies; they are quite as important as your certainties.'

'I had a vague idea that it was someone connected with my forgotten dream, someone who had been at me in my sleep, someone of great strength and great ability—and I was certain too—a woman.'

'A good woman?' asked John Silence quietly.

Pender started a little at the question and his sallow face flushed; it seemed to surprise him. But he shook his head quickly with an indefinable look of horror.

'Evil,' he answered briefly, 'appallingly evil, and yet mingled with the sheer wickedness of it was also a certain perverseness—the perversity of the unbalanced mind.'

He hesitated a moment and looked up sharply at his interlocutor. A shade of suspicion showed itself in his eyes.

'No,' laughed the doctor, 'you need not fear that I'm merely humouring you, or think you mad. Far from it. Your story interests me exceedingly and you furnish me unconsciously with a number of clues as you tell it. You see, I possess some knowledge of my own as to these psychic byways.'

'I was shaking with such violent laughter,' continued the narrator, reassured in a moment, 'though with no clear idea what was amusing me, that I had the greatest difficulty in getting up for the matches, and was afraid I should frighten the servants overhead with my explosions. When the gas was lit I found the room empty, of course, and the door locked as usual. Then I half dressed and went out on to the landing, my hilarity better under control, and proceeded to go downstairs. I wished to record my sensations. I stuffed a handkerchief into my mouth so as not to scream aloud and communicate my hysterics to the entire household.'

'And the presence of this—this?'

'It was hanging about me all the time,' said Pender, 'but for the moment it seemed to have withdrawn. Probably, too, my laughter killed all other emotions.'

'And how long did you take getting downstairs?'

'I was just coming to that. I see you know all my "symptoms" in advance, as it were; for, of course, I thought I should never get to the bottom. Each step seemed to take five minutes, and crossing the narrow hall at the foot of the stairs—well, I could have sworn it was half an hour's journey had not my watch certified that it was a few seconds. Yet I walked fast and tried to push on. It was no good. I walked apparently without advancing, and at that rate it would have taken me a week to get down Putney Hill.'

'An experimental dose radically alters the scale of time and space sometimes—'

'But, when at last I got into my study and lit the gas, the change came horridly, and sudden as a flash of lightning. It was like a douche of icy water, and in the middle of this storm of laughter—'

'Yes; what?' asked the doctor, leaning forward and peering into his eyes.

'—I was overwhelmed with terror,' said Pender, lowering his reedy voice at the mere recollection of it.

He paused a moment and mopped his forehead. The scared, hunted look in his eyes now dominated the whole face. Yet, all the time, the corners of his mouth hinted of possible laughter as though the recollection of that merriment still amused him. The combination of fear and laughter in his face was very curious, and lent great conviction to his story; it also lent a bizarre expression of horror to his gestures.

'Terror, was it?' repeated the doctor soothingly.

'Yes, terror; for, though the Thing that woke me seemed to have gone, the memory of it still frightened me, and I collapsed into a chair. Then I locked the door and tried to reason with myself, but the drug made my movements so prolonged that it took me five minutes to reach the door, and another five to get back to the chair again. The laughter, too, kept bubbling up inside me—great wholesome laughter that shook me like gusts of wind—so that even my terror almost made me laugh. Oh, but I may tell you, Dr Silence, it was altogether vile, that mixture of fear and laughter, altogether vile!

'Then, all at once, the things in the room again presented their funny side to me and set me off laughing more furiously than ever. The bookcase was ludicrous, the arm-chair a perfect clown, the way the clock looked at me on the mantelpiece too comic for words; the arrangement of papers and inkstand on the desk tickled me till I roared and shook and held my sides and the tears streamed down my cheeks. And that footstool! Oh, that absurd footstool!'

He lay back in his chair, laughing to himself and holding up his hands at the thought of it, and at the sight of him Dr Silence laughed too.

'Go on, please,' he said, 'I quite understand. I know something myself of the hashish laughter.'

The author pulled himself together and resumed, his face growing quickly grave again.

'So, you see, side by side with this extravagant, apparently causeless merriment there was also an extravagant, apparently causeless terror. The drug produced the laughter, I knew; but what brought in the terror I could not imagine. Everywhere behind the fun lay the fear. It was terror masked by cap and bells; and I became the playground for two opposing emotions, armed and fighting to the death. Gradually, then, the impression grew in me that this fear was caused by the invasion—so you called it just now—of the "person" who had wakened me: she was utterly evil; inimical to my soul, or at least to all in me that wished for good. There I stood, sweating and trembling, laughing at everything in the room, yet all the while with this white terror mastering my heart. And this creature was putting—putting her—'

He hesitated again, using his handkerchief freely.

'Putting what?'

'—putting ideas into my mind,' he went on glancing nervously about the room. 'Actually tapping my thought-stream so as to switch off the usual current and inject her own. How mad that sounds! I know it, but it's true. It's the only way I can express it. Moreover, while the operation terrified me, the skill with which it was accomplished filled me afresh with laughter at the clumsiness of men by comparison. Our ignorant, bungling methods of teaching the minds of others, of inculcating ideas, and so on, overwhelmed me with laughter when I understood this superior and diabolical method. Yet my laughter seemed hollow and ghastly, and ideas of evil and tragedy trod close upon the heels of the comic. Oh, doctor, I tell you again, it was unnerving!'

John Silence sat with his head thrust forward to catch every word of the story which the other continued to pour out in nervous, jerky sentences and lowered voice.

'You saw nothing—no one—all this time?' he asked.

'Not with my eyes. There was no visual hallucination. But in my mind there began to grow the vivid picture of a woman—large, dark-skinned, with white teeth and masculine features, and one eye—the left—so drooping as to appear almost closed. Oh, such a face— !'

'A face you would recognize again?'

Pender laughed dreadfully.

'I wish I could forget it,' he whispered, 'I only wish I could forget it!' Then he sat forward in his chair suddenly, and grasped the doctor's hand with an emotional gesture.

'I must tell you how grateful I am for your patience and sympathy,' he cried, with a tremor in his voice, 'and—that you do not think me mad. I have told no one else a quarter of all this, and the mere freedom of speech—the relief of sharing my affliction with another—has helped me already more than I can possibly say.'

Dr Silence pressed his hand and looked steadily into the frightened eyes. His voice was very gentle when he replied.

'Your case, you know is very singular, but of absorbing interest to me,' he said, 'for it threatens, not your physical existence, but the temple of your psychical existence—the inner life. Your mind would not be permanently affected here and now, in this world; but in the existence after the body is left behind, you might wake up with your spirit so twisted, so distorted, so befouled, that you would be *spiritually insane*—a far more radical condition than merely being insane here.'

There came a strange hush over the room, and between the two men sitting there facing one another.

'Do you really mean—Good Lord!' stammered the author as soon as he could find his tongue.

'What I mean in detail will keep till a little later, and I need only say now that I should not have spoken in this way unless I were quite positive of being able to help you. Oh, there's no doubt as to that, believe me. In the first place, I am very familiar with the workings of this extraordinary drug, this drug which has had the chance effect of opening you up to the forces of another region; and, in the second, I have a firm belief in the reality of super-sensuous occurrences as well as considerable knowledge of psychic processes acquired by long and painful experiment. The rest is, or should be, merely sympathetic treatment and practical application. The hashish has partially opened another world to you by increasing your rate of psychical vibration, and thus rendering you abnormally sensitive. Ancient forces attached to this house have attacked you. For the moment I am only puzzled as to their precise nature; for were they of an ordinary character, I should myself be psychic enough to feel them. Yet I am conscious of feeling nothing as yet. But now, please continue, Mr Pender, and tell me the rest of your wonderful story; and when you have finished, I will talk about the means of cure.'

Pender shifted his chair a little closer to the friendly doctor and then went on in the same nervous voice with his narrative.

'After making some notes of my impressions I finally got upstairs again to bed. It was four o'clock in the morning. I laughed all the way up—at the grotesque banisters, the droll physiognomy of the staircase window, the burlesque grouping of the furniture, and the memory of that outrageous footstool in the room below; but nothing more happened to alarm or disturb me, and I woke late in the morning after a dreamless sleep, none the worse for my experiment except for a slight headache and a coldness of the extremities due to lowered circulation.'

'Fear gone, too?' asked the doctor.

'I seemed to have forgotten it, or at least ascribed it to mere nervousness. Its reality had gone, anyhow for the time, and all that day I wrote and wrote and wrote. My sense of laughter seemed wonderfully quickened and my characters acted without effort out of the heart of true humour. I was exceedingly pleased with the result of my experiment. But when the stenographer had taken her departure and I came to read over the pages she had typed out, I recalled her sudden glances of surprise and the odd way she had looked up at me while I was dictating. I was amazed at what I read and could hardly believe I had uttered it.'

'And why?'

'It was so distorted. The words were mine so far as I could remember, but the meanings seemed strange. It frightened me. The sense was so altered. At the very places where my characters were intended to tickle the ribs, only curious emotions of sinister amusement resulted. Dreadful innuendoes had managed to creep into the phrases. There was laughter of a kind, but it was bizarre, horrible, distressing; and my attempt at analysis only increased my dismay. The story, as it read then, made me shudder, for by virtue of these slight changes it had come somehow to hold the soul of horror, or horror disguised as merriment. The framework of humour was there, if you understand me, but the characters had turned sinister, and their laughter was evil.'

'Can you show me this writing?'

The author shook his head.

'I destroyed it,' he whispered. 'But in the end, though of course much perturbed about it, I persuaded myself that it was due to some after-effect of the drug, a sort of reaction that gave a twist to my mind and made me read macabre interpretations into words and situations that did not properly hold them.'

'And, meanwhile, did the presence of this person leave you?'

'No; that stayed more or less. When my mind was actively employed I forgot it, but when idle, dreaming, or doing nothing in particular, there she was beside me, influencing my mind horribly—'

'In what way, precisely?' interrupted the doctor.

'Evil, scheming thoughts came to me, visions of crime, hateful pictures of wickedness, and the kind of bad imagination that so far has been foreign, indeed impossible, to my normal nature—'

'The pressure of the Dark Powers upon the personality,' murmured the doctor, making a quick note.

'Eh? I didn't quite catch—'

'Pray go on. I am merely making notes; you shall know their purport fully later.'

'Even when my wife returned I was still aware of this Presence in the house; it associated itself with my inner personality in most intimate fashion; and outwardly I always felt oddly constrained to be polite and respectful towards it—to open doors, provide chairs and hold myself carefully deferential when it was about. It became very compelling at last, and, if I failed in any little particular, I seemed to know that it pursued me about the house from one room to another haunting my very soul in its inmost abode. It certainly came before my wife so far as my attentions were concerned.

'But, let me first finish the story of my experimental dose, for I took it again the third night, and underwent a very similar experience, delayed like the first in coming, and then carrying me off my feet when it did come with a rush of this false demon-laughter. This time, however, there was a reversal of the changed scale of space and time; it shortened instead of lengthened, so that I dressed and got downstairs in about twenty seconds, and the couple of hours I stayed and worked in the study passed literally like a period of ten minutes.'

'That is often true of an overdose,' interjected the doctor, 'and you may go a mile in a few minutes, or a few yards in a quarter of an hour. It is quite incomprehensible to those who have never experienced it, and is a curious proof that time and space are merely forms of thought.'

'This time,' Pender went on, talking more and more rapidly in his excitement, 'another extraordinary effect came to me, and I experienced a curious changing of the senses, so that I perceived external things through one large main sense-channel instead of through the five divisions known as sight, smell, touch, and so forth. You will, I know, understand me when I tell you that I *heard* sights and *saw* sounds. No language can make this comprehensible, of course, and I can only say, for instance, that the striking of the clock I saw as a visible picture in the air before me. I saw the sounds of the tinkling bell. And in precisely the same way I heard the colours in the room, especially the colours of those books in the shelf behind you. Those red bindings next to them made a shrill, piercing note not unlike the chattering of starlings. That brown bookcase muttered, and those green curtains opposite kept up a constant sort of rippling sound like the lower notes of a wood-horn. But I only was conscious of these sounds when I looked steadily at the different objects, and thought about them. The room, you understand, was not full of a chorus of notes; but when I concentrated my mind upon a colour, I heard, as well as saw, it.'

'That is a known, though rarely-obtained, effect of *Cannabis indica*,' observed the doctor. 'And it provoked laughter again, did it?'

'Only the muttering of the cupboard-bookcase made me laugh. It was so like a great animal trying to get itself noticed, and made me think of a performing bear—which is full of a kind of pathetic humour, you know. But this mingling of the senses produced no confusion in my brain. On the contrary, I was unusually clear-headed and experienced an intensification of consciousness, and felt marvellously alive and keen-minded.

'Moreover, when I took up a pencil in obedience to an impulse to sketch—a talent not normally mine—I found that I could draw nothing but heads, nothing, but one head—always the same—the head of a dark-skinned woman, with huge and terrible features and a very drooping left eye; and so well drawn, too, that I was amazed, as you may imagine—'

'And the expression of the face—?'

Pender hesitated a moment for words, casting about with his hands in the air and hunching his shoulders. A perceptible shudder ran over him.

'What I can only describe as—*blackness*,' he replied in a low tone; 'the face of a dark and evil soul.'

'You destroyed that, too?' queried the doctor sharply.

'No; I have kept the drawings,' he said, with a laugh, and rose to get them from a drawer in the writing-desk behind him.

'Here is all that remains of the pictures, you see,' he added, pushing a number of loose sheets under the doctor's eyes; 'nothing but a few scrawly lines. That's all I found the next morning. I had really drawn no heads at all—nothing but those lines and blots and wriggles. The pictures were entirely subjective, and existed only in my mind which constructed them out of a few wild strokes of the pen. Like the altered scale of space and time it was a complete delusion. These all passed, of course, with the passing of the drug's effects. But the other thing did not pass. I mean, the presence of that Dark Soul remained with me. It is here still. It is real. I don't know how I can escape from it.'

'It is attached to the house, not to you personally. You must leave the house.'

'Yes. Only I cannot afford to leave the house, for my work is my sole means of support, and—well, you see, since this change I cannot even write. They are horrible, these mirthless tales I now write, with their mockery of laughter, their diabolical suggestion. Horrible! I shall go mad if this continues.'

He screwed his face up and looked about the room as though he expected to see some haunting shape.

'The influence in this house, induced by my experiment, has killed in a flash, in a sudden stroke, the sources of my humour, and though I still go on writing funny tales—I have a certain name, you know—my inspiration has dried up, and much of what I write I have to burn—yes, doctor, to burn, before anyone sees it.'

'As utterly alien to your own mind and personality?'

'Utterly! As though someone else had written it—'

'Ah!'

'And shocking!' He passed his hand over his eyes a moment and let the breath escape softly through his teeth. 'Yet most damnably clever in the consummate way the vile suggestions are insinuated under cover of a kind of high drollery. My stenographer left me, of course—and I've been afraid to take another—'

John Silence got up and began to walk about the room leisurely without speaking; he appeared to be examining the pictures on the wall and reading the names of the books lying about. Presently he paused on the hearthrug, with his back to the fire, and turned to look his patient quietly in the eyes. Pender's face was gray and drawn; the hunted expression dominated it; the long recital had told upon him.

'Thank you, Mr Pender,' he said, a curious glow showing about his fine, quiet face, 'thank you for the sincerity and frankness of your account. But I think now there is nothing further I need ask you.' He indulged in a long scrutiny of the author's haggard features, drawing purposely the man's eyes to his own and then meeting them with a look of power and confidence calculated to inspire even the feeblest soul with courage. 'And to begin with,' he added, smiling pleasantly, 'let me assure you without delay that you need have no alarm, for you are no more insane or deluded than I myself am—'

Pender heaved a deep sigh and tried to return the smile.

'—and this is simply a case, so far as I can judge at present, of a very singular psychical invasion, and a very sinister one, too, if you perhaps understand what I mean—'

'It's an odd expression; you used it before, you know,' said the author wearily, yet eagerly listening to every word of the diagnosis, and deeply touched by the intelligent sympathy which did not at once indicate the lunatic asylum.

'Possibly,' returned the other, 'and an odd affliction too, you'll allow, yet one not unknown to the nations of antiquity, nor to those moderns, perhaps, who recognize the freedom of action under certain pathogenic conditions between this world and another.'

'And you think,' asked Pender hastily, 'that it is all primarily due to the *Cannabis?* There is nothing radically amiss with myself—nothing incurable, or—?'

'Due entirely to the overdose,' Dr Silence replied emphatically, 'to the drug's direct action upon your psychical being. It rendered you ultra-sensitive and made you respond to an increased rate of vibration. And, let me tell you, Mr Pender, that your experiment might have had results far more dire. It has brought you into touch with a somewhat singular class of Invisible, but of one, I think, chiefly human in character. You might, however, just as easily have been drawn out of human range altogether, and the results of such a contingency would have been exceedingly terrible. Indeed, you would not now be here to tell the tale. I need not alarm you on that score, but mention it as a warning you will not misunderstand or underrate after what you have been through.

'You look puzzled. You do not quite gather what I am driving at and it is not to be expected that you should, for you, I suppose are the nominal Christian with the nominal Christian's lofty standard of ethics, and his utter ignorance of spiritual possibilities. Beyond a somewhat childish understanding of "spiritual wickedness in high places," you probably have no conception of what is possible once you break down the slender gulf that is mercifully fixed between you and that Outer World. But my studies and training have taken me far outside these orthodox trips, and I have made experiments that I could scarcely speak to you about in language that would be intelligible to you.'

He paused a moment to note the breathless interest of Pender's face and manner. Every word he uttered was calculated; he knew exactly the value and effect of the emotions he desired to waken in the heart of the afflicted being before him.

'And from certain knowledge I have gained through various experiences,' he continued calmly, 'I can diagnose your case as I said before to be one of psychical invasion.'

'And the nature of this—er—invasion?' stammered the bewildered writer of humorous tales.

'There is no reason why I should not say at once that I do not yet quite know,' replied Dr Silence. 'I may first have to make one or two experiments—'

'On me?' gasped Pender, catching his breath.

'Not exactly,' the doctor said, with a grave smile, 'but with your assistance, perhaps. I shall want to test the conditions of the house—to ascertain, if possible, the character of the forces, of this strange personality that has been haunting you—'

'At present you have no idea exactly who—what—why—' asked the other in a wild flurry of interest, dread and amazement.

'I have a very good idea, but no proof rather,' returned the doctor. 'The effects of the drug in altering the scale of time and space, and merging the senses have nothing primarily to do with the invasion. They come to any one who is fool enough to take an experimental dose. It is the other features of your case that are unusual. You see, you are now in touch with certain violent emotions, desires, purposes, still active in this house, that were produced in the past by some powerful and evil personality that lived here. How long ago, or why they still persist so forcibly, I cannot positively say. But I should judge that they are merely forces acting automatically with the momentum of their terrific original impetus.'

'Not directed by a living being, a conscious will you mean?'

'Possibly not—but none the less dangerous on that account, and more difficult to deal with. I cannot explain to you in a few minutes the nature of such things, for you have not made the studies that would enable you to follow me; but I have reason to believe that on the dissolution at death of a human being, its forces may still persist and continue to act in a blind, unconscious fashion. As a rule they speedily dissipate themselves, but in the case of a very powerful personality they may last a long time. And, in some cases—of which I incline to think this is one—these forces may coalesce with certain non-human entities who thus continue their life indefinitely and increase their strength to an unbelievable degree. If the original personality was evil, the beings attracted to the left-over forces will also be evil. In this case, I think there has been an unusual and dreadful aggrandizement of the thoughts and purposes left behind long ago by a woman of consummate wickedness and great personal power of character and intellect. Now, do you begin to see what I am driving at a little?'

Pender stared fixedly at his companion, plain horror showing in his eyes. But he found nothing to say, and the doctor continued:

'In your case, predisposed by the action of the drug, you have experienced the rush of these forces in undiluted strength. They wholly obliterate in you the sense of humour, fancy, imagination—all that makes for cheerfulness and hope. They seek, though perhaps automatically only, to oust your own thoughts and establish themselves in their place. You are the victim of a psychical invasion. At the same time, you have become clairvoyant in the true sense. You are also a clairvoyant victim.'

Pender mopped his face and sighed. He left his chair and went over to the fireplace to warm himself.

'You must think me a quack to talk like this, or a madman,' laughed Dr Silence. 'But never mind that. I have come to help you, and I can help you if you will do what I tell you. It is very simple: you must leave this house at once. Oh, never mind the difficulties; we will deal with those together. I can place another house at your disposal, or I would take the lease here off your hands, and later have it pulled down. Your case interests me greatly, and I mean to see you through, so that you have no anxiety, and can drop back into your old groove of work tomorrow! The drug has provided you, and therefore me, with a short-cut to a very interesting experience. I am grateful to you.'

The author poked the fire vigorously, emotion rising in him like a tide. He glanced towards the door nervously.

'There is no need to alarm your wife or to tell her the details of our conversation,' pursued the other quietly. 'Let her know that you will soon be in possession again of your sense of humour and your health, and explain that I am lending you another house for six months. Meanwhile I may have the right to use this house for a night or two for my experiment. Is that understood between us?'

'I can only thank you from the bottom of my heart,' stammered Pender, unable to find words to express his gratitude.

Then he hesitated for a moment, searching the doctor's face anxiously.

'And your experiment with the house?' he said at length.

'Of the simplest character, my dear Mr Pender. Although I am myself an artificially trained psychic and consequently aware of the presence of discarnate entities as a rule, I have so far felt nothing here at all. This makes me sure that the forces acting here are of an unusual description. What I propose to do is to make an experiment with a view of drawing out this evil, coaxing it from its lair, so to speak, in order that it may *exhaust itself through me* and become dissipated for ever. I have already been inoculated,' he added; 'I consider myself to be immune.'

'Heavens above!' gasped the author, collapsing on to a chair.

'Hell beneath! might be a more appropriate exclamation,' the doctor laughed. 'But, seriously, Mr Pender, this is what I propose to do—with your permission.'

'Of course, of course,' cried the other, 'you have my permission and my best wishes for success. I can see no possible objection, but—'

'But what?'

'I pray to Heaven you will not undertake this experiment alone, will you?'

'Oh dear, no; not alone.'

'You will take a companion with good nerves, and reliable in case of disaster, won't you?'

'I shall bring two companions,' the doctor said.

'Ah, that's better. I feel easier. I am sure you must have among your acquaintances men who—'

'I shall not think of bringing men, Mr Pender.'

The other looked up sharply.

'No, or women either; or children.'

'I don't understand. Who will you bring, then?'

'Animals,' explained the doctor, unable to prevent a smile at his companion's expression of surprise—'two animals, a cat and a dog.'

Pender stared as if his eyes would drop out upon the floor, and then led the way without another word into the adjoining room where his wife was awaiting them for tea.

II

A few days later the humorist and his wife, with minds greatly relieved, moved into a small furnished house placed at their free disposal in another part of London; and John Silence, intent upon his approaching experiment, made ready to spend a night in the empty house on the top of Putney Hill. Only two rooms were prepared for occupation: the study on the ground floor and the bedroom immediately above it; all other doors were to be locked, and no servant was to be left in the house. The motor had orders to call for him at nine o'clock the following morning.

And, meanwhile, his secretary had instructions to look up the past history and associations of the place, and learn everything he could concerning the character of former occupants, recent or remote.

The animals, by whose sensitiveness he intended to test any unusual conditions in the atmosphere of the building, Dr Silence selected with care and judgment. He believed (and had already made curious experiments to prove it) that animals were more often, and more truly, clairvoyant than human beings. Many of them, he felt convinced, possessed powers of perception far superior to that mere keenness of the senses common to all dwellers in the wilds where the senses grow specially alert; they had what he termed 'animal clairvoyance,' and from his experiments with horses, dogs, cats, and even birds, he had drawn certain deductions, which, however, need not be referred to in detail here.

Cats, in particular, he believed, were almost continuously conscious of a larger field of vision, too detailed even for a photographic camera, and quite beyond the reach of normal human organs. He had, further, observed that while dogs were usually terrified in the presence of such phenomena, cats on the other hand were soothed and satisfied. They welcomed manifestations as something belonging peculiarly to their own region.

He selected his animals, therefore, with wisdom so that they might afford a differing test, each in its own way, and that one should not merely communicate its own excitement to the other. He took a dog and a cat.

The cat he chose, now full grown, had lived with him since kittenhood, a kittenhood of perplexing sweetness and audacious mischief. Wayward it was and fanciful, ever playing its own mysterious games in the corners of the room, jumping at invisible nothings, leaping sideways into the air and falling with tiny mocassined feet on to another part of the carpet, yet with an air of dignified earnestness which showed that the performance was necessary to its own well-being, and not done merely to impress a stupid human audience. In the middle of elaborate washing it would look up, startled, as though to stare at the approach of some Invisible, cocking its little head sideways and putting out a velvet pad to inspect cautiously. Then it would get absent-minded, and stare with equal intentness in another direction (just to confuse the onlookers), and suddenly go on furiously washing its body again, but in quite a new place. Except for a white patch on its breast it was coal black. And its name was—Smoke.

'Smoke' described its temperament as well as its appearance. Its movements, its individuality, its posing as a little furry mass of concealed mysteries, its elfin-like elusiveness, all combined to justify its name; and a subtle painter might have pictured it as a wisp of floating smoke, the fire below betraying itself at two points only—the glowing eyes.

All its forces ran to intelligence—secret intelligence, the wordless, incalculable intuition of the Cat. It was, indeed, *the* cat for the business in hand.

The selection of the dog was not so simple, for the doctor owned many; but after much deliberation he chose a collie, called Flame from his yellow coat. True, it was a trifle old, and stiff in the joints, and even beginning to grow deaf, but, on the other hand, it was a very particular friend of Smoke's, and had fathered it from kittenhood upwards so that a subtle understanding existed between them. It was this that turned the balance in its favour, this and its courage. Moreover, though good-tempered, it was a terrible fighter, and its anger when provoked by a righteous cause was a fury of fire, and irresistible.

It had come to him quite young, straight from the shepherd, with the air of the hills yet in its nostrils, and was then little more than skin and bones and teeth. For a collie it was sturdily built, its nose blunter than most, its yellow hair stiff rather than silky, and it had full eyes, unlike the slit eyes of its breed. Only its master could touch it, for it ignored strangers, and despised their pattings—when any dared to pat it. There was something patriarchal about the old beast. He was in earnest, and went through life with tremendous energy and big things in view, as though he had the reputation of his whole race to uphold. And to watch him fighting against odds was to understand why he was terrible.

In his relations with Smoke he was always absurdly gentle; also he was fatherly; and at the same time betrayed a certain diffidence or shyness. He recognised that Smoke called for strong yet respectful management. The cat's circuitous methods puzzled him, and his elaborate pretences perhaps shocked the dog's liking for direct, undisguised action. Yet, while he failed to comprehend these tortuous feline mysteries, he was never contemptuous or condescending; and he presided over the safety of his furry black friend somewhat as a father, loving but intuitive, might superintend the vagaries of a wayward and talented child. And, in return, Smoke rewarded him with exhibitions of fascinating and audacious mischief.

And these brief descriptions of their characters are necessary for the proper understanding of what subsequently took place.

With Smoke sleeping in the folds of his fur coat, and the collie lying watchful on the seat opposite, John Silence went down in his motor after dinner on the night of November 15th.

And the fog was so dense that they were obliged to travel at quarter speed the entire way.

It was after ten o'clock when he dismissed the motor and entered the dingy little house with the latchkey provided by Pender. He found the hall gas turned low, and a fire in the study. Books and food had also been placed ready by the servant according to instructions. Coils of fog rushed in after him through the opened door and filled the hall and passage with its cold discomfort.

The first thing Dr Silence did was to lock up Smoke in the study with a saucer of milk before the fire, and then make a search of the house with Flame. The dog ran cheerfully behind him all the way while he tried the doors of the other rooms to make sure they were locked. He nosed about into corners and made little excursions on his own account. His manner was expectant. He knew there must be something unusual about the proceeding, because it was contrary to the habits of his whole life not to be asleep at this hour on the mat in front of the fire. He kept looking up into his master's face, as door after door was tried, with an expression of intelligent sympathy, but at the same time a certain air of disapproval. Yet everything his master did was good in his eyes, and he betrayed as little impatience as possible with all this unnecessary journeying to and fro. If the doctor was pleased to play this sort of game at such an hour of the night, it was surely not for him to object. So he played it too; and was very busy and earnest about it into the bargain.

After an uneventful search they came down again to the study, and here Dr Silence discovered Smoke washing his face calmly in front of the fire. The saucer of milk was licked dry and clean; the preliminary examination that cats always make in new surroundings had evidently been satisfactorily concluded. He drew an arm-chair up to the fire, stirred the coals into a blaze, arranged the table and lamp to his satisfaction for reading, and then prepared surreptitiously to watch the animals. He wished to observe them carefully without their being aware of it.

Now, in spite of their respective ages, it was the regular custom of these two to play together every night before sleep. Smoke always made the advances, beginning with grave impudence to pat the dog's tail, and Flame played cumbrously, with condescension. It was his duty rather than pleasure; he was glad when it was over, and sometimes he was very determined and refused to play at all.

And this night was one of the occasions on which he was firm.

The doctor, looking cautiously over the top of his book, watched the cat begin the performance. It started by gazing with an innocent expression at the dog where he lay with nose on paws and eyes wide open in the middle of the floor. Then it got up and made as though it meant to walk to the door, going deliberately and very softly. Flame's eyes followed it until it was beyond the range of sight, and then the cat turned sharply and began patting his tail tentatively with one paw. The tail moved slightly in reply, and Smoke changed paws and tapped it again. The dog, however, did not rise to play as was his wont, and the cat fell to patting it briskly with both paws. Flame still lay motionless.

This puzzled and bored the cat, and it went round and stared hard into its friend's face to see what was the matter. Perhaps some inarticulate message flashed from the dog's eyes into its own little brain, making it understand that the programme for the night had better not begin with play. Perhaps it only realised that its friend was immovable. But, whatever the reason, its usual persistence thenceforward deserted it, and it made no further attempts at persuasion.

Smoke yielded at once to the dog's mood; it sat down where it was and began to wash.

But the washing, the doctor noted, was by no means its real purpose; it only used it to mask something else; it stopped at the most busy and furious moments and began to stare about the room. Its thoughts wandered absurdly. It peered intently at the curtains; at the shadowy corners; at empty space above; leaving its body in curiously awkward positions for whole minutes together. Then it turned sharply and stared with a sudden signal of intelligence at the dog, and Flame at once rose somewhat stiffly to his feet and began to wander aimlessly and restlessly to and fro about the floor. Smoke followed him, padding quietly at his heels. Between them they made what seemed to be a deliberate search of the room.

And, here, as he watched them, noting carefully every detail of the performance over the top of his book, yet making no effort to interfere, it seemed to the doctor that the first beginnings of a faint distress betrayed themselves in the collie, and in the cat the stirrings of a vague excitement.

He observed them closely. The fog was thick in the air, and the tobacco smoke from his pipe added to its density; the furniture at the far end stood mistily, and where the shadows congregated in hanging clouds under the ceiling, it was difficult to see clearly at all; the lamplight only reached to a level of five feet from the floor, above which came layers of comparative darkness, so that the room appeared twice as lofty as it actually was. By means of the lamp and the fire, however, the carpet was everywhere clearly visible.

The animals made their silent tour of the floor, sometimes the dog leading, sometimes the cat; occasionally they looked at one another as though exchanging signals; and once or twice, in spite of the limited space, he lost sight of one or other among the fog and the shadows. Their curiosity, it appeared to him, was something more than the excitement lurking in the unknown territory of a strange room; yet so far, it was impossible to test this, and he purposely kept his mind quietly receptive lest the smallest mental excitement on his part should communicate itself to the animals and thus destroy the value of their independent behaviour.

They made a very thorough journey, leaving no piece of furniture unexamined, or unsmelt. Flame led the way, walking slowly with lowered head, and Smoke followed demurely at his heels, making a transparent pretence of not being interested, yet missing nothing. And, at length, they returned, the old collie first, and came to rest on the mat before the fire. Flame rested his muzzle on his master's knee, smiling beatifically while he patted the yellow head and spoke his name; and Smoke, coming a little later, pretending he came by chance, looked from the empty saucer to his face, lapped up the milk when it was given him to the last drop, and then sprang upon his knees and curled round for the sleep it had fully earned and intended to enjoy.

Silence descended upon the room. Only the breathing of the dog upon the mat came through the deep stillness, like the pulse of time marking the minutes; and the steady drip, drip of the fog outside upon the window-ledges dismally testified to the inclemency of the night beyond. And the soft crashings of the coals as the fire settled down into the grate became less and less audible as the fire sank and the flames resigned their fierceness.

It was now well after eleven o'clock, and Dr Silence devoted himself again to his book. He read the words on the printed page and took in their meaning superficially, yet without starting into life the correlations of thought and suggestion that should accompany interesting reading. Underneath, all the while, his mental energies were absorbed in watching, listening, waiting for what might come. He was not over sanguine himself, yet he did not wish to be taken by surprise. Moreover, the animals, his sensitive barometers, had incontinently gone to sleep.

After reading a dozen pages, however, he realised that his mind was really occupied in reviewing the features of Pender's extraordinary story, and that it was no longer necessary to steady his imagination by studying the dull paragraphs detailed in the pages before him. He laid down his book accordingly, and allowed his thoughts to dwell upon the features of the Case. Speculations as to the meaning, however, he rigorously suppressed, knowing that such thoughts would act upon his imagination like wind upon the glowing embers of a fire.

As the night wore on the silence grew deeper and deeper, and only at rare intervals he heard the sound of wheels on the main road a hundred yards away, where the horses went at a walking pace owing to the density of the fog. The echo of pedestrian footsteps no longer reached him, the clamour of occasional voices no longer came down the side street. The night, muffled by fog, shrouded by veils of ultimate mystery, hung about the haunted villa like a doom. Nothing in the house stirred. Stillness, in a thick blanket, lay over the upper storeys. Only the mist in the room grew more dense, he thought, and the damp cold more penetrating. Certainly, from time to time, he shivered.

The collie, now deep in slumber, moved occasionally,—grunted, sighed, or twitched his legs in dreams. Smoke lay on his knees, a pool of warm, black fur, only the closest observation detecting the movement of his sleek sides. It was difficult to distinguish exactly where his head and body joined in that circle of glistening hair; only a black satin nose and a tiny tip of pink tongue betrayed the secret.

Dr Silence watched him, and felt comfortable. The collie's breathing was soothing. The fire was well built, and would burn for another two hours without attention. He was not conscious of the least nervousness. He particularly wished to remain in his ordinary and normal state of mind, and to force nothing. If sleep came naturally, he would let it come—and even welcome it. The coldness of the room, when the fire died down later, would be sure to wake him again; and it would then be time enough to carry these sleeping barometers up to bed. From various psychic premonitions he knew quite well that the night would not pass without adventure; but he did not wish to force its arrival; and he wished to remain normal, and let the animals remain normal, so that, when it came, it would be unattended by excitement or by any straining of the attention. Many experiments had made him wise. And, for the rest, he had no fear.

Accordingly, after a time, he did fall asleep as he had expected, and the last thing he remembered, before oblivion slipped up over his eyes like soft wool, was the picture of Flame stretching all four legs at once, and sighing noisily as he sought a more comfortable position for his paws and muzzle upon the mat.

It was a good deal later when he became aware that a weight lay upon his chest, and that something was pencilling over his face and mouth. A soft touch on the cheek woke him. Something was patting him.

He sat up with a jerk, and found himself staring straight into a pair of brilliant eyes, half green, half black. Smoke's face lay level with his own; and the cat had climbed up with its front paws upon his chest.

The lamp had burned low and the fire was nearly out, yet Dr Silence saw in a moment that the cat was in an excited state. It kneaded with its front paws into his chest, shifting from one to the other. He felt them prodding against him. It lifted a leg very carefully and patted his cheek gingerly. Its fur, he saw, was standing ridgewise upon its back; the ears were flattened back somewhat; the tail was switching sharply. The cat, of course, had wakened him with a purpose, and the instant he realised this, he set it upon the arm of the chair and sprang up with a quick turn to face the empty room behind him. By some curious instinct, his arms of their own accord assumed an attitude of defence in front of him, as though to ward off something that threatened his safety. Yet nothing was visible. Only shapes of fog hung about rather heavily in the air, moving slightly to and fro.

His mind was now fully alert, and the last vestiges of sleep gone. He turned the lamp higher and peered about him. Two things he became aware of at once: one, that Smoke, while excited, was *pleasurably* excited; the other, that the collie was no longer visible upon the mat at his feet. He had crept away to the corner of the wall farthest from the window, and lay watching the room with wide-open eyes, in which lurked plainly something of alarm.

Something in the dog's behaviour instantly struck Dr Silence as unusual, and, calling him by name, he moved across to pat him. Flame got up, wagged his tail, and came over slowly to the rug, uttering a low sound that was half growl, half whine. He was evidently perturbed about something, and his master was proceeding to administer comfort when his attention was suddenly drawn to the antics of his other four-footed companion, the cat.

And what he saw filled him with something like amazement.

Smoke had jumped down from the back of the arm-chair and now occupied the middle of the carpet, where, with tail erect and legs stiff as ramrods, it was steadily pacing backwards and forwards in a narrow space, uttering, as it did so, those curious little guttural sounds of pleasure that only an animal of the feline species knows how to make expressive of supreme happiness. Its stiffened legs and arched back made it appear larger than usual, and the black visage wore a smile of beatific joy. Its eyes blazed magnificently; it was in an ecstasy.

At the end of very few paces it turned sharply and stalked back again along the same line, padding softly, and purring like a roll of little muffled drums. It behaved precisely as though it were rubbing against the ankles of some one who remained invisible. A thrill ran down the doctor's spine as he stood and stared. His experiment was growing interesting at last.

He called the collie's attention to his friend's performance to see whether he too was aware of anything standing there upon the carpet, and the dog's behaviour was significant and corroborative. He came as far as his master's knees and then stopped dead, refusing to investigate closely. In vain Dr Silence urged him; he wagged his tail, whined a little, and stood in a half-crouching attitude, staring alternately at the cat and at his master's face. He was, apparently, both puzzled and alarmed, and the whine went deeper and deeper down into his throat till it changed into an ugly snarl of awakening anger.

Then the doctor called to him in a tone of command he had never known to be disregarded; but still the dog, though springing up in response, declined to move nearer. He made tentative motions, pranced a little like a dog about to take to water, pretended to bark, and ran to and fro on the carpet. So far there was no actual fear in his manner, but he was uneasy and anxious, and nothing would induce him to go within touching distance of the walking cat. Once he made a complete circuit, but always carefully out of reach; and in the end he returned to his master's legs and rubbed vigorously against him. Flame did not like the performance at all: that much was quite clear.

For several minutes John Silence watched the performance of the cat with profound attention and without interfering. Then he called to the animal by name.

'Smoke, you mysterious beastie, what in the world are you about?' he said, in a coaxing tone.

The cat looked up at him for a moment, smiling in its ecstasy, blinking its eyes, but too happy to pause. He spoke to it again. He called to it several times, and each time it turned upon him its blazing eyes, drunk with inner delight, opening and shutting its lips, its body large and rigid with excitement. Yet it never for one instant paused in its short journeys to and fro.

He noted exactly what it did: it walked, he saw, the same number of paces each time, some six or seven steps, and then it turned sharply and retraced them. By the pattern of the great roses in the carpet he measured it. It kept to the same direction and the same line. It behaved precisely as though it were rubbing against something standing there on that strip of carpet, something invisible to the doctor, something that alarmed the dog, yet caused the cat unspeakable pleasure.

'Smokie!' he called again, 'Smokie, you black mystery, what is it excites you so?'

Again the cat looked up at him for a brief second, and then continued its sentry-walk, blissfully happy, intensely preoccupied. And, for an instant, as he watched it, the doctor was aware that a faint uneasiness stirred in the depths of his own being, focusing itself for the moment upon this curious behaviour of the uncanny creature before him.

There rose in him quite a new realisation of the mystery connected with the whole feline tribe, but especially with that common member of it, the domestic cat—their hidden lives, their strange aloofness, their incalculable subtlety. How utterly remote from anything that human beings understood lay the sources of their elusive activities. As he watched the indescribable bearing of the little creature mincing along the strip of carpet under his eyes, coquetting with the powers of darkness, welcoming, maybe, some fearsome visitor, there stirred in his heart a feeling strangely akin to awe. Its indifference to human kind, its serene superiority to the obvious, struck him forcibly with fresh meaning; so remote, so inaccessible seemed the secret purposes of its real life, so alien to the blundering honesty of other animals. Its absolute poise of bearing brought into his mind the opium-eater's words that 'no dignity is perfect which does not at some point ally itself with the mysterious'; and he became suddenly aware that the presence of the dog in this foggy, haunted room on the top of Putney Hill was uncommonly welcome to him. He was glad to feel that Flame's dependable personality was with him. The savage growling at his heels was a pleasant sound. He was glad to hear it. That marching cat made him uneasy.

Finding that Smoke paid no further attention to his words, the doctor decided upon action. Would it rub against his leg, too? He would take it by surprise and see.

He stepped quickly forward and placed himself upon the exact strip of carpet where it walked.

But no cat is ever taken by surprise! The moment he occupied the space of the Intruder, setting his feet on the woven roses midway in the line of travel, Smoke suddenly stopped purring and sat down. It lifted up its face with the most innocent stare imaginable of its green eyes. He could have sworn it laughed. It was a perfect child again. In a single second it had resumed its simple, domestic manner; and it gazed at him in such a way that he almost felt Smoke was the normal being, and *his* was the eccentric behaviour that was being watched. It was consummate, the manner in which it brought about this change so easily and so quickly.

'Superb little actor!' he laughed in spite of himself, and stooped to stroke the shining black back. But, in a flash, as he touched its fur, the cat turned and spat at him viciously, striking at his hand with one paw. Then, with a hurried scutter of feet, it shot like a shadow across the floor and a moment later was calmly sitting over by the window-curtains washing its face as though nothing interested it in the whole world but the cleanness of its cheeks and whiskers.

John Silence straightened himself up and drew a long breath. He realised that the performance was temporarily at an end. The collie, meanwhile, who had watched the whole proceeding with marked disapproval, had now lain down again upon the mat by the fire, no longer growling. It seemed to the doctor just as though something that had entered he room while he slept, alarming the dog, yet bringing happiness to the cat, had now gone out again, leaving all as it was before. Whatever it was that excited its blissful attentions had retreated for he moment.

He realised this intuitively. Smoke evidently realised it, too, for presently he deigned to march back to the fireplace and jump upon his master's knees. Dr Silence, patient and determined, settled down once more to his book. The animals soon slept; the fire blazed cheerfully; and the cold fog from outside poured into the room through every available chink and crannie.

For a long time silence and peace reigned in the room and Dr Silence availed himself of the quietness to make careful notes of what had happened. He entered for future use in other cases an exhaustive analysis of what he had observed, especially with regard to the effect upon the two animals. It is impossible here, nor would it be intelligible to the reader unversed in the knowledge of the region known to a scientifically trained psychic like Dr Silence, to detail these observations. But to him it was clear, up to a certain point—and for the rest he must still wait and watch. So far, at least, he realised that while he slept in the chair—that is, while his will was dormant—the room had suffered intrusion from what he recognised as an intensely active Force, and might later be forced to acknowledge as something more than merely a blind force, namely, a distinct personality.

So far it had affected himself scarcely at all, but had acted directly upon the simpler organisms of the animals. It stimulated keenly the centres of the cat's psychic being, inducing a state of instant happiness (intensifying its consciousness probably in the same way a drug or stimulant intensifies that of a human being); whereas it alarmed the less sensitive dog, causing it to feel a vague apprehension and distress.

His own sudden action and exhibition of energy had served to disperse it temporarily, yet he felt convinced—the indications were not lacking even while he sat there making notes—that it still remained near to him, conditionally if not spatially, and was, as it were, gathering force for a second attack.

And, further, he intuitively understood that the relations between the two animals had undergone a subtle change: that the cat had become immeasurably superior, confident, sure of itself in its own peculiar region, whereas Flame had been weakened by an attack he could not comprehend and knew not how to reply to. Though not yet afraid, he was defiant—ready to act against a fear that he felt to be approaching. He was no longer fatherly and protective towards the cat. Smoke held the key to the situation; and both he and the cat knew it.

Thus, as the minutes passed, John Silence sat and waited, keenly on the alert, wondering how soon the attack would be renewed, and at what point it would be diverted from the animals and directed upon himself.

The book lay on the floor beside him, his notes were complete. With one hand on the cat's fur, and the dog's front paws resting against his feet, the three of them dozed comfortably before the hot fire while the night wore on and the silence deepened towards midnight.

It was well after one o'clock in the morning when Dr Silence turned the lamp out and lighted the candle preparatory to going up to bed. Then Smoke suddenly woke with a loud sharp purr and sat up. It neither stretched, washed nor turned: it listened. And the doctor, watching it, realised that a certain indefinable change had come about that very moment in the room. A swift readjustment of the forces within the four walls had taken place—a new disposition of their personal equations. The balance was destroyed, the former harmony gone. Smoke, most sensitive of barometers, had been the first to feel it, but the dog was not slow to follow suit, for on looking down he noted that Flame was no longer asleep. He was lying with eyes wide open, and that same instant he sat up on his great haunches and began to growl.

Dr Silence was in the act of taking the matches to re-light the lamp when an audible movement in the room behind made him pause. Smoke leaped down from his knee and moved forward a few paces across the carpet. Then it stopped and stared fixedly; and the doctor stood up on the rug to watch.

As he rose the sound was repeated, and he discovered that it was not in the room as he first thought, but outside, and that it came from more directions than one. There was a rushing, sweeping noise against the window-panes, and simultaneously a sound of something brushing against the door—out in the hall. Smoke advanced sedately across the carpet, twitching his tail, and sat down within a foot of the door. The influence that had destroyed the harmonious conditions of the room had apparently moved in advance of its cause. Clearly, something was about to happen.

For the first time that night John Silence hesitated; the thought of that dark narrow hall-way, choked with fog, and destitute of human comfort, was unpleasant. He became aware of a faint creeping of his flesh. He knew, of course, that the actual opening of the door was not necessary to the invasion of the room that was about to take place, since neither doors nor windows, nor any other solid barriers could interpose an obstacle to what was seeking entrance. Yet the opening of the door would be significant and symbolic, and he distinctly shrank from it.

But for a moment only. Smoke, turning with a show of impatience, recalled him to his purpose, and he moved past the sitting, watching creature, and deliberately opened the door to its full width.

What subsequently happened, happened in the feeble and flickering light of the solitary candle on the mantelpiece.

Through the opened door he saw the hall, dimly lit and thick with fog. Nothing, of course, was visible—nothing but the hat-stand, the African spears in dark lines upon the wall and the high-backed wooden chair standing grotesquely underneath on the oilcloth floor. For one instant the fog seemed to move and thicken oddly; but he set that down to the score of the imagination. The door had opened upon nothing.

Yet Smoke apparently thought otherwise, and the deep growling of the collie from the mat at the back of the room seemed to confirm his judgment.

For, proud and self-possessed, the cat had again risen to his feet, and having advanced to the door, was now ushering some one slowly into the room. Nothing could have been more evident. He paced from side to side, bowing his little head with great *empressement* and holding his stiffened tail aloft like a flagstaff. He turned this way and that, mincing to and fro, and showing signs of supreme satisfaction. He was in his element. He welcomed the intrusion, and apparently reckoned that his companions, the doctor and the dog, would welcome it likewise.

The Intruder had returned for a second attack.

Dr Silence moved slowly backwards and took up his position on the hearthrug, keying himself up to a condition of concentrated attention.

He noted that Flame stood beside him, facing the room, with body motionless, and head moving swiftly from side to side with a curious swaying movement. His eyes were wide open, his back rigid, his neck and jaws thrust forward, his legs tense and ready to leap. Savage, ready for attack or defence, yet dreadfully puzzled and perhaps already a little cowed, he stood and stared, the hair on his spine and sides positively bristling outwards as though a wind played through them. In the dim firelight he looked like a great yellow-haired wolf, silent, eyes shooting dark fire, exceedingly formidable. It was Flame, the terrible.

Smoke, meanwhile, advanced from the door towards the middle of the room, adopting the very slow pace of an invisible companion. A few feet away it stopped and began to smile and blink its eyes. There was something deliberately coaxing in its attitude as it stood there undecided on the carpet, clearly wishing to effect some sort of introduction between the Intruder and its canine friend and ally. It assumed its most winning manners, purring, smiling, looking persuasively from one to the other, and making quick tentative steps first in one direction and then in the other. There had always existed such perfect understanding between them in everything. Surely Flame would appreciate Smoke's intentions now, and acquiesce.

But the old collie made no advances. He bared his teeth, lifting his lips till the gums showed, and stood stockstill with fixed eyes and heaving sides. The doctor moved a little farther back, watching intently the smallest movement, and it was just then he divined suddenly from the cat's behaviour and attitude that it was not only a single companion it had ushered into the room, but *several*. It kept crossing over from one to the other, looking up at each in turn. It sought to win over the dog to friendliness with them all. The original Intruder had come back with reinforcements. And at the same time he further realised that the Intruder was something more than a blindly acting force, impersonal though destructive. It was a Personality, and moreover a great personality. And it was accompanied for the purposes of assistance by a host of other personalities, minor in degree, but similar in kind.

He braced himself in the corner against the mantelpiece and waited, his whole being roused to defence, for he was now fully aware that the attack had spread to include himself as well as the animals, and he must be on the alert. He strained his eyes through the foggy atmosphere, trying in vain to see what the cat and dog saw; but the candlelight threw an uncertain and flickering light across the room and his eyes discerned nothing. On the floor Smoke moved softly in front of him like a black shadow, his eyes gleaming as he turned his head, still trying with many insinuating gestures and much purring to bring about the introductions he desired.

But it was all in vain. Flame stood riveted to one spot, motionless as a figure carved in stone.

Some minutes passed, during which only the cat moved, and then there came a sharp change. Flame began to back towards the wall. He moved his head from side to side as he went, sometimes turning to snap at something almost behind him. *They* were advancing upon him, trying to surround him. His distress became very marked from now onwards, and it seemed to the doctor that his anger merged into genuine terror and became overwhelmed by it. The savage growl sounded perilously like a whine, and more than once he tried to dive past his master's legs, as though hunting for a way of escape. He was trying to avoid something that everywhere blocked the way.

This terror of the indomitable fighter impressed the doctor enormously; yet also painfully; stirring his impatience; for he had never before seen the dog show signs of giving in, and it distressed him to witness it. He knew, however, that he was not giving in easily, and understood that it was really impossible for him to gauge the animal's sensations properly at all. What Flame felt, and saw, must be terrible indeed to turn him all at once into a coward. He faced something that made him afraid of more than his life merely. The doctor spoke a few quick words of encouragement to him, and stroked the bristling hair. But without much success. The collie seemed already beyond the reach of comfort such as that, and the collapse of the old dog followed indeed very speedily after this.

And Smoke, meanwhile, remained behind, watching the advance, but not joining in it; sitting, pleased and expectant, considering that all was going well and as it wished. It was kneading on the carpet with its front paws—slowly, laboriously, as though its feet were dipped in treacle. The sound its claws made as they caught in the threads was distinctly audible. It was still smiling, blinking, purring.

Suddenly the collie uttered a poignant short bark and leaped heavily to one side. His bared teeth traced a line of whiteness through the gloom. The next instant he dashed past his master's legs, almost upsetting his balance, and shot out into the room, where he went blundering wildly against walls and furniture. But that bark was significant; the doctor had heard it before and knew what it meant: for it was the cry of the fighter against odds and it meant that the old beast had found his courage again. Possibly it was only the courage of despair, but at any rate the fighting would be terrific. And Dr Silence understood too, that he dared not interfere. Flame must fight his own enemies in his own way.

But the cat, too, had heard that dreadful bark; and it, too, had understood. This was more than it had bargained for. Across the dim shadows of that haunted room there must have passed some secret signal of distress between the animals. Smoke stood up and looked swiftly about him. He uttered a piteous meow and trotted smartly away into the greater darkness by the windows. What his object was only those endowed with the spirit-like intelligence of cats might know. But, at any rate, he had at last ranged himself on the side of his friend. And the little beast meant business.

At the same moment the collie managed to gain the door. The doctor saw him rush through into the hall like a flash of yellow light. He shot across the oilcloth, and tore up the stairs, but in another second he appeared again, flying down the steps and landing at the bottom in a tumbling heap, whining, cringing, terrified. The doctor saw him slink back into the room again and crawl round by the wall towards the cat. Was, then, even the staircase occupied? Did *They* stand also in the hall? Was the whole house crowded from floor to ceiling?

The thought came to add to the keen distress he felt at the sight of the collie's discomfiture. And, indeed, his own personal distress had increased in a marked degree during the past minutes, and continued to increase steadily to the climax. He recognised that the drain on his own vitality grew steadily, and that the attack was now directed against himself even more than against the defeated dog, and the too much deceived cat.

It all seemed so rapid and uncalculated after that—the events that took place in this little modern room at the top of Putney Hill between midnight and sunrise—that Dr Silence was hardly able to follow and remember it all. It came about with such uncanny swiftness and terror; the light was so uncertain; the movements of the black cat so difficult to follow on the dark carpet, and the doctor himself so weary and taken by surprise—that he found it almost impossible to observe accurately, or to recall afterwards precisely what it was he had seen or in what order the incidents had taken place. He never could understand what defect of vision on his part made it seem as though the cat had duplicated itself at first, and then increased indefinitely, so that there were at least a dozen of them darting silently about the floor, leaping softly on to chairs and tables, passing like shadows from the open door to the end of the room, all black as sin, with brilliant green eyes flashing fire in all directions. It was like the reflections from a score of mirrors placed round the walls at different angles. Nor could he make out at the time why the size of the room seemed to have altered, grown much larger, and why it extended away behind him where ordinarily the wall should have been. The snarling of the enraged and terrified collie sounded sometimes so far away; the ceiling seemed to have raised itself so much higher than before, and much of the furniture had changed in appearance and shifted marvellously.

It was all so confused and confusing, as though the little room he knew had become merged and transformed into the dimensions of quite another chamber, that came to him, with its host of cats and its strange distances, in a sort of vision.

But these changes came about a little later, and at a time when his attention was so concentrated upon the proceedings of Smoke and the collie, that he only observed them, as it were, subconsciously. And the excitement, the flickering candlelight, the distress he felt for the collie, and the distorting atmosphere of fog were the poorest possible allies to careful observation.

At first he was only aware that the dog was repeating his short dangerous bark from time to time, snapping viciously at the empty air, a foot or so from the ground. Once, indeed, he sprang upwards and forwards, working furiously with teeth and paws, and with a noise like wolves fighting, but only to dash back the next minute against the wall behind him. Then, after lying still for a bit, he rose to a crouching position as though to spring again, snarling horribly and making short half-circles with lowered head. And Smoke all the while meowed piteously by the window as though trying to draw the attack upon himself.

Then it was that the rush of the whole dreadful business seemed to turn aside from the dog and direct itself upon his own person. The collie had made another spring and fallen back with a crash into the corner, where he made noise enough in his savage rage to waken the dead before he fell to whining and then finally lay still. And directly afterwards the doctor's own distress became intolerably acute. He had made a half movement forward to come to the rescue when a veil that was denser than mere fog seemed to drop down over the scene, draping room, walls, animals and fire in a mist of darkness and folding also about his own mind. Other forms moved silently across the field of vision, forms that he recognised from previous experiments, and welcomed not. Unholy thoughts began to crowd into his brain, sinister suggestions of evil presented themselves seductively. Ice seemed to settle about his heart, and his mind trembled. He began to lose memory—memory of his identity, of where he was, of what he ought to do. The very foundations of his strength were shaken. His will seemed paralysed.

And it was then that the room filled with this horde of cats, all dark as the night, all silent, all with lamping eyes of green fire. The dimensions of the place altered and shifted. He was in a much larger space. The whining of the dog sounded far away, and all about him the cats flew busily to and fro, silently playing their tearing, rushing game of evil, weaving the pattern of their dark purpose upon the floor. He strove hard to collect himself and remember the words of power he had made use of before in similar dread positions where his dangerous practice had sometimes led; but he could recall nothing consecutively; a mist lay over his mind and memory; he felt dazed and his forces scattered. The deeps within were too troubled for healing power to come out of them.

It was glamour, of course, he realised afterwards, the strong glamour thrown upon his imagination by some powerful personality behind the veil; but at the time he was not sufficiently aware of this and, as with all true glamour, was unable to grasp where the true ended and the false began. He was caught momentarily in the same vortex that had sought to lure the cat to destruction through its delight, and threatened utterly to overwhelm the dog through its terror.

There came a sound in the chimney behind him like wind booming and tearing its way down. The windows rattled. The candle flickered and went out. The glacial atmosphere closed round him with the cold of death, and a great rushing sound swept by overhead as though the ceiling had lifted to a great height. He heard the door shut. Far away it sounded. He felt lost, shelterless in the depths of his soul. Yet still he held out and resisted while the climax of the fight came nearer and nearer. . . . He had stepped into the stream of forces awakened by Pender and he knew that he must withstand them to the end or come to a conclusion that it was not good for a man to come to. Something from the region of utter cold was upon him.

And then quite suddenly, through the confused mists about him, there slowly rose up the Personality that had been all the time directing the battle. Some force entered his being that shook him as the tempest shakes a leaf, and close against his eyes—clean level with his face—he found himself staring into the wreck of a vast dark Countenance, a countenance that was terrible even in its ruin.

For ruined it was, and terrible it was, and the mark of spiritual evil was branded everywhere upon its broken features. Eyes, face and hair rose level with his own, and for a space of time he never could properly measure, or determine, these two, a man and a woman, looked straight into each other's visages and down into each other's hearts.

And John Silence, the soul with the good, unselfish motive, held his own against the dark discarnate woman whose motive was pure evil, and whose soul was on the side of the Dark Powers.

It was the climax that touched the depth of power within him and began to restore him slowly to his own. He was conscious, of course, of effort, and yet it seemed no superhuman one, for he had recognised the character of his opponent's power, and he called upon the good within him to meet and overcome it. The inner forces stirred and trembled in response to his call. They did not at first come readily as was their habit, for under the spell of glamour they had already been diabolically lulled into inactivity, but come they eventually did, rising out of the inner spiritual nature he had learned with so much time and pain to awaken to life. And power and confidence came with them. He began to breathe deeply and regularly, and at the same time to absorb into himself the forces opposed to him, and to *turn them to his own account.* By ceasing to resist, and allowing the deadly stream to pour into him unopposed, he used the very power supplied by his adversary and thus enormously increased his own.

For this spiritual alchemy he had learned. He understood that force ultimately is everywhere one and the same; it is the motive behind that makes it good or evil; and his motive was entirely unselfish. He knew—provided he was not first robbed of self-control—how vicariously to absorb these evil radiations into himself and change them magically into his own good purposes. And, since his motive was pure and his soul fearless, they could not work him harm.

Thus he stood in the main stream of evil unwittingly attracted by Pender, deflecting its course upon himself; and after passing through the purifying filter of his own unselfishness these energies could only add to his store of experience, of knowledge, and therefore of power. And, as his self-control returned to him, he gradually accomplished this purpose, even though trembling while he did so.

Yet the struggle was severe, and in spite of the freezing chill of the air, the perspiration poured down his face. Then, by slow degrees, the dark and dreadful countenance faded, the glamour passed from his soul, the normal proportions returned to walls and ceiling, the forms melted back into the fog, and the whirl of rushing shadow-cats disappeared whence they came.

And with the return of the consciousness of his own identity John Silence was restored to the full control of his own will-power. In a deep, modulated voice he began to utter certain rhythmical sounds that slowly rolled through the air like a rising sea, filling the room with powerful vibratory activities that whelmed all irregularities of lesser vibrations in its own swelling tone. He made certain sigils, gestures and movements at the same time. For several minutes he continued to utter these words, until at length the growing volume dominated the whole room and mastered the manifestation of all that opposed it. For just as he understood the spiritual alchemy that can transmute evil forces by raising them into higher channels, so he knew from long study the occult use of sound, and its direct effect upon the plastic region wherein the powers of spiritual evil work their fell purposes. Harmony was restored first of all to his own soul, and thence to the room and all its occupants.

And, after himself, the first to recognise it was the old dog lying in his corner. Flame began suddenly uttering sounds of pleasure, that 'something' between a growl and a grunt that dogs make upon being restored to their master's confidence. Dr Silence heard the thumping of the collie's tail against the ground. And the grunt and the thumping touched the depth of affection in the man's heart, and gave him some inkling of what agonies the dumb creature had suffered.

Next, from the shadows by the window, a somewhat shrill purring announced the restoration of the cat to its normal state. Smoke was advancing across the carpet. He seemed very pleased with himself, and smiled with an expression of supreme innocence. He was no shadow-cat, but real and full of his usual and perfect self-possession. He marched along, picking his way delicately, but with a stately dignity that suggested his ancestry with the majesty of Egypt. His eyes no longer glared; they shone steadily before him; they radiated, not excitement, but knowledge. Clearly he was anxious to make amends for the mischief to which he had unwittingly lent himself owing to his subtle and electric constitution.

Still uttering his sharp high purrings he marched up to his master and rubbed vigorously against his legs. Then he stood on his hind feet and pawed his knees and stared beseechingly up into his face. He turned his head towards the corner where the collie still lay, thumping his tail feebly and pathetically.

John Silence understood. He bent down and stroked the creature's living fur, noting the line of bright blue sparks that followed the motion of his hand down its back. And then they advanced together towards the corner where the dog was.

Smoke went first and put his nose gently against his friend's muzzle, purring while he rubbed, and uttering little soft sounds of affection in his throat. The doctor lit the candle and brought it over. He saw the collie lying on its side against the wall; it was utterly exhausted, and foam still hung about its jaws. Its tail and eyes responded to the sound of its name, but it was evidently very weak and overcome. Smoke continued to rub against its cheek and nose and eyes, sometimes even standing on its body and kneading into the thick yellow hair. Flame replied from time to time by little licks of the tongue, most of them curiously misdirected.

But Dr Silence felt intuitively that something disastrous had happened, and his heart was wrung. He stroked the dear body, feeling it over for bruises or broken bones, but finding none. He fed it with what remained of the sandwiches and milk, but the creature clumsily upset the saucer and lost the sandwiches between its paws, so that the doctor had to feed it with his own hand. And all the while Smoke meowed piteously.

Then John Silence began to understand. He went across to the farther side of the room and called aloud to it.

'Flame, old man! come!'

At any other time the dog would have been upon him in an instant, barking and leaping to the shoulder. And even now he got up, though heavily and awkwardly, to his feet. He started to run, wagging his tail more briskly. He collided first with a chair, and then ran straight into a table. Smoke trotted close at his side, trying his very best to guide him. But it was useless. Dr Silence had to lift him up into his own arms and carry him like a baby. For he was blind.

III

It was a week later when John Silence called to see the author in his new house, and found him well on the way to recovery and already busy again with his writing. The haunted look had left his eyes, and he seemed cheerful and confident.

'Humour restored?' laughed the doctor, as soon as they were comfortably settled in the room overlooking the Park.

'I've had no trouble since I left that dreadful place,' returned Pender gratefully; 'and thanks to you——'

The doctor stopped him with a gesture.

'Never mind that,' he said, 'we'll discuss your new plans afterwards, and my scheme for relieving you of the house and helping you settle elsewhere. Of course it must be pulled down, for it's not fit for any sensitive person to live in, and any other tenant might be afflicted in the same way you were. Although, personally, I think the evil has exhausted itself by now.'

He told the astonished author something of his experiences in it with the animals.

'I don't pretend to understand,' Pender said, when the account was finished, 'but I and my wife are intensely relieved to be free of it all. Only I must say I should like to know something of the former history of the house. When we took it six months ago I heard no word against it.'

Dr Silence drew a typewritten paper from his pocket.

'I can satisfy your curiosity to some extent,' he said, running his eye over the sheets, and then replacing them in his coat; 'for by my secretary's investigations I have been able to check certain information obtained in the hypnotic trance by a "sensitive" who helps me in such cases. The former occupant who haunted you appears to have been a woman of singularly atrocious life and character who finally suffered death by hanging, after a series of crimes that appalled the whole of England and only came to light by the merest chance. She came to her end in the year 1798, for it was not this particular house she lived in, but a much larger one that then stood upon the site it now occupies, and was then, of course, not in London, but in the country. She was a person of intellect, possessed of a powerful, trained will, and of consummate audacity, and I am convinced availed herself of the resources of the lower magic to attain her ends. This goes far to explain the virulence of the attack upon yourself, and why she is still able to carry on after death the evil practices that formed her main purpose during life.'

'You think that after death a soul can still consciously direct——' gasped the author.

'I think, as I told you before, that the forces of a powerful personality may still persist after death in the line of their original momentum,' replied the doctor; 'and that strong thoughts and purposes can still react upon suitably prepared brains long after their originators have passed away.

'If you knew anything of magic,' he pursued, 'you would know that thought is dynamic, and that it may call into existence forms and pictures that may well exist for hundreds of years. For, not far removed from the region of our human life, is another region where floats the waste and drift of all the centuries, the limbo of the shells of the dead; a densely populated region crammed with horror and abomination of all descriptions, and sometimes galvanised into active life again by the will of a trained manipulator, a mind versed in the practices of lower magic. That this woman understood its vile commerce I am persuaded, and the forces she set going during her life have simply been accumulating ever since, and would have continued to do so had they not been drawn down upon yourself, and afterwards discharged and satisfied through me.

'Anything might have brought down the attack, for, besides drugs, there are certain violent emotions, certain moods of the soul, certain spiritual fevers, if I may so call them, which directly open the inner being to a cognisance of this astral region I have mentioned. In your case it happened to be a peculiarly potent drug that did it.

'But now, tell me,' he added, after a pause, handing to the perplexed author a pencil-drawing he had made of the dark countenance that had appeared to him during the night on Putney Hill—'tell me if you recognise this face?'

Pender looked at the drawing closely, greatly astonished. He shuddered a little as he looked.

'Undoubtedly,' he said, 'it is the face I kept trying to draw—dark, with the great mouth and jaw, and the drooping eye. That is the woman.'

Dr Silence then produced from his pocket-book an old-fashioned woodcut of the same person which his secretary had unearthed from the records of the Newgate Calendar. The woodcut and the pencil drawing were two different aspects of the same dreadful visage. The men compared them for some moments in silence.

'It makes me thank God for the limitations of our senses,' said Pender quietly, with a sigh; 'continuous clairvoyance must be a sore affliction.'

'It is indeed,' returned John Silence significantly, 'and if all the people nowadays who claim to be clairvoyant were really so, the statistics of suicide and lunacy would be considerably higher than they are. It is little wonder,' he added, 'that your sense of humour was clouded, with the mind-forces of that dead monster trying to use your brain for their dissemination. You have had an interesting adventure, Mr Felix Pender, and, let me add, a fortunate escape.'

The author was about to renew his thanks when there came a sound of scratching at the door, and the doctor sprang up quickly.

'It's time for me to go. I left my dog on the step, but I suppose——'

Before he had time to open the door, it had yielded to the pressure behind it and flew wide open to admit a great yellow-haired collie. The dog, wagging his tail and contorting his whole body with delight, tore across the floor and tried to leap up upon his owner's breast. And there was laughter and happiness in the old eyes; for they were clear again as the day.

Certainly the most dominant personality in occult circles at this period was the self-proclaimed 'Great Beast 666' and 'Master Therion', *Aleister Crowley* (1875-1947), now an international cult figure among the young who have seen him as a fore-runner of the 'Beats' and 'hippies'. Crowley, whose excesses of sex, mystical rites and drug-taking earned him the legend 'The Wickedest Man in the World' was, for all his showmanship, deeply versed in occultism and recorded in his diaries some of the most detailed and effective accounts of ritual magic (or 'Magick' as Crowley called it) written in modern times.

Born the child of strict Plymouth Brethren parents, he was a rebel against conformity and society virtually from his teens, a brilliant yet unstable student, and an indulger in physical and mental excesses from his university days. His first contact with the occultism which was to be the focus of his life, appears to have come while he was at Cambridge, and it was here, too, that he first experimented with opium and hashish and awakened the interest in stimulants which was to remain with him until his death. From university he joined The Hermetic Order of the Golden Dawn, which, apart from W. B. Yeats, numbered Arthur Machen and Dion Fortune among its members. However, this group very soon ceased to satisfy the restless Crowley who began to seek more exotic pleasures and experiments elsewhere. He was an inveterate traveller, sampling drugs and women in Europe, America, Mexico (where he first tried peyote), India and the Far East until he found his 'mission' in Cairo in 1904. Here, in the land where opium growing and usage had traditionally begun,[1] he proclaimed himself a Magus and said that his 'Holy Guardian Angel', a spirit called 'Aiwass', had dictated to him 'The Book of the Law' which contained 'the quintessence of my philosophy'. Crowley, as

[1] At the turn of the century, Egypt was the most popular centre for Europeans and Americans eager to 'discover' the pleasures and pains of opium. While the Egyptians themselves continued to smoke their hookahs with as little fuss as they had done for many generations, tourists flocked to the country, and Cairo in particular, to sample the drug. Part of this attraction

has been indicated, saw himself as a rebel against all the standards of his time, and in this book formulated his objective in the resounding phrase, 'Do What Thou Wilt Shall Be The Whole Of The Law.' For his 'work' he then proceeded to indulge himself in sex and drugs, linking them to his search for occult secrets, and recording the results in the books which have subsequently been published by his literary executor John Symonds as *The Magical Record of the Beast 666* and *The Confessions of Aleister Crowley.*

He took hashish, opium, ether, heroin, cocaine and peyote and firmly believed he could control any of their effects with his mind. 'The action of hashish is as varied as life itself,' he wrote in 1920, 'and seems to be determined almost entirely by the will or mood of the "assassin" and that within the hedges of his mental and moral form. I can get fantastic visions, or power of mind-analysis, or spiritual exaltation, or sexual excitement of various kinds, or ravenous hunger, or vigour of imagination, whichever I please, absolutely at will, on a minute dose of the Parke Davis extract. This is simply because I have discovered the theory and perfected the practice of the instrument.' He believed, too, in combining certain of the drugs such as morphine and heroin for re-doubled effect and advanced his own estimation of drug-taking as a whole: 'The "drug-fiend" is the result of an attempt of men to progress on lines which have not been prepared by centuries of variation and selection. I cannot doubt that he is momentarily at least an advance on the normal man; and I think he does it, as a magician would say, by "invoking one of his 'spirits'". He concentrates upon and calls forth, certain sections of his brain, while he quiets the rest.' Crowley endeavoured to expand this philosophy in 1922 in a novel, *The Diary of a Drug Fiend,* and from its sensational pages ('Full of base and bestial horrors', the *Sunday Express* said) grew the beginnings of his legend.

At this time he had created a community of followers in Sicily. There all of them indulged in sex and drug orgies until the authorities finally deported them, after rumours began to grow about the practise of Black Magic and human sacrifice. Back in England, Crowley declined rapidly into old age, still writing constantly of his experiences

was undoubtedly caused by the strange and bizarre stories which were told of opium and the other stimulants and which are to be found in abundance in much of the popular fiction and travel books of the late nineteenth and early twentieth century. The rich, the jaded, the seekers-after-excitement, all flocked to the Middle East in search of something new and the Egyptians were often happy to oblige in the contrived manner now often demonstrated by the Spaniards with some of their bullfights—a taste of danger without actual involvement. But, nonetheless, real danger did lurk just beneath the surface and opium and hashish 'addicts' were as real in Egypt as anywhere else in the world.

but wracked by pain and dependent on heroin to the extent of seven or eight grains a day. Much of Crowley's later work reflects his interest in the famous drug-writers, and he constantly refers to Coleridge, Poe and Baudelaire as 'the pioneers of the drug road to heaven'. In one diary entry he noted: 'Their achievements should encourage us, their errors warn us; but we should aim to improve on their crude engines, trim their unstable balance, guard against repetition of their accidents, instead of abusing them, persecuting their successors, denying the possibility of their machine, treating the whole affair as "shocking" or "wicked" and "immoral".'

Much that Crowley wrote was obviously influenced by, if not actually written under, the effects of the drugs he took. One might note particularly 'The Opium Pipe', inspired by Claud Farrère's novel, *Fumées d'Opium*, his cocaine poem 'Graymalkin' and the heroin essay, 'Liber Jugorum: An Instruction for the Control of Speech, Action and Thought'. 'The Stratagem' is perhaps the most interesting of all his short stories, however, and Crowley himself has recorded how it came to be written in his 'Confessions': 'I must mention one incident of my workings as being of general interest, outside technical Magick. During the operation I had a bad attack of influenza which settled down to very severe bronchitis. I was visited one evening by an old friend of mine and her young man, who very kindly and sensibly suggested that I should find relief if I smoked a few pipes of opium. They accordingly brought the apparatus from their apartment and we began. (Opium by the way is sacred to Jupiter, and to *Chesed,* Mercy, as being sovereign against pain, and also as enabling the soul to free itself from its gross integument and realise its majesty.) My bronchitis vanished; I went off to sleep; my guests retiring without waking me. In my sleep I dreamt; and when I awoke the dream remained absolutely perfect in my consciousness, down to the minutest details. It was a story, a subtle exposure of English stupidity, set in a framework of the craziest and most fantastically gorgeous workmanship. Ill as I was, I jumped out of bed and wrote down the story offhand. I called it "The Stratagem". No doubt it was inspired by Jupiter, for it was the first short story that I had ever written which was accepted at once. More : I was told—and nothing in my life ever made me prouder—that Joseph Conrad said it was the best short story he had read in ten years.'

*

I have tried the hashish life, the opium life, the cocaine life, the ether life, the heroin life, none of them has held me for a moment or interfered with any of the other lives.

Diary entry, 1920

The Stratagem
ALEISTER CROWLEY

The fellow-travellers climbed down on to the fiery sand of the platform. It was a junction, a junction of that kind where there is no town for miles, and where the resources of the railway and its neighbourhood compare unfavourably with those of the average quarantine station.

The first to descend was a man unmistakably English. He was complaining of the management even while he extracted his hand-baggage from the carriage with the assistance of his companion. 'It is positively a disgrace to civilisation,' he was saying, 'that there should be no connection at such a station as this, an important station, sir, let me tell you, the pivot—if I may use the metaphor—of the branch which serves practically the whole of Muckshire south of the Tream. And we have certainly one hour to wait, and Heaven knows it's more likely to be two, and perhaps three. And, of course, there's not as much as a bar nearer than Fatloam; and if we got there we should find no drinkable whisky. I say, sir, the matter is a positive and actual disgrace to the railway that allows it, to the country that tolerates it, to the civilisation that permits that such things should be. The same thing happened to me here last year, sir, though luckily on that occasion I had but half-an-hour to wait. But I wrote to *The Times* a strong half-column letter on the subject, and I'm damned if they didn't refuse to print it. Of course, our independent press, etc.; I might have known. I tell you, sir, this country is run by a ring, a dirty ring, a gang of Jews, Scotchmen, Irish, Welsh—where's the good old jolly True Blue Englishman? In the cart, sir, in the cart.'

The train gave a convulsive backward jerk, and lumbered off in imitation of the solitary porter who, stationed opposite the guard's van, had witnessed without emotion the hurling forth of two trunks like rocks from a volcano, and after a moment's contemplation had, with screwed mouth, mooched along the platform to his grub, which he would find in an isolated cottage some three hundred yards away.

In strong contrast to the Englishman, with his moustache afforesting a whitish face, marked with deep red rings on neck and forehead, his impending paunchiness and his full suit of armour, was the small, active man with the pointed beard whom fate had thrown first into the same compartment, and then into the same hour of exile from all their fellows.

His eyes were astonishingly black and fierce; his beard was grizzled and his face heavily lined and obviously burnt by tropical suns; but that face also expressed intelligence, strength, and resourcefulness in a degree which would have made him an ideal comrade in a forlorn hope, or the defence of a desperate village. Across the back of his left hand was a thick and heavy scar. In spite of all this, he was dressed with singular neatness and correctness; which circumstance, although his English was purer than that of his companion in distress, made the latter secretly incline to suspect him of being a Frenchman. In spite of the quietness of his dress and the self-possession of his demeanour, the sombre glitter of those black eyes, pin-points below shaggy eyebrows, inspired the large man with a certain uneasiness. Not at all a chap to quarrel with, was his thought. However, being himself a widely-travelled man—Boulogne, Dieppe, Paris, Switzerland, and even Venice—he had none of that insularity of which foreigners accuse some Englishmen, and he had endeavoured to make conversation during the journey. The small man had proved a poor companion, taciturn to a fault, sparing of words where a nod would satisfy the obligations of courtesy, and seemingly fonder of his pipe than of his fellow-man. A man with a secret, thought the Englishman.

The train had jolted out of the station and the porter had faded from the landscape. 'A deserted spot,' remarked the Englishman, whose name was Bevan, 'especially in such fearful heat. Really, in the summer of 1911, it was hardly as bad. Do you know, I remember once at Boulogne——' He broke off sharply, for the brown man, sticking the ferrule of his stick repeatedly in the sand, and knotting his brows came suddenly to a decision. 'What do you know of heat?' he cried, fixing Bevan with the intensity of a demon. 'What do you know of desolation?' Taken aback, as well he might be, Bevan was at a loss to reply. 'Stay,' cried the other. 'What if I told you my story? There is no one here but ourselves.' He glared menacingly at Bevan, seemed to seek to read his soul. 'Are you a man to be trusted?' he barked, and broke off short.

At another time Bevan would most certainly have declined to become the confidant of a stranger; but here the solitude, the heat, not a little boredom induced by the previous manner of his companion, and even a certain mistrust of how he might take a refusal, combined to elicit a favourable reply.

Stately as an oak, Bevan answered, 'I was born an English gentleman, and I trust that I have never done anything to derogate from that estate.' 'I am a Justice of the Peace,' he added after a momentary pause.

'I knew it,' cried the other excitedly. 'The trained legal mind is that of all others which will appreciate my story. Swear, then,' he went on with sudden gravity, 'swear that you will never whisper to any living soul the smallest word of what I am about to tell you. Swear by the soul of your dead mother.'

'My mother is alive,' returned Bevan.

'I knew it,' exclaimed his companion, a great and strange look of god-like pity illuminating his sunburnt face. It was such a look as one sees upon many statues of Buddha, a look of divine, of impersonal compassion.

'Then swear by the Lord Chancellor.'

Bevan was more than ever persuaded that the stranger was a Frenchman. However, he readily gave the required promise.

'My name,' said the other, 'is Duguesclin. Does that tell you my story?' he asked impressively. 'Does that convey anything to your mind?'

'Nothing at all.'

'I knew it,' said the man from the tropics. 'Then I must tell you all. In my veins boils the fiery blood of the greatest of the French warriors, and my mother was the lineal descendant of the Maid of Saragossa.'

Bevan was startled, and showed it.

'After the siege, sir, she was honourably married to a nobleman,' snapped Duguesclin. 'Do you think a man of my ancestry will permit a stranger to lift the shadow of an eyebrow against the memory of my great-grandmother?'

The Englishman protested that nothing had been further from his thoughts.

'I suppose so,' proceeded the other more quietly, 'And the more, perhaps, that I am a convicted murderer.'

Bevan was now fairly alarmed.

'I am proud of it,' continued Duguesclin. 'At the age of twenty-five my blood was more fiery than it is to-day. I married. Four years later I found my wife in the embraces of a neighbour. I slew him. I slew her. I slew our three children, for vipers breed only vipers. I slew the servants; they were accomplices of the adultery; or if not, they should at any rate not witness their master's shame. I slew the gendarmes who came to take me—servile hirelings of a corrupt republic. I set my castle on fire, determined to perish in the ruins. Unfortunately, a piece of masonry, falling, struck me on the arm. My rifle dropped. The accident was seen, and I was rescued by the firemen. I determined to live; it was my duty to my ancestors to continue the family of which I was the sole direct scion. It is in search of a wife that I am travelling in England.'

He paused, and gazed proudly on the scenery, with the air of a Selkirk. Bevan suppressed the obvious comment on the surprising termination of the Frenchman's narrative. He only remarked, 'Then you were not guillotined?'

'I was not, sir,' retorted the other passionately. 'At that time capital punishment was never inflicted in France, though not officially abrogated. I may say,' he added, with the pride of a legislator, 'that my action lent considerable strength to the agitation which led to its re-introduction.

'No, sir, I was not guillotined. I was sentenced to perpetual imprisonment in Devil's Island.' He shuddered. 'Can you imagine that accursed Isle? Can your fancy paint one tithe of its horror? Can nightmare itself shadow that inferno, that limbo of the damned? My language is strong, sir; but no language can depict that hell. I will spare you the description. Sand, vermin, crocodiles, venomous snakes, miasma, mosquitoes, fever, filth, toil, jaundice, malaria, starvation, foul undergrowth, weedy swamps breathing out death, hideous and bloated trees of poison, themselves already poisoned by their earth, heat unendurable, insufferable, intolerable, unbearable (as the *Daily Telegraph* said at the time of the Dreyfus case), heat continuous and stifling, no breeze but the pestilential stench of the lagoon, heat that turned the skin into a raging sea of irritation to which the very stings of the mosquitoes and centipedes came as a relief, the interminable task of the day beneath the broiling sun, the lash on every slightest infraction of the harsh prison rules, or even of the laws of politeness toward our warders, men only one degree less damned than we ourselves—all this was nothing. The only amusement of the governors of such a place is cruelty; and their own discomfort makes them more ingenious than all the inquisitors of Spain, than Arabs in their religious frenzy, than Burmans and Kachens and Shans in their Buddhist hatred of all living men, than even the Chinese in their cold lust of cruelty. The governor was a profound psychologist; no corner of the mind that he did not fathom, so as to devise a means of twisting it to torture.

'I remember one of us who took pleasure in keeping his spade bright —it was the regulation that spades must be kept bright, a torture in itself in such a place, where mildew grows on everything as fast almost as snow falls in happier climates. Well, sir, the governor found out that this man took a pleasure in the glint of the sun on the steel, and he forbade that man to clean his spade. A trifle, indeed. What do you know of what prisoners think of trifles? The man went raving mad, and for no other reason. It seemed to him that such detailed refinement of cruelty was a final proof of the innate and inherent devilishness of the universe. Insanity is the logical consequence of such a faith. No sir, I will spare you the description.'

Bevan thought that there had already been too much description, and in his complacent English way surmised that Duguesclin was exaggerating, as he was aware that Frenchmen did. But he only remarked that it must have been terrible. He would have given a good deal, now, to have avoided the conversation. It was not altogether nice to be on a lonely platform with a self-confessed multiple murderer, who had presumably escaped only by a further and extended series of crimes.

'But you ask,' pursued Duguesclin, 'you ask how I escaped? That, sir, is the story I propose to tell you. My previous remarks have been but preliminary; they have no pertinence or interest, I am aware; but they were necessary, since you so kindly expressed interest in my personality, my family history — heroic (I may claim it) as is the one, and tragic (no one will deny it) as is the other.'

Bevan again reflected that his interlocutor must be as bad a psychologist as the governor of Devil's Island was a good one; for he had neither expressed nor felt the slightest concern with either of these matters.

'Well, sir, to my story! Among the convicts there was one universal pleasure, a pleasure that could cease only with life or with the empire of the reason, a pleasure that the governor might (and did) indeed restrict, but could not take away. I refer to hope—the hope of escape. Yes, sir, that spark (alone of all its ancient fires) burnt in this breast—and in that of my fellow-convicts. And in this I did not look so much to myself as to another. I am not endowed with any great intellect,' he modestly pursued, 'my grandmother was pure English, a Higginbotham, one of the Warwickshire Higginbothams (what has that to do with his stupidity? thought Bevan) and the majority of my companions were men not only devoid of intelligence, but of education. The one pinnacled exception was the great Dodu—ha! you start?' Bevan had not done anything of the sort; he had continued to exhibit the most stolid indifference to the story.

'Yes, you are not mistaken; it was indeed the world-famous philosopher, the discoverer of Dodium, rarest of known elements, supposed only to exist in the universe to the extent of the thirty-thousand and fifth part of a milligramme, and that in the star called Pegasi; it was Dodu who has shattered the logical process of obversion, and reduced the quadrangle of oppositions to the condition of the British square at Abu-Klea. So much you know; but this perhaps you did not know, that, although a civilian, he was the greatest strategist of France. It was he who in his cabinet made the dispositions of the armies of the Ardennes; and the 1890 scheme of the fortifications of Lunéville was due to his genius alone. For this reason the Government were loth to condemn him, though public opinion revolted bitterly against his crime. You remember that, having proved that women after the age of fifty were a useless burden to the State, he had demonstrated his belief by decapitating and devouring his widowed mother. It was consequently the intention of the Government to connive at his escape on the voyage, and to continue to employ him under an assumed name in a flat in an entirely different quarter of Paris. However, the Government fell suddenly; a rival ousted him, and his sentence was carried out with as much severity as if he had been a common criminal.

'It was to such a man (naturally) that I looked to devise a plan for our escape. But rack my brains as I would—my grandmother was a Warwickshire Higginbotham—I could devise no means of getting into touch with him. He must, however, have divined my wishes; for, one day after he had been about a month upon the island (I had been there seven months myself) he stumbled and fell as if struck by the sun at a moment when I was close to him. And as he lay upon the ground he managed to pinch my ankle three times. I caught his glance—he hinted rather than gave me the sign of recognition of the fraternity of Freemasons. Are you a Mason?'

'I am Past Provincial Deputy Grand Sword-Bearer of this province,' returned Bevan. 'I founded Lodge 14,883, "Boetic" and Lodge 17,212, "Colenso." And I am Past Grand Haggai in my Provincial Grand Chapter.'

'I knew it!' exclaimed Duguesclin enthusiastically.

Bevan began to dislike this conversation exceedingly. Did this man —this criminal—know who he was? He knew he was a J.P., that his mother was alive, and now his Masonic dignities. He distrusted this Frenchman more and more. Was the story but a pretext for the demand of a loan? The stranger looked prosperous and had a first class ticket. More likely a blackmailer; perhaps he knew of other things—say that affair at Oxford—or the incident of the Edgware Road—or the matter of Esmé Holland. He determined to be more than ever on his guard.

'You will understand with what joy,' continued Duguesclin, innocent or careless of the sinister thoughts which occupied his companion, 'I received and answered this unmistakable token of friendship. That day no further opportunity of intercourse occurred, but I narrowly watched him on the morrow, and saw that he was dragging his feet in an irregular way. Ha! thought I, a drag for long, an ordinary pace for short. I imitated him eagerly, giving the Morse letter A. His alert mind grasped instantly my meaning; he altered his code (which had been of a different order) and replied with a Morse B on my own system. I answered C; he returned D. From that moment we could talk fluently and freely as if we were on the terrace of the Café de la Paix in our beloved Paris. However, conversation in such circumstances is a lengthy affair. During the whole march to our work he only managed to say, "Escape soon—please God." Before his crime he had been an atheist. I was indeed glad to find that punishment had brought repentance.'

Bevan himself was relieved. He had carefully refrained from admitting the existence of a French Freemason; that one should have repented filled him with a sense of almost personal triumph. He began to like Duguesclin, and to believe in him. His wrong had been hideous; if his vengeance seemed excessive and even indiscriminate, was not he a Frenchman? Frenchmen do these things! And after all Frenchmen were men. Bevan felt a great glow of benevolence; he remembered that he was not only a man, but a Christian. He determined to set the stranger at his ease.

'Your story interests me intensely,' said he. 'I sympathise deeply with you in your wrongs and in your sufferings. I am heartily thankful that you have escaped, and I beg of you to proceed with the narration of your adventures.'

Duguesclin needed no such encouragement. His attitude, from that of the listless weariness with which he had descended from the train, had become animated, sparkling, fiery; he was carried away by the excitement of his passionate memories.

'On the second day Dodu was able to explain his mind. "If we escape, it must be by a stratagem," he signalled. It was an obvious remark; but Dodu had no reason to think highly of my intelligence. "By a stratagem," he repeated with emphasis.

' "I have a plan," he continued. "It will take twenty-three days to communicate, if we are not interrupted; between three and four months to prepare; two hours and eight minutes to execute. It is theoretically possible to escape by air, by water, or by earth. But as we are watched day and night, it would be useless to try to drive a tunnel to the mainland; we have no aeroplanes or balloons, or means of making them. But if we could once reach the water's edge, which we must do in whatever direction we set out if we only keep in a straight line, and if we can find a boat unguarded, and if we can avoid arousing the alarm, then we have merely to cross the sea, and either find a land where we are unknown, or disguise ourselves and our boat and return to Devil's Island as shipwrecked mariners. The latter idea would be foolish. You will say that the Governor would know that Dodu would not be such a fool; but more, he would know also that Dodu would not be such a fool as to try to take advantage of that circumstance; and he would be right, curse him!"

'It implies the intensest depth of feeling to curse in the Morse code with one's feet—ah! how we hated him.

'Dodu explained to me that he was telling me these obvious things for several reasons: (1) to gauge my intelligence by my reception of them; (2) to make sure that if we failed it should be by my stupidity and not by his neglect to inform me of every detail; (3) because he had acquired the professorial habit as another man might have the gout.

'Briefly, however, this was his plan; to elude the guards, make for the coast, capture a boat, and put to sea. Do you understand? Do you get the idea?'

Bevan replied that it seemed to him the only possible plan.

'A man like Dodu,' pursued Duguesclin, 'takes nothing for granted. He leaves no precaution untaken; in his plans, if chance be an element, it is an element whose value is calculated to twenty-eight places of decimals.

'But hardly had he laid down these bold outlines of his scheme when interruption came. On the fourth day of our intercourse he signalled only "Wait. Watch me!" again and again.

'In the evening he manœuvred to get to the rear of the line of convicts, and only then dragged out "There is a traitor, a spy. Henceforth I must find a new means of communicating the details of my plan. I have thought it all out. I shall speak in a sort of rebus, which not even you will be able to understand unless you have all the pieces —and the key. Mind you engrave upon your memory every word I say."

'The following day: "Do you remember the taking of the old mill by the Prussians in '70? My difficulty is that I must give you the skeleton of the puzzle, which I can't do in words. But watch the line of my spade and my heelmarks, and take a copy."

'I did this with the utmost minuteness of accuracy and obtained this figure. At my autopsy,' said Duguesclin, dramatically, 'this should be found engraved upon my heart.'

He drew a notebook from his pocket, and rapidly sketched the subjoined figure for the now interested Bevan.

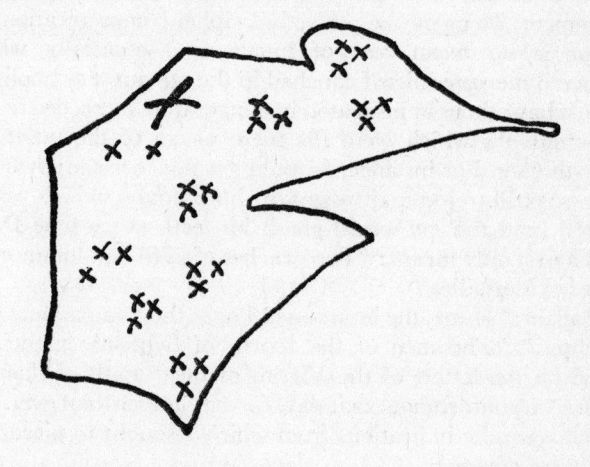

'You will note that the figure has eight sides, and that twenty-seven crosses are disposed in groups of three, while in one corner is a much larger and thicker cross and two smaller crosses not so symmetrical. This group represents the element of chance; and you will at least gain a hint of the truth if you reflect that eight is the cube of two, and twenty-seven of three.'

Bevan looked intelligent.

'On the return march,' continued Duguesclin, 'Dodu said, "The spy is on the watch. But count the letters in the name of Aristotle's favourite disciple." I guessed (as he intended me to do) that he did not mean Aristotle. He wished to suggest Plato, and so Socrates; hence I counted A-L-C-I-B-I-A-D-E-S = 10, and thus completely baffled the spy for that day. The following day he rapped out "Rahu" very emphatically, meaning that the next lunar eclipse would be the proper moment for our evasion, and spent the rest of the day in small talk, so as to lull the suspicions of the spy. For three days he had no opportunity of saying anything, being in the hospital with fever. On the fourth day: "I have discovered that spy is a damned swine of an opium-smoking lieutenant from Toulon. We have him; he doesn't know Paris. Now then—draw a line from the Gare de l'Est to the Etoile; erect an equilateral triangle on that line. Think of the name of the world-famous man who lives at the apex." (This was a touch of super-genius, as it forced me to use the English alphabet for the basis of the cipher, and the spy spoke no language but his own, except a little Swiss.) "From this time I shall communicate in a cipher of the direct additive numerical order, and the key shall be his name."

'It was only my incomparably strong constitution which enabled me to add the task of deciphering his conversation to that imposed by Government. To memorise perfectly a cipher communication of half-an-hour is no mean feat of mnemonics, especially when the deciphered message is itself couched in the obscurest symbolism. The spy must have thought his reason in danger if he succeeded in reading the hieroglyphs which were the mere pieces of the puzzle of the master-thinker. For instance, I would get this message; owhmomdvvtxskzvgcqxzllhtrejrgscpxjrmsgausrgwhbdxzldabe, which, when deciphered (and the spy would gnash his teeth every time Dodu signalled a W), only meant: "The peaches of 1761 are luminous in the gardens of Versailles."

'Or again: "Hunt; the imprisoned Pope; the Pompadour; the Stag and Cross." "The men of the fourth of September; their leader divided by the letters of the Victim of the Eighth of Thermidor." "Crillon was unfortunate that day, though braver than ever."

'Such were the indications from which I sought to piece together our plan of escape!

'Perhaps rather by intuition than by reason, I gathered from some two hundred of such clues that the guards Bertrand, Rolland, and Monet, had been bribed, and also promised advancement, and (above all) removal from the hated Island, should they connive at our escape. It seemed that the Government had still use for its first strategist. The eclipse was due some ten weeks ahead, and needed neither bribe nor promise. The difficulty was to ensure the presence of Bertrand as sentinel in our corridor, Rolland at the ring-fence, and Monet at the outposts. The chances against such a combination at the eclipse were infinitesimal, 99,487,306,294,236,873,489 to 1.

'It would have been madness to trust to luck in so essential a matter. Dodu set to work to bribe the Governor himself. This was unfortunately impossible; for (*a*) no one could approach the governor even by means of the intermediary of the bribed guards; (*b*) the offence for which he had been promoted to the governorship was of a nature unpardonable by any Government. He was in reality more a prisoner than ourselves; (c) he was a man of immense wealth, assured career, and known probity.

'I cannot now enter into his history, which you no doubt know in any case. I will only say that it was of such a character that these facts (of so curiously contradictory appearance—on the face of it) apply absolutely. However the tone of confidence which thrilled in Dodu's messages, "Pluck grapes in Burgundy; press vats in Cognac; ha!" "The soufflé with the nuts in it is ready for us by the Seine," and the like, showed me that his giant brain had not only grappled with the problem, but solved it to his satisfaction. The plan was perfect; on the night of the eclipse those three guards would be on duty at such and such gates; Dodu would tear his clothes into strips, bind and gag Bertrand, come and release me. Together we would spring on Rolland, take his uniform and rifle, and leave him bound and gagged. We should then dash for the shore, do the same with Monet, and then, dressed in their uniforms, take the boat of an octopus-fisher, row to the harbour, and ask in the name of the governor for the use of his steam yacht to chase an escaped fugitive. We should then steam into the tracks of ships and set fire to the yacht, so as to be "rescued" and conveyed to England, whence we could arrange with the French Government for rehabilitation.

'Such was the simple yet subtle plan of Dodu. Down to the last detail was it perfected—until one fatal day.

'The spy, stricken by yellow fever, dropped suddenly dead in the fields before noon "Cease work" had sounded. Instantly, without a moment's hesitation, Dodu strode across to me and said, at the risk of the lash; 'The whole plan which I have explained to you in cipher these last four months is a blind. That spy knew all. His lips are sealed in death. I have another plan, the real plan, simpler and surer. I will tell it to you to-morrow."'

The whistle of an approaching engine interrupted this tragic episode of the adventures of Duguesclin.

'"Yes," said Dodu' (continued the narrator), ' "I have a better plan. I have a stratagem. I will tell it you tomorrow."'

The train which was to carry the narrator and his hearer to Mudchester came round the corner.

'That morrow,' glowered Duguesclin, 'that morrow never came. The same sun that slew the spy broke the great brain of Dodu; that very afternoon, a gibbering maniac, they thrust him in the padded room, never again to emerge.'

The train drew up at the platform of the little junction. He almost hissed in Bevan's face.

'It was not Dodu at all,' he screamed, 'it was a common criminal, an epileptic; he should never have been sent to Devil's Island at all. He had been mad for months. His messages had no sense at all; it was a cruel practical joke!'

'But how,' said Bevan getting into his carriage and looking back, 'how did you escape in the end?'

'By a stratagem,' replied the Irishman, and jumped into another compartment.